IN THIS WORLD BUT NOT OF IT

~

A Journey from Enslavement to Enlightenment

by
Paul Henderson

All rights reserved
Copyright Paul Henderson ©2013

Paul Henderson is hereby identified as author of this work in accordance with Section 77 of the Copyright, Designs and Patents Act 1988

The book cover Design is by
Nick Buchanan

This book is sold subject to the conditions that it shall not, by way of trade or otherwise, be lent, resold, hired out or otherwise circulated without the author's prior consent in any form of binding or cover other than that in which it is published and without a similar condition including this condition being imposed on the subsequent purchaser

A CIP record for this book is available from the British Library

ISBN 978-1-291-37424-7

Author's Notes

The inspiration for this book came as a result of an incredible journey, a voyage through both shadow and light. Many of the experiences outlined are true life events.

My dearest wish is that you utilize the information herein to free yourself from the inhibiting residues of the past and embrace the infinite wisdom of the Universal Mind.

Reflections

Have you ever had the feeling that life is void of meaning?

Do you perceive yourself as a passive bystander on the freeway of life?

Has your growth been thwarted as a result of childhood abuse?

Do you know that your internal world is populated by many different characters who predispose you to act in rigid ways?

Do you know that you re-enact past relationships in the present?

Do you understand the unconscious mechanisms that draw you to your partners?

Do you know that the physical world is a mass illusion?

Do you know that you co-create your life?

Do you understand the true nature of love?

Do you understand the power of intent?

Would you like to be free of the inhibiting residues of the past?

Would you like to recognise your true potential and fulfill your life's purpose?

If you are intrigued by any of these questions then this book is designed especially for you. **IN THIS WORLD BUT NOT OF IT**, *A Journey from Enslavement to Enlightenment*, is a unique novel, offering a wealth of psychological and esoteric knowledge; information that is designed to inspire, challenge and practically transform your life. Whether you wish to explore the inhibiting residues of your childhood, or traverse the infinite expanse of the Universal Mind, the forthcoming pages will satisfy your appetite.

This book is not meant as a mere novel, it is a reference book rich with tried and tested psychological tools and spiritual practices that will enhance your quality of life. Once you have read it through, my advice is that you revisit and reflect on the chapters that appeal to your present level of growth.

As a recovering alcoholic, I sought answers to many of the questions outlined above. For many years I was faced with the disconcerting proposition that life was void of meaning. Then, in the summer of 1996, a succession of powerful psychic experiences initiated an alchemical process that brought about radical change. During this period, my physical senses became subservient to my subtle senses and I found myself coalescing with the 'unseen realms'. As my awareness entered this fourth dimension of existence, I awakened to the fact that the space around me was imbued with intelligence. Within this so called *nothingness* existed many levels of experience. Subsequently, I formed an intimate bond with two disincarnate guides who revealed my life's purpose. In preparation to teach and heal I studied and practiced psychology, spiritual healing techniques, clinical hypnotherapy, and psychodynamic counselling. For the past few years I have been facilitating holistic development workshops throughout the country.

Through developing my own personal psyche - the mental, emotional and spiritual aspects of myself - I have come to realise that the part of myself I call 'I' is a mere appendage of something far greater. To quote my spirit guide, Theodore:

We are all unique cells within one unified body, inimitable waves in the same ocean. Each of us has a singular purpose and that purpose is designed to serve the whole.

We are one.

As well as extending my heart-felt love to my soul family, both incarnate and discarnate - Anita, Ian, Steve, Gordon, Nick, Theodore, Esba and Galfridus - who enabled this book to manifest, I would like to extend an invitation to each and every one of you:

Please join us and let's unite as one; for where unity prevails separation can't exist and from separation stems all conflict. Let us walk hand-in-hand towards our destiny. Let's seek out that place where you, I, and all that is, converge as one

- for that place is our true home.

With Love and Light

Paul

Contents

Chapter		Page
1	Violet's Demise	11
2	Signposts	17
3	Reality Returns	20
4	Phil's Story: Chaos to Clarity	30
5	Authenticating the Signposts	39
6	The Physical World: A Mass Illusion	53
7	Subtle Anatomy	64
8	A Prophecy	77
9	The Universal Mind: An Infinite Expanse of Consciousness	87
10	Unveiling the Hidden Realms	107
11	Unconscious Dynamics of Relationships: The Past is Buried Alive	118
12	Coalescing with Spirit Guide – Theodore	144
13	Uni-Verse: One Song	165
14	Reflections	178
15	Past-Life Influences	184
16	Light dispels Darkness	193
17	Romantic Revelation	201
18	Synergy of Worlds	210
19	Growing Pains and Insight	214
20	Black Christmas	221
21	Recap with a Disincarnate Entity	228

Chapter		Page
22	Abused from Beyond the Grave	234
23	Synchronistic Science	236
24	A Family Reunion	239
25	Devastating Effects of Psychic Abuse	246
26	Prophecy of a Romany	250
27	Observations from the Unseen Realms	257
28	The Physicist Awakens	264
29	Inner and Outer Direction	267
30	Progression: A Journey into the Future	278
31	Ullswater: The Mystical Lady	284
32	Destiny by Divination	293
33	Two People – One Heart	299
34	Spirit Clearance	308
35	Radical Transformation of a Dedicated Human Being	313
36	Engaged in Fear	321
37	Happiness to Heart-Ache: A Lesson in Unconditional Love	326
38	A Child is Born?	329
39	Soul Mates Separate	334
40	Destined to Deliver	338
41	Freedom: A Jester Holds the Key	340
42	The Homecoming	344
Epilogue	Rebirth at Rainbow's End	349

Let Your Journey commence

~

Within your depths, obscured from view
A promised land awaits for you
When stormy days, where shadows cast
Subside to bring the sun alas
This world appears, from depths ascends
And this is where your rainbow ends

Galfridus

Chapter 1

Violet's demise

Vi gazed nonchalantly out of the window into the garden. It was a beautiful spring day. The flowers and plants were covered in a morning dew and each dew drop sparkled like a diamond as it reflected the sunlight. A tall tree reached out into the clear blue sky and the birds sang with the joy of a new day.

Vi perceived this scene as grey and dreary, reflecting the way she felt inside: fatigued and desperate. Her slender figure and long dark flowing hair exhibited her natural beauty but the strain of life had severely taken its toll. A grey pallor eclipsed her skin and her pronounced features were drawn. Bereft of meaning and emotionally bankrupt, the distraught thirty-five year old assumed the countenance of a much older woman.

Vi had lived with partner, Tom, for twelve years at their bungalow in the suburbs of Lancaster, north-west England. She had fond memories of the former part of their relationship but somewhere along the way they had drifted apart. She had considered leaving him on several occasions but had a large investment in the safety and security the set-up provided: a fundamental need stemming from a turbulent childhood. The situation had become one of pure convenience: two people sharing the same house but never at home. Tom, though lacking charisma and enterprise, was a quiet, trustworthy man to whom Vi felt indebted. He had been a caring advocate during a traumatic period of her life. Despite this, she spent most of her time avoiding him. He was apt to be extremely negative and inert. Vi's many attempts to counter his incessant pessimism had been to no avail: they constantly left her feeling drained and depleted, her zest for life asphyxiated. She would often fly into rage, hurtling furniture across the room, as her frustration spiralled out of control. These episodes were further exacerbated by vestiges of her past lurking in the dark chasms of her mind, forever reminding her of the mistreatment she was subjected to as a child.

Throughout childhood, Vi witnessed and experienced a great deal of violence. Her father frequently administered horrific beatings to all the members of the family and she became very protective towards her mother and three younger siblings. Her slight frame was misleading: she had the heart of a lion. She would kick, punch, bite and gouge her father in an attempt to protect her family. Unfortunately, on many occasions, this led to further beatings.

At the age of seven she was clad in adult clothing, taking on the responsibilities normally associated with the head of the household. There was very little money but Vi was innovative and ensured there was food on the table. As her father lay slumped in a drunken stupor, she would take money from his pockets and hide it to buy groceries. Her mother fell into deep depression as a result of her experiences; Vi tended to her and the household chores. She would don a stern face in front of the family pretending she wasn't affected by the domestic situation but, at night, in the sanctity of her bedroom, she would cry herself to sleep clutching a little crocheted doll her beloved grandmother had made for her. She was a tower of strength to her family, but the price, unfortunately, was her childhood.

Despite all her efforts to keep the family together, the domestic situation continued to deteriorate; her mother fell deeper into depression and her father's alcoholism escalated. The children rarely attended school and neighbours became increasingly concerned about them. Eventually the authorities were informed and after a thorough investigation, they were taken into care.

Initially they were kept together at a local Salvation Army care home. One by one, however, they were fostered out and new homes found for them. Vi was placed with an elderly couple who were brother and sister. She was heart-broken at being separated from her family. Every night she would stare up at the sky and ask to be re-united with them in a happy, loving home. Everything she had ever loved, it would seem, had been taken away from her.

As time elapsed, she began to accept her foster home and was thankful for the relative safety it provided. Her foster parents were a good deal older than parents of other children her age and unable to participate in the normal leisure activities associated with family life, so Vi spent a great deal of time interacting with her crocheted doll and imaginary friend - Sally. Tragically, however, benevolence turned to barbarity as she became the target of sporadic bouts of sexual abuse perpetrated by her foster-father, something she never dared disclose for fear of reprisals and rejection. She banished these experiences to the outermost regions of her mind, pretending they had never happened. Though out of sight, they remained active deep within the realms of her unconscious, causing problems for many years to come.

At school she was made to feel different from other children. She wore hand-me-down clothes provided by the welfare, small round national health spectacles and was issued with a different colour meal ticket from that of the other children, advertising the fact that she was in receipt of free meals. She became the target of cruel taunts from her peers and responded in the only way she knew how: aggressively. Circumstance and experience had left her with no self-esteem and a serious inability to form intimate relationships. The next few years saw her very withdrawn and hermitized.

A few days after her eighteenth birthday, whilst taking a walk, she noticed an advertisement for a martial arts club. She thought this would be a good way to release her pent up anger and provide a means to defend herself from any further attacks. The following Monday she went along and commenced training. After a couple of weeks she was befriended by a young man named Rob who had also had a disastrous childhood. They quickly formed a bond and a relationship ensued. At first, it was wonderful: they went for meals, to shows, for drinks and to the cinema. A whole new world opened up to Vi. Two years into their relationship, however, Rob started to act strange. He started to have severe mood swings: one day he was jovial, the next introverted and irritable. Vi began to suspect he was using drugs. Her suspicions were confirmed when she inadvertently caught him injecting heroin. She pleaded with him to get help but within twelve months he was dead from an overdose. During the subsequent mourning period she met current partner, Tom.

The culmination of these tumultuous experiences had led Vi to a place of desolation, a dark abyss and there was seemingly only one way out. She turned from the window, her eyes red and glazed, and took several shaky steps over to the dining room table where she sat down. Staring vacuously into space, she contemplated taking a lethal cocktail of alcohol and painkillers which lay on the table before her. Hands trembling, she picked up a note pad and pen and began to write:

My body is tired and weak and my mind a cesspool. I have no fight left in me, it's time to surrender. Forgive me, but I need to find a place to belong. This world offers me no such place.

Sobbing uncontrollably, she reached for the painkillers. Vivid images of her family flashed across the screen of her mind plunging her into a mire of guilt. The room began to spin. Everything became dark. Malicious voices emerged from the depths of her unconscious, reverberating round her mind: 'USELESS', 'COWARD', 'WORTHLESS', 'SHAME ON YOU', 'NOBODY

WANTS YOU ANYWAY', 'FAILURE' followed by chants of DIE', 'DIE', 'DIE', 'DIE'. Her body began to convulse with sheer terror. The room began to spin faster and faster. Then she slumped over and passed out.

Some time passed before she started to regain consciousness. When she came to, the crescendo of voices had diminished and her mind was strangely tranquil. A peacefulness permeated the room and stillness descended. Vi felt as though something was cradling her, holding her in gentle repose. Then, emerging from the silence of her mind, came a soft whisper:

I hear your cries dear child and respond with love… there's much you don't understand at present but I will enlighten you… have trust… your seemingly tempestuous life has been orchestrated for a reason which will become apparent to you shortly…your life is about to take on new meaning, propelling you into a fourth dimension of existence…don't despair: the best days of your life lie ahead of you… now it's time to awaken and consolidate. You have an important mission.

Vi froze for a moment then asked 'Who are you?' her voice breaking up as shudders of sorrow rippled through her body.

I am your Uniqueness, the soft voice replied.

Vi lifted her head to see if she had gulped down any of the vodka. She needed a rational explanation and quick, but the seal was still in tact.

'I don't understand. My *Uniqueness*?' she said, in somewhat disbelief.

Yes child. The voice of your truth. A higher aspect of your being, your wisdom.. your eternal essence.

'What do you want?… my life has been orchestrated for a reason, ah! What rubbish, it's been a nightmare,' Vi snapped, as a surge of residual anger leapt up to dominate her response.

I want to enlighten you dear one… assist you on your journey home…grant your wish and take you to that place where you belong…that place you seek so desperately...I want to act as a midwife and birth you into the reality you are destined for. A world of purpose, love, meaning, joy and fulfilment... I want to help you resolve the vestiges of your past and set you free...I want to aid in the transformation of your life and endow you with the tools to reach and heal others ...today is the first day of the rest of your life.

The gentle whisper began to reach Vi's innermost centre; she started to mellow.

'Whoever you are, help me, I am desperate,' she said pleadingly.

I intend to dear one... rest now... I will visit soon... **look out for the signposts**.

Vi sat totally dazed. *I must be going mad*, she thought, but there was something distinctly different about her - she emanated a glow. Slowly, she rose to her feet, picked up the deathly solution and flushed it down the toilet. She then went into the garden and burnt the suicide note. Finally, she fell into bed and drifted into a deep sleep.

Chapter 2

Signposts

The following morning Vi awoke at 5.30am having slept for nearly nineteen hours. She lay in bed, clasped her hands behind her head and began to recall a strange dream she'd experienced during the night.

She was standing in a dark thicket when several beams of sunlight broke through the trees and illuminated two flowers in front of her. A voice whispered 'choose this flower and you will wither away through lack of sunshine, choose the other and you will blossom in a field of dreams, a magical place where you truly belong.' The voice faded and Vi, to her disillusionment, couldn't remember which flower she was suppose to choose.

She pondered for a moment, thinking how meaningful this dream was. Her life at present wasn't working. She felt as if she had come to a dead end: literally. However, this dream suggested another pathway was open to her, a pathway which would lead her to that elusive place where she truly belonged. She was at a crossroads but didn't know which way to go.

'Look out for the signposts' my Uniqueness said. 'What did she mean by that?'

Just at that moment the room began to assume a familiar stillness and the soft whisper returned.

Good morning, you enquire about signposts do you not?

'How did you know what I was thinking?' replied Vi, startled.

At my level of existence there is no physicality, just pure consciousness. Here we communicate solely through thought, so it's natural for me to read your thoughts.

'Oh!' Vi replied, feeling somewhat exposed. 'We - who's *we*? You said *we* communicate solely through thought.'

Perhaps I can answer your question and explain signposts at the same time…

..Your being exists at several different levels simultaneously. You might view these as different levels of consciousness or layers of the mind. I am your Uniqueness, which is that part of you that mediates between your Soul and your earthly self or ego. If you like, I am that part of your Soul that is manifest in your physical body. Whereas your ego is infected and conditioned by life's ups and downs, I remain completely unblemished, maintaining my roots in the unconditional love and wisdom of your Soul. Your Soul is powerful and wise, encapsulating the totality of your eternal experiences and orchestrating your current life from the non-physical realms. As you interact with other people, so your Soul interacts with other spiritual entities. Some of these entities are highly evolved and act as guides and healers to those lost and suffering on the earthly plane. So in answer to your first question – who's we? I communicate with your Soul and, in turn, your Soul communicates with a large network of other spiritual entities…

…We are all aspects of a great ocean of consciousness often referred to as the Universe, Universal Mind or Source. Though this is ultimately one unified body, it differentiates and experiences through localised complexes of energy known to you as the individualised Soul. Your Soul emerges from the oneness of the Source and creates your earthly self in order to further its experience and evolve. As your Soul is an extension of the Universal Mind, so your earthly self is an extension of your Soul; your ego, your Uniqueness, your Soul and the Universal Mind are all aspects of your 'self' existing at different levels of consciousness: **everything is simply an unfolding of consciousness. The Universe is coming to know itself through all its differentiated aspects…**

... Before incarnation, your Soul determines a purpose for its child, your earthly self. The child is given free will and generally loses sight of its purpose when it becomes enmeshed in the chaos of the physical world. Many of these children or earthly selves never regain sight of their purpose and become lost, confused and totally disconnected from their Uniqueness and hence, their Soul and the Universe...

*...Now in answer to your second question – what are signposts? When human beings become lost, their Souls, in conjunction with other spiritual entities, create circumstances and events to help them regain direction. These happenings are called '***signposts***'. Signposts come in many forms: dreams, lines and passages from books, other people, meaningful songs, chance events. They can come in almost any guise. To recognise signposts you must remain wide awake and sustain a high level of awareness as they often come in subtle form. Humans are continuously given signposts but are so hypnotised by life's demands that they fail to see them. Many humans never awaken and become so deeply entrenched in the turmoil of life that they never discern the purpose behind the mirage of misery.*

The whisper dissipated and the room fell into silence. The experience had left Vi feeling a little dazed and bewildered, yet something had shifted within her. Yesterday she was desperate and suicidal; now she had a tiny glimmer of hope. She reached for her private notebook in which she occasionally wrote down her innermost thoughts and feelings, recorded her mystical experiences, then lay back and perused them.

My dream was a signpost, she mused. *Metaphorically speaking, I must find out which flower to choose and this will become apparent if I pay attention to the signposts.*

Chapter 3

Reality Returns

Vi spent the next few days visiting her family. Although circumstance had separated them earlier in life, the emotional bond had never been severed and they were now closer than ever. Vi resumed her parental role, taking it upon herself to resolve any family problems and disputes. Despite the huge burden it bestowed on her, this role gave her a sense of self-worth, something in which she was seriously lacking. Her mother, now divorced, lived alone after two subsequent relationships had ended catastrophically. Brothers, Tim and Joe, were married with families of their own. They were good men but prone to terrible mood swings, occasionally leading to aggression and trouble with the law. Vi was always there to bail them out. Her sister, Val, had a seven year old daughter, Charlie, to a man who had long since left for another woman. She now lived with partner, Ron. Vi idolised Charlie, often acting as a surrogate mother to her. Charlie was a little old woman who constantly sent her into fits of laughter: a welcomed oasis in the baron wasteland of life. With the exception of Vi, all the family still had occasional contact with their father whose health was rapidly deteriorating due to years of chronic alcohol abuse.

Vi had visited her mother and Joe earlier that afternoon and decided to make her last port of call sister Val's. Charlie spotted her walking up the path, dashed out and flung her arms around her.

'I'm going to have a new brother or sister auntie Vi,' she said bursting with excitement.

'I know sweetheart, isn't that wonderful,' replied Vi, giving Charlie a kiss on the forehead.

Val had been very concerned about her sister and was obviously relieved to see her. Vi kept a religious vigil over the family, never letting forty eight hours go by without contact. Yet Val had heard nothing from her for over a fortnight.

'Where have you been? I've been trying to contact you,' cried Val, as she ran up the path to greet her sister.

Vi's defence system immediately sprang into action. 'Oh, just caught up in the mundane things of life,' she replied, shrugging off her sister's question.

Val gave her a hug and invited her inside for a cup of tea. 'What's wrong, Vi?' she asked, with eyebrows raised. 'You don't fool me. You haven't been yourself for some time now.'

Vi began to fidget; her eyes fell to the floor. 'Oh, just the usual thing, I've been arguing with Tom.'

Val got up from her chair and sat beside her on the settee. 'I know Tom is a decent man, Vi, but these episodes seem to repeat themselves continuously. You don't seem to have much of a life together - do you?' she probed.

Vi remained evasive, promptly diverting the course of conversation. 'Well what about this new baby then?' she replied, her smile covering a river of tears.

The sisters spent some time discussing names and clothes for the new baby, then Val invited Vi to take a look at the nursery she had been preparing over the last few weeks. The dressing table was bedecked with soft toys. A small crib with lace drapes stood in the corner and the light blue wallpaper was filled with little smiling teddy bears.

'It's lovely, Val,' said Vi, a tinge of sadness edging her voice.

Val walked over to the dressing table where, amidst the soft toys, a heart-shaped musical box stood.

'Listen to this.' She lifted the lid and the melody of 'Hush Little Baby Don't Say a Word' rang around the room.

Vi's eyes glossed over; her stomach sank. She harboured a deep yearning for a baby of her own but didn't want to introduce a child into the disharmony of her home environment. The nursery scene was a little overwhelming, putting her right back in touch with her deepest desires.

She quickly regained her composure and complimented Val on her work, feeling an inner warmth as she watched her sister glow at the prospect of having a playmate for Charlie. *At least something's going right in our family. Maybe this baby will be the start of a new era, a rebirth so to speak.*

'Well, Val, I must be off now. Would you like me to take Charlie to the cinema tonight?'

'Oh, would you mind?'

'It'll be my pleasure; I'll pick her up at seven.'

Vi returned home to find Tom cooking dinner, one of the very few activities which interested him. 'I'll have mine later,' she muttered, inwardly planning her escape route for that evening.

'Where are you going?'

'I'm taking Charlie to the cinema.'

'Going out again? Don't you think you should stay in and save some money? The car tax is due in a couple of weeks.'

Vi felt an inferno of anger building up inside. After her father, she swore never to let another man exercise control over her. 'Don't speak to me like a child; I'll do what I want. Anyway, Val needs to rest,' she countered furiously.

Tom reverted to emotional blackmail. 'You think more of them than you do of me. I've got no friends and you're never in lately. Is there something wrong with me? Stay in and let's spend some time together.'

'Stay in with you and do what! Listen to your sermons about saving bloody money! Listen to you drone on about bloody work! I'm sick of this house, I'm sick of having no money and I'm sick of you telling me how to run my bloody life,' roared Vi as she picked up a cup and hurled it at the wall.

'You're just like your father,' Tom said antagonistically, realising his manipulative ploy wasn't working.

Vi saw red at his comment. Several other items of crockery went careering across the room, one just missing Tom's head by a hair's whisker. She then stormed off up the stairs crying.

After a cooling off period she lay on the bed contemplating.

Where does all this anger come from? It's as though something takes over me. I don't know what gets into me at times. Perhaps I have inherited some of my father's traits.

Feeling rather guilty, she went downstairs and sheepishly cleared up the mess, taking particular care not to let Tom see her remorse. The atmosphere could have been cut with a knife; not a single word was exchanged.

When she'd finished, she took a shower and was getting dressed when the phone rang.

'Vi!' Tom shouted, a sense of urgency in his voice. 'Ron's on the phone and he doesn't sound too good to me.'

Vi rushed downstairs and picked up the phone. 'Hi Ron, what's the matter?'

'She's lost the baby, Vi. Just after you left she started having pains and began to bleed. She's distraught. I don't know what to do. Can you come and see her? We're at the hospital.'

23

No sooner had Ron got the words out of his mouth than Vi was on her way to the hospital. Ron met her at the entrance and the pair made their way to the ward. Vi perched herself on the edge of the bed, embraced her tearful sister and gently rocked her back and forward. 'It'll be ok, you'll see honey,' she whispered, inwardly seething at the injustice of life. She too was fighting back tears as her eyes made contact with Charlie who stood there expressionless.

Later that night Val was discharged from the hospital and Vi spent the remainder of the night consoling her. When she returned home in the early hours of the morning the house was in darkness. She crept up the stairs, passed the spare bedroom where Tom was sound asleep, and quietly got into bed.

The last few days epitomise the whole of my life – a total disaster. Why do some people reap the benefits of life, finding love and happiness while others have to toil their way through trauma and sadness?

Immediately the energy in the room began to change and the whisper of her Uniqueness returned.

Some Souls choose a more difficult path for their earthly selves, but on awakening, their earthly counterpart realises the opportunities presented by such traumatic events and, like the alchemist, starts the process of transforming their misfortunes into their wealth.

'There goes my vivid imagination again. I won't be seduced by the trickery of my mind this time,' Vi scowled.

It saddens invisible aspects of the Source to be dismissed by human beings as imagination. People who are in tune with their higher senses are often ridiculed or even feared. People say, 'don't be stupid. It's all in the mind.' Of course it's all in the mind. The mind is the only medium through which we can communicate. Anything that transcends the physical senses on your planet is dismissed as unreal as you are conditioned away from your higher senses during childhood. Our communications are subtle and can feel very much like imagination. Yet they are as real as anything you experience through your physical senses… trust me…… Now you want to help heal your family do you not?

'Why yes, of course I do.'

Then begin with healing her.

A vivid image began to form in Vi's mind's eye. A bedraggled little girl with a tear stained face, looking solemn and abandoned.

'Who is she?'

She is your dear inner child and she needs you. Your internal world is populated by many different characters who have affected her: shamed, abused, and abandoned her. **Past relationships are not dead and buried: they are buried alive.** *They infiltrate your psyche and remain active deep within the unconscious realm of your mind. These internal relationships are often re-enacted externally; they cause you to think, feel and act in rigid ways. They're the negative forces that thwart your growth and impede your happiness presently. They need to be worked with and dissolved or you will remain all alone, an emotional hermit, frightened to let anyone close. Your inner child needs to be nurtured to gain trust in people again. She longs for love and affection but is terrified because every time she loves she gets badly hurt. She's convinced herself she has no need for love, when in reality she is crying out for it. True love is the seed from which she will blossom. The elusive place you seek, the place where you truly belong, is not made from bricks and mortar, it is an energy having the foundation of true love.*

Vi's mind became still. She lay in silence for a while, contemplating.

Okay this child is me, years ago. I understand that, but what's happened has happened. I can't do much about it. I can't change the past. Anyway, it can't possibly affect me now. And love, uh! I can do without that. It hasn't done much for me so far. And look where it got my mother! As for my misfortune becoming my wealth, I don't think so. It's best forgotten about, it's depressing.

Despite her cynicism, she recorded the night's events in her notebook and re-read her earlier encounters. When she'd finished, she leant over to switch off the bedside lamp. As she did, an envelope slipped out from between some books on the bookshelf: it had a hypnotic effect on her, everything else fading into insignificance. She got up, opened it and found a card inside. The verse on the front immediately caught her attention:

Thunderous clouds turn to free flowing rivers,

when meaning is found in the trials life delivers.

Concealed within heartache, frustration and woe,

are the signposts that tell you which way you should go.

So rise to each challenge, let fear abate,

flow with the current of wisdom – innate.

Surge to the ocean where all grief's repealed,

a vast sea of spirit where all is revealed.

Silence.

Two points of light entered the surrounding space, radiating harmonic vibrations into the ether. An effulgent glow suffused the room. Vi's scepticism suddenly assuaged as the destructive aspirants of her internal world fell into silence. She entered a deep ruminative state, absorbing the essence of the verse assiduously. As she did, latent forces stirred deep within her being. The dross of life melted away like snow on a spring day. An effervescent spring coursed through every cell of her body. A river of inspiration swept her awareness to a sea of limitless possibilities. She immersed herself, capitulating to the all-pervading ablution of mind, body and spirit.

Concealed within the ether, the celestial beings responsible for her liberating sense of expansion emitted concentric circles of refined light into the atmosphere. As the subtle emanations caressed Vi's energy field, her psychic senses ignited. Her 'third-eye' drew in the celestial light and started to demodulate the information. Her inner screen lit up. Out of the *no-thing* that contains *every-thing*, a phrase appeared, each letter composed of diaphanous light.

Providence has intervened let it proceed.

Vi stood entranced: bewildered. 'What does this mean?' she mused.

A single word echoed through her mind - *signposts*.

She remained in deep thought; mezmerized by the psychic phenomenon. Several minutes passed before she broke the silence. 'But I don't understand, in which direction does it point?'

No response.

Time elapsed. She started to become irritable. A sense of anxiety edged her voice. 'Destiny has stepped in, follow it,' she paraphrased, 'but where to?'

As the energy in the room intensified, something quite extraordinary happened: the initial letter of each word seemed to reach out to her.

Providence Has Intervened Let It Proceed.

She stared with mouth agape: the name, **Philip**, emblazoned in her mind. Then suddenly, as if cued by an inaudible directive, her internal screen went dark.

Visibly disoriented, she opened her eyes. As she did, her gaze fixed on the card that now lay open on the table before her: the message inside left her spellbound:

Listen to the pleadings of your heart.

With love and light

Phil x

Verging on hypnotic trance, she contemplated the serendipitous happening. *Phil, how is it that every time I'm feeling low you seem to show up?*

Her celestial visitors dissipated back into the nothingness.

*

Two days later Vi returned to work in the finance department of the local university, receiving a warm welcome from her colleagues. She avoided getting into any deep discussion as to the reasons for her absence. No-one was to know about her near suicide attempt, including her doctor who gave her a note for stress. After reading her backlog of emails she glanced at the clock to find it was 9.15am.

'Is Phil on holiday?' she enquired, noticing the chair next to her was still empty.

'No,' replied Heather. 'He went off ill just after you and we haven't heard anything from him since.'

Managing to conceal her sense of disappointment, Vi responded empathetically. 'Oh, I do hope he's okay, he's been pushing himself so hard lately. He was looking so tired.'

The weeks passed by and there was still no sign of Phil. Vi fell back into her mechanical routine: shopping at lunch times, attending the gym Monday and Wednesday nights, teaching martial arts Tuesdays and Thursdays and sorting out the family affairs of a weekend. She left no time to relax and contemplate. Whenever there was a lull in her relentless schedule she faced the realities of her situation and that was painful, so she ploughed her way through life hoping all her problems would disappear. As scepticism set back in, her faith in Uniqueness began to wane and her mystical experiences were reduced to lavish fantasies. Once again, she looked tired, drawn, and disillusioned.

Chapter 4

Phil's Story:
Chaos to Clarity

Phil had led a varied life. Born and raised in Liverpool he was no stranger to the challenges of growing up in the inner city. Although he'd mastered the survival techniques warranted to fend off hostile predators in the uncertain terrain of the urban jungle, he was inherently gentle in nature. His childhood home resembled a menagerie as his love of animals infiltrated many rooms: turtles, terrapins, hamsters, goldfish, tropical fish, budgerigars, zebra finches, a rabbit, and his faithful but somewhat mischievous Labrador, 'Pal', made up his extended family. When he wasn't preoccupied with his pets, his formative years had been spent pursuing another major interest – music. By the age of seventeen he had great hopes of fulfilling his dream of becoming a pop star. He formed a band with some school friends and travelled the country performing at night clubs, bars and festivals. During the summer of 1988 they landed a contract with a small recording company and were about to set off for Germany on a tour of American army bases when two love-struck members of the band opted out. The group disbanded and for the next few years Phil performed solo on the cabaret circuits. Eventually the novelty wore off and he wondered what to do with the rest of his life, feeling totally empty inside. He tried his hand at various jobs, re-educated himself and had a string of relationships in an attempt to fill this incessant void, but nothing worked and he became increasingly restless and frustrated.

Attempting to escape the disconcerting proposition that life was devoid of meaning, he turned to alcohol. Initially it seemed the perfect antidote to his dismal existence, creating a colourful fantasy world in which he could play any role. However, within a short period of time his newfound ally turned foe, equipped with an arsenal of fear, terror, bewilderment and guilt, mounting an assault on his life that would leave a trail of devastation and heartache. His fantasy world gave way to a hell in which the only role was that of sinner. He despised himself for the destruction his two bottle-a-day habit was causing to his loved ones and on many occasions pledged never to drink again, only to find himself continually defeated by his cunning adversary. Brawls and arguments ensued as his inner frustration spilled over into the outside world; erratic behaviour led to arrests and probation. Ending up totally paranoid, fearing everything and everybody, he felt safe only in the confines of a hospital ward or rehabilitation centre. On several occasions he took overdoses with the sole intention of being admitted into hospital, twice having his life saved by the swift response and expertise of the hospital staff. Drink had robbed him of his pride, his family, his hopes and aspirations: now it wanted his life. Secretly he hoped that the doctor's prognosis was right and his days on this planet were numbered.

Intervention finally arrived during a period of detoxification when an ex-drinking partner visited him. John's experience of alcohol was similar to that of his own, but here he stood, immaculately dressed, looking the picture of health and highly contented.

'How did you do it?' asked Phil curiously.

'I joined the twelve step program of Alcoholics Anonymous.'

The pair talked for nearly three hours after which Phil agreed to attend some meetings with John. His subsequent recovery was rocky. Relapse followed sobriety in cycles, but eventually he surrendered to a life of abstinence.

After making amends to those he had hurt during his years of active alcoholism, city life appeared totally abhorrent to him. He decided to move to the country, securing steady employment and establishing a new circle of friends. Logically he knew he should have been grateful for this miraculous transformation but he still had an unremitting thorn in his side. The true purpose of life still evaded him. Something called to him but he was just out of earshot. He had an uncanny sense that the part of himself he called 'I' was a mere appendage of something far greater. Every night, in the privacy of his own home, he would remove the clown's mask he wore for public viewing and ask in all earnest for the meaning of his life to be unveiled. For months nothing happened. Finally, late one night, he sat quietly in the peaceful ambience of his candle lit meditation room when what could only be described as a loving presence embraced him. The energy in the room became imbued with peace and tranquility. His mind stilled, a sense of anticipation pulsated throughout the whole his body and a wave of love swept over him. A deluge of thoughts and images pierced the peripheries of his mind with the velocity of a shower of meteors hurtling through space projecting his life onto his internal screen. He was shown that he was no passive bystander on the freeway of life but an explorer with the power to determine his own destiny. His traumatic experiences had been no chance happenings; they had been orchestrated from the unseen realms for the purposes of growth and evolution. His life had unfolded according to a spiritual blueprint agreed upon before incarnation and imprinted into the depths of his Soul. His purpose was to teach and heal but first he had to experience the sufferings of other human beings in order to empathize. The key to transformation lay in the recognition that he wasn't one of life's victims but rather a crusader on a quest to turn darkness into light.

Fulfilment of his purpose hinged on his exploring the darker side of earthly life and transforming it into light through the process of spiritual alchemy. He saw his future vividly: he was destined to pen a bestselling novel and use the proceeds to found a residential holistic development centre set in an area of great natural beauty. Although he had resigned himself to never having children, he was to father a very special child, a prodigy who would take his legacy into future generations.

These powerful experiences continued every night for three months. People began to see a vast improvement in his general demeanour. He emanated a glow, his eyes reflecting the joy of his Soul. He spoke with both purpose and humility, becoming wise, tender and sensitive as he absorbed the energy of the two guides responsible for his awakening, 'Theodore' and 'Esba'. He channelled these two nurturing entities religiously, assimilating their teachings, digesting their wisdom, embracing their love and basking in their healing presence.

For three years he felt totally liberated and the thorn in his side disappeared. He meditated, channelled, qualified as a hypnotherapist, became a Reiki master and studied for a degree in Psychology. He expended vast amounts of time and energy on manifesting his vision and was relentless in its pursuit.

Things started to deteriorate when his attempts to write a book failed dismally. He had envisaged himself sitting down and channelling the information effortlessly but this just hadn't happened. He desperately needed funds to establish the centre so he shelved the book and took on extra work. Driving himself harder and harder, beyond any reasonable limits, his fevered mind began to fracture and he started to experience dreadful panic attacks. His awareness plummeted, his beloved guides appeared to have deserted him and his weary body struggled to carry out even the most menial of tasks. Becoming more withdrawn, he isolated himself in his caravan in the Lake District and was rapidly heading towards crisis point.

*

Phil arrived at the caravan feeling as if his head was home to a swarm of bees. He gathered his belongings from the car, threw them into the van and collapsed totally exhausted on the bed. *What's happening to me?* he cried inwardly, searching desperately for a place of solace in the tempest of his mind. Tossing and turning, saturated in sweat and enmeshed in a ceaseless flow of perplexity, he felt like a drifting raft at the mercy of turbulent rapids, culminating only in an eddy of ever deepening despair. Several grotesque faces leapt out of the darkness startling him. He jumped up, switched on the bedside lamp and lay with eyes fixed on the crimson curtains, like a corpse about to enter the funeral pyre. Paralyzed with fear, he felt his life force was inexorably ebbing away.

Suddenly, his consciousness ejected from his body and he found himself suspended between two worlds, neither of which looked inviting. Below was a swarthy cloud of mist which he intuited as symbolising his current earthly state: lost, lonely and confused. Above was a mirror image, another dark cloud. His attention vacillated from one cloud to the other as he tried to elicit the meaning behind the scene. Slowly he realised that he was being given a choice: renounce his earthly life and return to the realms of the disincarnate or return to earth and re-establish his path. The thought of escaping his pain was very tempting yet the dark cloud above told him there was no escape. If he returned 'home' before his time, deserting his purpose, he would have to face his failure in the higher realms. He had to return to his corporeal state and re-establish his path. He felt an almighty thud as his spirit abruptly re-entered his body. Then he slipped into a welcomed state of oblivion.

Morpheus had intervened and eased his troubled state. He had slept for six hours. On awakening he felt somewhat refreshed. Lacing his fingers behind his head he began to contemplate a past life experience that had presented itself in the form of a dream.

*

He found himself in a small village sometime in the 17th century. His home was a small stone cottage which he shared with his parents. As the scene materialised, he noticed his parents were engrossed in a somewhat heated conversation regarding his future. War had broken out at the frontier and he had been summoned to join the infantry. By nature he was a pacifist and didn't want to participate in the violence. His father talked about the disgrace he would bring upon his family if he refused to fight. His mother agonized over the prospect of losing her beloved son but was too fearful to challenge her husband's authority so, reluctantly, she sided with him.

There was a parade in the village as a band of young boys dressed in dark blue uniforms with white cross-bands and red epaulettes marched off to war. A bloody battle commenced and Phil found himself in the midst of a holocaust. Destruction filled his entire field of vision and the stench of death filled the air. He found himself engaged in face-to-face combat with another young boy who fell to the ground during a struggle: they stared at each other intently through terrified eyes. His adversary reached for his sword. In sheer panic Phil removed his sword from its scabbard and plunged it straight into the heart of his opponent, watching in sickly disbelief as the life drained out of him.

After the battle ended several of them were to be commended for bravery and service to their country. The thought of being commended for taking the life of an innocent young boy repulsed Phil. The day the ceremony was due to take place he deserted and went deep into the desert. Immersed in guilt, he couldn't erase that young boy's face from his mind. After several months of complete solitude he became extremely adept at self hatred and resigned himself to a life of isolation.

Early one evening as the sun was setting, he spotted the lonesome figure of a young woman approaching. As she neared he could hear her soft and gentle voice whispering *'all your future battles will be fought with love, my friend.'* She oozed compassion and appeared to have a very deep understanding of him. She took his hand and they walked toward the beautiful sunset. The scene concluded as the sunlight changed into a radiant white light into which they both dissolved.

*

Phil was sufficiently versed in these matters by now to pay close attention to such an intense dream. He knew that dreams often portrayed other realities rather than mere fantasies. Theodore had taught him that streams of energy flow from the Soul during sleep bringing the unseen into the seen. Phil also recalled that Theodore had said that everybody has experienced thousands of past lives, the memories of which are stored in a large reservoir at the highest level of the Soul. The Soul encapsulates the totality of an individual's eternal experiences. The Higher Self, that part of the Soul that is manifest in the physical body, retains only a handful of these past life memories from which one's current life's purpose is born.

This past life's been shown to me for a significant reason; it's trying to inform me of something.

His mind began to drift.

There are many parallels with my current life……the recurring theme of guilt has dogged me.

He slipped into a deeper state of rumination.

The cruelty of the battle reminds me of the toxic shaming that took place amongst my peer group during adolescence, the penetrating weapons being vicious words, ruthless taunts that left deep scars.

His mind continued to wander. He began to recall distant memories of his cousin, a role model during his formative years, forcing him to fight another boy to prove he wasn't a coward. Inwardly, he didn't want fight; he despised violence, but yet he knew he'd be shamed and ostracized if he refused. Gangs of youths congregated round them in the park chanting 'fight, fight, fight, fight.' The violent clash lasted about half an hour. Although he won the fight, he seemingly still hadn't done enough to prove himself. As the other boy walked home crying, his cousin urged him to 'go and give it to him again.'

Is this so different from being forced to go to war out of fear of bringing shame on the family? He thought.

Tears filled his eyes as he acknowledged the extent to which young impressionable people are constantly corrupted in the name of pride, coerced to conform to the expectations of a society immersed in fear.

No wonder this world is so screwed up. How can we deal with all this anger and violence? Fighting violence with violence is barbaric. How can we bring peace to this world?

His thoughts turned to the young woman in the dream.

Who is she? She's vaguely familiar. 'All your future battles will be fought with love,' she said. What did she mean by that?

Immediately, an air of peace began to pervade the surrounding space and a vivid image of the beautiful young woman reappeared in his mind's eye. Her long dark flowing hair complemented her porcelain-like skin and she smiled coyly. Her essence was almost angelic. He felt a lightness sweep throughout the whole of his body as her healing presence appeared to permeate every cell, bone and tissue. Her radiance lit up the dark denizens of his internal world as he stared in awe of her elegance. Then, in one brief instant, and with the graciousness of a ballerina, she turned through one hundred and eighty degrees and completely vanished.

He lay stunned for a moment, then began to mull over the experience.

Who is she? I know her, I'm sure I know her.

A few minutes elapsed before the identity of the woman became clear.

It's Vi! She looked so different but it was most definitely her.

Thoughts raced through his brain.

Why Vi? She's a good friend but I only see her at work. We laugh and joke and occasionally confide in each other but nothing too deep. I never envisaged her in this capacity before. Stop Phil! You're giving in to logical analysis now. You should know better, have faith.

His confusion quickly dispersed and a sense of excitement swept over him as he strongly suspected his guides had returned and been the animating force behind these experiences: these were no meaningless coincidences - they were far too powerful.

My guides have put this dream and vision into my mind for a good reason: they are signposts. I have to get back to work as soon as possible. I must talk to Vi.

Chapter 5

Authenticating the Signposts

The following Monday Phil returned to work, arriving early, knowing that Vi was always in the office half an hour before anybody else. He entered the building, said a cheerful 'good morning' to the porter and made his way along the corridor, a real sense of anticipation in the pit of his stomach. When he reached the office, he quietly opened the door and tip-toed up behind Vi who was deeply engrossed in her computer.

'Good morning!' he said, startling her.

'Phil!' Her face beamed with delight. 'It's great to see you, I've really missed you.'

'I've missed you too, Vi.' he replied, giving her a warm hug.

'How's things?' she asked.

'It's a long story, but I'm okay now….and you?'

'Well…the truth?'

'Yes, the truth,' Phil insisted, knowing Vi was inclined to be evasive.

Her brow furrowed. 'Not too good really.'

'I'm sorry to hear that, Vi. Would you like to talk about it?'

'I suppose I ought to,' she replied hesitantly.

'Listen, the others will be in soon. We can't talk here. Are you doing anything at lunchtime?'

'I was going to go shopping but it can wait.'

Vi, being a strict vegetarian, tucked into her salad, whilst Phil wrestled with his spaghetti bolognaise. Vi laughed heartily as she watched Phil rolling strands of spaghetti round his fork and shovelling them down the front of his clean white shirt. Her delight pinnacled when he decided to go to the toilet to clean himself up and entered the door marked Senioras! The chemistry between the pair had been highly apparent since they first met, their dry senses of humour often leading to witty exchanges and childish pranks.

Phil returned from the ladies' toilets to the rapturous applause of a number of fellow diners. Realising his mistake, he smiled at them impishly and acknowledged them with a frivolous bow. When the merriment settled down his mood began to change.

'How are you, Vi?' he asked, compassionately.

Her eyes averted, a vacant expression swept across her face and momentarily silence fell.

'To be perfectly honest, Phil, I've been awful,' she replied, her voice beginning to falter.

'What is it, Vi? What's troubling you?'

'I just feel so messed up. A few weeks ago, I was totally distraught, in fact....' she stared at Phil somberly, her eyes becoming moist, '...I was suicidal.'

A solitary tear trickled down her cheek.

Phil reached across the table and placed his hand on top of hers. 'It's okay, Vi. I understand; I assure you. I've been there myself.'

Vi's eyes roved aimlessly around the room and her foot tapped nervously on the floor.

'So much has happened in my life,' she continued, her voice now barely audible. 'Everything just got on top of me. I just felt as if I couldn't cope anymore. It seemed like the only solution.'

'And now.. are these thoughts still with you?'

'No, not anymore.' She paused for a moment as though in deep thought.

'Something really strange happened.'

Phil looked at her curiously. 'Strange, in what way?'

'A voice,' she replied. 'A voice in my mind.'

Beginning to feel a little vulnerable, she turned to Phil for reassurance.

'Do go on, Vi, there's nothing strange in what you're saying.'

'Well,' she continued, somewhat uneasily, 'the morning I contemplated the end, my mind went into a spin. I started to feel dizzy and passed out. When I came to, everything seemed so different. My mind was strangely calm and I felt that I wasn't alone. Then something started whispering to me - not in the normal audible sense, a trail of thought running through my mind.'

She glanced at Phil again.

'What did the voice say, Vi? Do you remember?'

'Yes, I wrote it down…. All my life, I've had this feeling of not belonging, always felt out of place. The voice spoke of taking me to a special place, a place where I truly belong. She claimed to be my Uniqueness, part of my Soul, and urged me to follow the signposts. It all felt really special at the time but now I just put it down to my imagination.'

'No, Vi, it's not your imagination at all, or let's say imagination is grossly misunderstood in our society. I've had experiences similar to these for eight years and know the impact that they have on our lives. Think about it. This voice intervened at a crucial moment in time, saving your life. That's quite extraordinary isn't it?'

'I suppose so,' she replied, thoughtfully.

'Do you believe in spirit guidance?'

'Yes, I've always believed in that sort of thing.'

'Then can you accept the possibility that what you experienced was guidance from a higher aspect of yourself: a level of your consciousness that's wise and can see what you're unable to see?'

'Oh, I don't know,' she sighed. 'There's been no improvement in my life whatsoever.'

'There are no magic wands, Vi. Your Uniqueness has given you a vision, but you have to be prepared to put in the work and this can be difficult. Spirit will work *with* us, not *for* us. Spirit guides and higher aspects of ourselves don't remove our pain. If they did we would never grow. They facilitate our growth by imparting wisdom that enables us to understand our lives from a much higher perspective. Ultimately, we have to ground their teachings, apply them to our lives and be prepared to make the necessary changes ourselves.'

'But how can I be certain my experience wasn't some sort of elaborate fantasy?' Vi retorted.

At that moment Phil began to drift, becoming distant and somewhat spacey.

'What is it?' inquired Vi, noticing the change in him.

'Mary,' he whispered, in a low sotto tone. 'There's a lady with me by the name of Mary.' He paused for moment, closing his eyes, his speech becoming slow and pronounced. 'She tells me she's your grandmother and expresses great concern for you… she wants to help…I can feel her sadness…She is placing imagery in my mind…I see you as a young child, seated on a motorcycle, being pushed around a garden by a man.'

The imagery began to fade and Phil slowly returned to his ordinary state of awareness. On opening his eyes, he stared intently across the table at Vi. 'Does this make any sense?'

Vi looked astonished. 'How could you possibly know that?'

Phil tilted his head and glared at her.

'Mary was my father's mother. She died before I was born. That scene you described actually happened. When I was very young, my father would push me around the garden on his motorbike.'

A wave of sadness came over her as she recalled a time, very early on in life, when she loved her father.

'What happened, Phil?'

'Exactly what happened to you when you had your experiences with your Uniqueness. I began to sense an energy around me then a voice began to whisper in my mind. If I hadn't known better I would have dismissed it as imagination because it took place at a subtle level, but things like this have happened to me before.'

A warm smile came to Phil's face. 'I guess someone's trying to disperse your doubts about the authenticity of subtle communication.'

'I don't know what to say, it's incredible. I don't know whether to laugh or cry but it's certainly given me hope. Did it feel like your imagination?'

'Yes, Vi, this is what is meant by "subtle". The language that bridges the veil between our world and the spirit world is that of thought: visual, auditory and kinesthetic thought processes known as *clairvoyance, clairaudience* and *clairsentience*. When you had your experiences the thoughts you had were quite distinct from your own, right?'

'Yes,' replied Vi.

'Then what you experienced was clairaudience: literally, clear hearing. When the spirit world speaks to us, it's most unusual to hear voices audibly, although, on occasions, it does happen. Clairaudience is normally experienced as a distinct trail of thought running through the mind, just as it did with you.'

Vi's scepticism began to lift; she began to resonate with what Phil was saying. 'Come to think of it, I could never have personally come up with the information my Uniqueness relayed to me. It must have come from elsewhere. So what are clair…..erm?'

'Clairvoyance,' Phil intervened, 'literally means "clear seeing" and describes what a psychic sees on a subtle level - in other words, sees in the mind's eye. In addition to thoughts, the spirit world communicates by imprinting symbols and imagery into our minds. These visionary experiences are seen with our "psychic eye" or "third-eye chakra" as it is commonly called and projected onto our inner screen.'

'During my experiences,' Vi interrupted enthusiastically, 'I had a vision of a little girl. Was this an example of clairvoyance?'

'Describe what happened.'

'My Uniqueness spoke about my inner child and the vision of a little girl appeared in my mind.'

'Yes, Vi, this is your third-eye chakra at work transforming psychic energy into imagery that you can perceive and work with. Here your mind is clothing energy from the spirit world into imagery. Our minds are wonderful things. They're invested with the power to transform the unseen energy of the spirit world into tangible form. In actual fact, the word "fantasy" is derived from the Ancient Greek word "phantasia" which means "to make visible". Our intellectual ancestors deemed phantasia to be the mechanism through which the spirit world spoke to the human mind, bringing the unseen into vision.'

'I see, this is all beginning to make much more sense now.'

'Excellent, Vi. Now remind me of what you felt during your experiences.'

'Mmm, that's quite difficult. I felt all sorts of things: anger, frustration, hope, love, you name it, I felt it. But most of all I remember feeling an incredible warmth and having a sense of being embraced.'

'Well, clairsentience means clear feeling, our ability to sense energy around us. We do this naturally on a daily basis. We sense how other people are feeling without verbally communicating with them. We are constantly exchanging energy with other people and this can affect the way we feel. Some people's energies leave us feeling inspired, refreshed and vibrant whilst others leave us feeling drained and depleted. Similarly, when we have encounters with spirit guides or higher parts of ourselves, we sense their energies around us. We literally feel their presence. The love, warmth and feeling of being embraced you experienced are all typical signs of the presence of spirit guides; the anger and frustration, I would suggest, came from within you.'

'That's right, Phil. I was angry with the whole world, but the presence I felt was gentle, loving and warm.'

'I know exactly how it feels, Vi, believe me. I've had many such experiences.'

'So you think my Uniqueness was real? She wasn't just a figment of my imagination?'

'That's an ambiguous question. The answer to the first part is categorically "yes". I do believe your Uniqueness is real. The part about her being a figment of your imagination needs some further explanation.

'Modern day society dismisses anything that transcends the physical senses as unreal, using phrases like "it's just your imagination" when, in truth, the imagination can act as a mechanism to transcend the world of matter and link us to other levels of existence. The word "imagination" stems from the Latin word "imago" which literally means "image". In its truest sense, the imagination is the image forming capacity of the mind. It is the faculty of the mind that transforms invisible energy into images we can perceive. Some of these images come from within us and some come from the world of spirit.'

'This is really interesting, Phil. How do you know all this stuff?'

'Like you, in the beginning I had many unanswered questions, but having a curious nature I decided to do some homework and this is the information I uncovered.'

Phil glanced at his watch. 'There's so much more I'd like to share with you, Vi, but we have to be back at work soon. Would you like to get together one evening this week after work?'

'Yes, as soon as possible?' said Vi, an increasing sense of hope and enthusiasm in her voice.

'How about tomorrow?'

'Yes, that's fine.'

*

The two ambled along a meandering path under an ever-changing verdant canopy. The fallen leaves formed an absorbent cushion beneath their feet, the silence broken only by the occasional snap of a twig. Butterflies were in profusion illuminated by shafts of light of varying intensity which penetrated through the leafy mantle. The air was permeated with the sweet heady incense of pine, moss and fern. Emerging from the wood, they found themselves in a pastoral expanse and strolled alongside a small stream that led down to a lake.

'It's beautiful,' said Vi, staring at her reflection in the mirror-like surface.

'It certainly is,' replied Phil. 'It's one of my favourite places.'

They stood in silence for a while, absorbing the tranquility of the idyllic setting then took a seat on a fallen tree that lay adjacent to the lake.

'That wood Phil, it reminded me of a dream I had recently.'

'Would you like to share it? Dreams can tell us a great deal about our lives.'

Vi reached down and removed her notebook from her bag. 'Let me look in here. I wrote down what I could remember. Here it is - I was in a small dark wood when the sunlight broke through the trees and illuminated two flowers in front of me. A voice said something like "choose this flower and your life will be awful. Choose the other and you will find the place where you truly belong." The voice faded and I couldn't remember which flower I was supposed to choose.'

'What did you feel the dream was trying to tell you?' inquired Phil.

'I've given this a lot of thought and this is what I've come up with. The dream told me that I had an option. I didn't have to resign myself to the life I had and I didn't have to end my life to find the place where I belong. The act of choosing the right flower was metaphorical, indicating I was at a crossroads. The voice in the dream was that of my Uniqueness. She pointed me in the right direction, but in my confusion I forgot which way to go. I remembered what she'd said the previous morning: "follow the signposts", so I figured I had to wait to be shown the right direction. It's funny because a couple of nights later, I was lying in bed, back in the depths of despair, when an envelope slipped out from between some books. It was a card you sent me last year. I read it and it seemed to awaken something within me. That night I had quite a few strange experiences. Since then, Phil, I've felt very close to you. When I returned to work and found you were absent, I really began to miss you. Every morning I would stare at the office door hoping you'd walk in. I know we've been good friends for a few years but something felt really different.'

'I knew it,' Phil said, in a low, thoughtful tone. 'Signposts.'

'What do you mean? What exactly are signposts?'

'Meaningful events that are orchestrated from the spirit world to guide us on our way. I feel we're sitting here right now because of such events. The card Vi, tell me how you felt when you set eyes on it?'

'It was almost hypnotic, like it was the only thing in the room.'

'That's a perfect example of a signpost. Let me tell you about some of my experiences…..Eight years ago, I started having experiences similar to the ones you have had recently. My awareness locked into to a stream of energy from the spirit world, although I didn't understand this at the time. On the first occasion, images and thoughts shot through my mind making sense of the whole of my life. The feelings I had were quite indescribable: love, excitement, humility, bliss, all rolled into one. My whole view of life changed. During the subsequent weeks and months a very wise and gentle voice entered my mind speaking of both personal and worldly issues. Some months later the voice identified himself as "Theodore", a teacher and philosopher from the higher realms. Sometimes the voice was accompanied by the shimmering outline of a monk in my mind's eye. Two years later the vivid image of a young Indian squaw entered my mind and identified herself as "Esba", a teacher and healer from the higher realms. Over the years, these two guides have become my friends, nurturing me, offering compassion, wisdom and understanding, enabling me to reframe my whole experience of life. They never remove my lessons but they enable me to view difficult circumstances from a much higher perspective…

... Recently I inadvertently veered off course and hit rock bottom. Like you, I thought my life was about to end. During this experience my consciousness entered an alternative state - another world. As the scene unfolded I realised

I was being given a choice: let go of my physicality and return to the spirit world, or pursue my purpose. I instantly knew I had to pursue my purpose but didn't know which direction to go in. That night I had a profound dream in which a young woman rescued me from a life of desolation. This dream, I knew, portrayed a past life. When I awoke the identity of the woman evaded me yet I vaguely recognised her. I asked myself repeatedly, "who is she?" Then your image appeared vividly on my inner screen. I knew it was a signpost and after what you've told me about your experiences, things are becoming much clearer. I feel we're being ushered together for a reason. What that reason is, as yet, I don't know. All that I know is that my visions of you gave me a sense of renewal and ended a seven week disaster.'

'Why, what happened to you?'

'I'd taken on external accounts to raise money to start a holistic development centre which I believe to be part of my destiny. I frequently worked until three or four in the morning. The sheer demand of my workload led to a near breakdown. When my mind cleared, I realised that even this unwelcomed state was a signpost. I was going in the wrong direction and my guides intervened, stopping me in my tracks, forcing me to re-evaluate my life. Signposts are not always welcome events: sometimes they're sent to shake us up. When this happens we shouldn't adopt the victim mentality; we should raise our awareness and identify areas of our lives that warrant change. I guess that day you contemplated suicide seemed like the worst day of your life, but it may have been a much needed event that will act as a catalyst to propel you forward.'

'That makes sense, Phil. I've been desperately unhappy for a long time now. I know I have to make changes in my life.'

'Perhaps that's why we've been brought together: To help each other in the next stage of our journey. Let's think again about what's brought us here - the signposts. You were lost and suicidal and your Uniqueness intervened speaking of taking you to your true home. You dreamt of an alternative pathway and knew you had to follow the signposts. The card pointed you in my direction and I was able to authenticate your experiences and clarify some of your misgivings. I too had become lost and was experiencing a great deal of upheaval. I dreamt that you had rescued me from a life of desolation, taking me by the hand and leading me into the light. The subsequent visions I had of you had a profound healing effect on me. The following day I felt both physically and mentally renewed despite having suffered panic attacks and eating very little for the previous seven weeks. Like you, I felt something had changed between us. Now we're sitting here, in these beautiful surroundings, sharing intimate details of our lives that we've never previously discussed. Can you see how certain forces are working to bring us together?'

'Yes, Phil. At first I thought it was all a load of idealistic nonsense - cuckoo land. But now I'm starting to see the practical implications of it all; I really do feel a renewed sense of hope.'

The two smiled at each other appreciatively and engaged in a warm embrace.

'Now, all this talking has built up my appetite. I'm starving. Shall we go and find something to eat?' asked Phil.

Vi reached down into her bag, pulled out some pre-packed sandwiches, a couple of apples and a flask of hot coffee. 'Dinner is served, my friend,' she said, a radiant smile on her face.

'You're a princess,' replied Phil, reciprocating her smile.

After ravenously demolishing their food, the pair sat and sipped coffee.

'Vi, do you remember asking me to have a word with Graham a few of months ago when you were quite concerned about him?'

'Yes.'

'Well, before I went off ill, we met up on a couple of occasions and you were right, he was going through the mill. At first he was reluctant to talk but eventually he opened up. Through the course of our conversations I revealed my spiritual beliefs and experiences and he was eager to learn more about the process of channelling.

'Channelling....... what's that?' Vi intervened.

'Well, clinically speaking, channelling is described as the process of using your physical body as a conduit for higher parts of yourself or spirit guides to communicate through. These wise and loving entities have no physical attributes. They are beings of pure consciousness and rely on our bodies to act as vessels to bring through their teachings. I prefer to think of channelling as simply the merging of two consciousnesses. When you had your experiences you were naturally channelling your Uniqueness or Higher Self.'

'So channelling is just like a spiritual telephone cable, connecting us to spirit guides?'

'Yes, but the messages come in the forms I described yesterday and can sometimes be abstract and open to interpretation.'

'Do you think it could help me, too?'

'Yes. Nurturing our ability to channel can have a profound affect on our everyday life. As we absorb the love and wisdom of our higher selves and spirit guides, their energies filter down to our mental and emotional levels and we naturally begin to change.'

'I'd like to learn more about channelling too, Phil.'

'Well, Graham and I are going to my caravan for a four day break. We're going a week Friday. Would you like to join us?'

'Let me think. I don't think I've anything on that weekend. Yes, count me in. If there's anything I've forgotten, I'll cancel it. I feel I need to go. I can't go on as I am.'

'Great, Vi. You'll never regret your decision I promise you. There is no magical panacea. This path can have its ups and downs but ultimately it'll take you to that place where you belong.'

The two had been totally engrossed in conversation for several hours and darkness had crept up on them unawares. A myriad of stars and the crescent moon lit up the dark velvet sky and several shooting stars arced across their field of vision.

'It's beautiful, Phil. I wish it could be like this for ever,' said Vi, mesmerized by the spectacular heavenly light show. As she turned to face Phil he appeared distant, exuding an air of utter tranquility. Unknown to her, he had slipped into a trance-like state and was in deep communication with another sphere of consciousness, that of his guide, Theodore.

You have emerged from a beautiful ocean of consciousness, dear one, and one day you will return to that blissful state. For now you must anchor yourself deep in this ocean of love for the surface is about to become tempestuous. This maelstrom emanates from the great inhibitor fear and can only be annulled by the light of love. Expand your awareness, explore your true nature and listen to the language of your heart.

Chapter 6

The Physical World: A Mass Illusion

Blue sky, punctuated by fast moving banks of cloud, scudded overhead, skimming the crest of the hills which were swathed in an opaque blue haze making their topographical features difficult for the eye to discern. Occasionally the sun burst through this ménage of textures, depths and colours that varied from pure white to menacing black, sending its rays cascading down from the clear sky that reigned supreme above. As the light descended on the hillside the blue haze dissolved and details of the trees, rocks and streams were clearly discernable within its lens. The immediate location of the caravan fitted perfectly into this pastoral scene. The caravans were all painted green in concordance with nature's hues. Phil's van was situated in proximity to a river edged by over hanging trees and bushes. Due to heavy rainfall during the previous week, the water had washed away soil and stones from the bank and its level were now starting to fall, but the sound of the rushing, tumbling, torrent was sheer music to the ears.

'Welcome to Walthwaite,' said Phil. 'I hope it lives up to your expectations.'

'It's perfect,' replied Graham. 'A total contrast to that cradle of civilization we call the city.' His sardonic tone and wry smile indicated his disdain for city life.

'I can't believe I'm here. The scenery is spectacular,' said Vi, engrossed in the panorama, looking like a little girl experiencing the wonder of her first ever holiday.

Phil took them inside and showed them to their rooms. Vi had the privacy of the master bedroom, Graham the bunk room and Phil the dining area which converted into a double bed. Although the caravan was twenty years old it had been well maintained and was equipped with all mod cons. Statuettes of all shapes and sizes adorned the dark wooden shelves. Jade stones inscribed with Reiki symbols surrounded a golden Buddha who was flanked by figure heads of Athena and Socrates. An array of uncut crystals along with several ornamental candles and incense holders lined the mahogany ledge below the window. A huge hand carved eagle glared down from the top of a tallman, its piercing eyes glaring through the mesh of a hand-made Indian dreamcatcher. In one corner stood another carving: a wolf, the power animal that visited Phil during his hours of sleep. The diverse collection of artifacts created an ambience that embraced an air of eastern mysticism, the serenity of a Buddhist temple and the magic of Aladdin's cave.

'This is a wonderful place, Phil. It's got real character and so cozy and warm.'

'Thanks, Vi, I'm glad you like it. Make yourself comfortable while I prepare us some breakfast.'

Graham, a six foot three gentle giant with the appetite of a horse, couldn't wait for the scrambled egg and tomatoes on toast. He sat in the lounge, ravenously devouring a large bowl of cornflakes.

'I'd never get through the day without my cornies,' he mumbled, smacking his lips and clanging his spoon against the bowl. 'They're delicious.'

'They sound nice!' said Vi, giggling away.

'Vi,' Phil called, a look of mischief on his face, 'could you get two plates from that cupboard for you and I while I nip into the field and get a trough for G.'

Laughter.

Graham picked up a coaster and launched it at Phil.

'Now boys, behave yourselves!'

'Listen to Miss Innocent over there! I do believe you're the one that started it all!' said Phil.

After breakfast Vi and G courteously washed up while Phil erected a gazebo and set out some garden furniture on the lawn. When the chores were all finished Phil invited the others to join him outside.

'I thought we could use the next few days as a mini-workshop, an introduction to psychic phenomena and consciousness. During the day I thought we'd cover some theory and tomorrow and Sunday evening do some experiential work, leaving tonight free to relax – how does that sound?'

'Excellent,' said Vi. 'I'm really looking forward to it.'

'Sounds good to me,' said G, who was now tucking into some malt loaf. 'Would anyone like another cup of coffee before we begin?'

'I'll make it,' insisted Vi.

After a short interval the three reconvened and the theory commenced.

'So, for the first lesson. The first thing to understand is that everything in existence consists of energy and that physicality is an illusion. If I said to you that your body is actually 99.99% empty space what would your reaction be?'

Graham and Vi glanced at each other and shrugged their shoulders.

'Relapse comes to mind. Maybe you've reverted to the bottle!' said Vi, an impish grin on her face.

'I wouldn't really blame you,' replied Phil, chuckling to himself. 'Or maybe it's that your 99.99% empty space is concentrated between ears!'

Laughter.

'Anyhow, enough of the joviality and on with our lesson in quantum physics. The building blocks of everything that exists at a material level, including our so- called *physical* bodies, are atoms. The body, for instance, consists of cells which, in turn, are built up of molecules and these molecules are made up of atoms. If we continue the process of peeling away the layers that make up what appear to be solid objects, we find that the atom is made up of minute particles that are shooting through empty space at lightning speeds……..now here's where things start to get really interesting. Modern science has found that these tiny particles have no solidity whatsoever; they are literally tiny fluctuations of energy impressed with different types of information. If our eyes were replaced with sub-atomic lenses we would see the world in a whole new light: a vast sea of energy and information known as the quantum field. **The physical world as we know it is a mass illusion. This table, the chairs we're sitting on, those trees and our bodies are literally vibrating patterns of energy.**'

Graham and Vi looked at each other puzzled.

'But how come everything appears solid to us?'

'That's what I was coming to next, Vi. The energy patterns we refer to as our physical bodies are equipped with a mechanism known as perception. It is this faculty of our physiology that magically transforms the energy and information of the quantum field into the three dimensional world we call reality – and this is how it happens. When patterns of energy impinge on our nerve receptors, signals are sent to the brain. The brain then interprets this information as the three dimensional world we take to be reality.'

'Are you saying that the three dimensional world we deem *reality* is actually a construct that takes place in our head?' inquired Graham.

'Exactly, G., a mass illusion. Material reality is not external to us, it's inside us, which means it's a level of consciousness. Nothing exists outside us except waves of energy and information that form themselves into patterns. When these patterns interact with our body, which itself is a pattern of energy, they are interpreted as chairs, tables, trees, physical bodies and so on. Everything that takes place in the material world is actually a result of energy interacting with energy at the quantum level.'

'Oh, you've lost me now,' said a disheartened Vi.

'It's a difficult concept to grasp at first. Let me give you another example. The air around us is filled with television signals containing sound and video information. We can't see or hear them because they vibrate at a frequency that's beyond the limitations of our physical senses. When these signals reach your television set they are decoded and interpreted into a form you can comprehend: sound and video. Are you with me so far, Vi?'

'Yes, I understand that.'

'The energy and information of the quantum field can be likened to the T.V. signal before it's decoded: patterns of invisible energy and information travelling through space. Our system of perception can be compared to the decoding equipment in that it transforms the invisible energy of the quantum field into the three dimensional reality we're experiencing right now. Whereas the television signals are projected onto your T.V. screen, the information and energy of the quantum field is projected onto your internal screen and deemed reality. Does that make it any clearer?'

'I think so. Is it similar to putting on a virtual reality headset?'

'That's an excellent analogy, Vi, and as our system of perception is an integral part of our physiology we can't remove it. Therefore, we are permanently immersed in the movie of life, the three dimensional world we call reality. The only way we can break free from this reality is in altered states of awareness. I'll come back to this point later. For now let me recap on the story so far.

'We have seen that the quantum field is vast ocean of energy and information that is translated into solid form through a faculty of our physiology known as perception. Our so-called physical bodies and everything in the physical Universe are literally fluctuating patterns of energy and information. The physical world we experience on a moment-to-moment basis is a construct that takes place in our mind and therefore, and this is crucial, *it is a level of consciousness*. Everything we experience through the physical senses of taste, touch, sound, feeling and sight is literally an internal interpretation resulting from energy interacting with energy...... And...may I add....this is not metaphysical jargon or mere speculation, it is scientific fact........ are you both happy so far?'

'Yes, I think I've got it,' said Vi.

'Me too,' said G.

'Excellent, now let's take this one stage further. I said to you earlier that our bodies are actually 99.99% percent empty space. In fact, every perceivable solid object consists of 99.99% empty space at the quantum level. This means that the quantum field is a vast ocean of energy and information floating around in a huge void of apparent nothingness - can you visualize this?'

'Yes, like a gigantic swarm of mosquitoes arranging themselves into shapes, forming a ghostly image of the physical world.'

'Yes, that's a good way of looking at it, Vi. Now recently, scientists have taken a great interest in this apparent nothingness out of which the quantum field has arisen - the empty space that surrounds us - and their findings have been astounding. In short, they have found that it appears to be impregnated with intelligence. In fact, they are beginning to suspect what psychics, mediums, ancient rishis and gurus have known for thousands of years — *this so called empty space is a matrix of intelligence that contains many different levels of existence.*

'The physical world emerges from the quantum field and constitutes one layer of reality. Beyond the quantum field, and still largely undetectable by modern day scientific equipment, are successive layers of energy that become more refined as they ascend in frequency. Each of these layers constitutes another reality.

'When we die, or to be exact, go through transition, we don't go anywhere physically. Our awareness ascends and becomes immersed in another ocean of energy and information that vibrates at a much higher frequency than that of the quantum field. The fabric of these layers is so refined that the word *energy* is substituted by the word *spirit* – hence, the spirit world. Are you getting the bigger picture?'

Vi and Graham looked slightly flummoxed.

'I sort of understand but can you explain it a bit more,' said Vi.

'OK, let's go back to the TV analogy I used earlier. Remember me saying that the air around us is filled with invisible TV signals containing sound and video information?'

'Yes.'

'Let's say a broadcasting station is transmitting seven movies simultaneously and so seven invisible TV signals are travelling through space towards your TV set. The energy and information of each movie is transmitted at a different frequency to stop them interfering with each other, much like the seven bands of a rainbow – with me so far?'

'Yes, that's clear enough.'

'For simplicity, let's number these frequencies one to seven. Now, you are sitting at home in front of your TV and decide to watch movie one which is to be shown on channel one. When you press the button for channel one what you're actually doing is tuning your TV aerial to resonate with invisible frequency one – are you still following?'

'Yes, but keep it nice and slow.'

'The decoding apparatus in your TV takes the invisible energy and information of frequency one and magically transforms it into movie one. Now, although you are tuned to channel one and engrossed in movie one, it doesn't mean to say that the other movies have ceased to exist. They're still out in the ether, invisible to the senses. If you want to view them then you just have to adjust your tuner – is this making sense?'

'Yes, I'm with you so far,' replied Vi.

'Good, now let's look at this in terms of dimensions of existence, or levels of consciousness. In the space around us are gateways to other dimensions of existence, dimensions that are totally inaccessible via the physical senses, just like the seven invisible TV signals. These dimensions are beyond time and space as we know it. In our ordinary state of awareness we are permanently tuned to the three dimensional world of matter, just as you were engrossed in movie one when tuned to channel one – still with me?'

'Yes.'

'Just because you are tuned to the world of matter doesn't mean to say that these other refined levels of experience don't exist. They're just out of view, hidden in the empty space around us. It's just that you're not tuned into them. – still keeping up?'

'Yes.'

'To access them you have to shift your internal tuner, in other words, your awareness, to another level. Whereas the energy and information of the quantum field is decoded by your system of perception, you have to rely on your extrasensory functions of clairvoyance, clairaudience and clairsentience to access these other realities.'

'Now I'm getting the picture,' said Vi, 'Ah! Do you get it, the picture!'

The other two looked at her with unappreciative wry smiles.

'It's easy to see how we adjust our TV tuner but how can we adjust our awareness?' she continued.

'We do this naturally through dreams and consciously through practices such as meditation, mediumship and channelling. We also inadvertently tune into them in moments of inspiration and sudden spiritual experience.'

'Oh, of course,' said Vi.

'The physical world tends to dominate our minds purely because its energy is much denser than the highly refined energies of these other dimensions. The information from the spirit world presents itself in a much more subtle, and often abstract form, like a movie that's not tuned in properly – does this make sense?'

'Yes, that's painted a real clear picture in my mind,' said G.

'Yes, absolutely, and it also makes sense of why we're apt to dismiss spirit communication as imagination. Because the energies of the spirit world are so refined, they don't manifest in our minds anywhere near as vivid or prominent as the energy from the quantum field.'

'Precisely, Vi.........and let's also remember that we not only communicate with other Souls from these other dimensions we also communicate with a part of ourselves that exists there too - and this part is?....'

'Our Soul.'

'No need to call me that, Vi!'

Laughter.

'Exactly, our eternal essence, the Soul. Tomorrow I'd like to take a closer look at these hidden dimensions and make them more tangible, seeing how they fit into the bigger picture, but for now, let's recap.

'The material world, in essence, is an illusion created by the limitations of our physical senses. Although we deem ourselves to be individuals, having defined boundaries and appearing separate from one another, in reality, we're all part of the same energy field - the quantum field. The quantum field is one level of existence within a matrix of many other realities…Part of ourselves exists at these other levels too…. Everyone got that?'

The others nodded in agreement.

'Right, time for a break I think. I don't want to overload your minds. There's an awful lot to take in.'

*

Vi decided to spend a little time alone, a luxury her relentless schedule often prohibited. She strolled into a nearby field and sat on the grass, her back resting against the trunk of a large oak tree.

This whole world is in my mind. All the people on this planet share a collective reality which is manifest only in their minds. We're all wearing the same virtual reality headset. Everything happens within our consciousness. Our system of perception makes things appear solid and gives the illusion that the material world lies beyond us, but it's a mirage. And hidden in the space around us, out of reach of our physical senses, are other realities. But these also manifest in our minds, it's just that they're so subtle we dismiss them. They consist of extremely refined energy or spirit and are only accessible via our subtle senses: clairaudience, clairvoyance and clairsentience. I remember being taught at school that 'energy is neither created nor destroyed,' it just changes form. This is what happens to us. We don't die, we just change form and enter another reality. We are eternal. In fact, a large part of us already exists in these higher realms.

Her mind suddenly became still and her whole being softened. The voice of her Uniqueness returned.

You begin to awaken to your true essence, my child. You're emerging from a coma induced by the trappings of your physical shell. You are indeed a child of the Universe composed of shimmering stardust, a magical unique expression of the omnipotent power of the Source. You are boundless and eternal and have the power to manifest your every desire. Be prepared to clear the debris that impedes your growth, pave a pathway to the Universe and enter the gateway to your wealth.

Chapter 7

Subtle Anatomy

After a light lunch the trio settled down for another session, the subject of the afternoon being the localised or personal energy field.

'This morning we have seen that our body is an energy field,' Phil continued. 'It is actually one of a series of interlocking energy fields that make up our being as a whole. Energy is fluid and we are permanently exchanging information with other human beings, our environment and the spirit world. When we interact with others, we imprint some of our energy onto them and vice versa; the more powerful the interaction, the greater the energy exchange. In essence, we are made up of bits and pieces of other people: we absorb their thoughts, beliefs, and emotions through transactions of energy. Through this process the idea of who we are arises, the concept of self, but this is quite illusionary, as we shall see later. In addition, we exchange energy with entities from other dimensions and this too can play a fundamental role in the emergence of the concept of self.

'All of us have a personal Universe, an energy field that encompasses the totality of our experience. It can be described as an ellipse of light enveloping body, mind and spirit; a transceiver for thoughts and emotions and a gateway to our true eternal essence and the spirit world.

'What's a transceiver?' interrupted G.

'A transceiver is similar to a radio except it not only receives information, it transmits it, too. Our subtle anatomy is that part of our being that receives, transmits, accurately deciphers and stores information about our earthly environment and the spirit world then relays its impressions to us in the form of emotions, thoughts, images and intuition – does that answer your question big man?'

'Yes, loud and clear.'

'Our aura is an extension of who we are, revealing our history and current emotional, mental and spiritual status. It portrays our personality, how we relate to others and how we perceive ourselves. Working with our subtle anatomy can improve our physical, mental and emotional well-being as well as expanding our awareness and revealing our path to contentment and happiness. The shape, size and colours that make up a person's subtle anatomy are a great source of knowledge revealing information pertaining to the emotional, mental and spiritual well-being of the individual. When we tune into someone psychically, we are sensing information held in their energy field which can tell us a great deal about them. Incidentally, this is part of what we'll be doing tomorrow – OK so far?'

'Just one thing, Phil, is our aura and our subtle anatomy one and the same thing?'

'Not exactly, Vi. Our aura is part of our subtle anatomy. Each level of the aura is associated with one of the major chakras, spinning vortices of energy that act as selective filters for various kinds of emotional, mental and spiritual information. The chakras are gateways through which we transmit and receive information. I'll return to this subject very soon but for now just understand that our subtle anatomy is comprised of the auric layers and these chakras.'

'Right, OK.'

'Now let's take a closer look at this energy field. Our subtle anatomy consists of seven bands of energy that interpenetrate and surround the physical body. These layers are connected to each other as well as the physical body and the outside world via energetical gateways known as chakras, each layer being associated with one of the major chakras. One way to envisage our auras is to think of them as a set of Russian dolls, our physical body being the innermost doll; the only difference being that the levels of the aura not only encapsulate each other, the larger ones also occupy the same space as those inside it. That is, they interpenetrate one another.'

'How can they do that?' inquired G.

'Because the energy becomes more refined with each successive layer. The reason I can't occupy the same space as you is that our physical bodies are vibrating in the same frequency spectrum. If I vibrated at the same frequency as, let's say, a radio wave, I could pass straight through you – does this make it any clearer?'

'Yes, got it.'

'In addition, this also explains why other levels of reality can occupy the space around us. As they vibrate at a much higher frequency than that of the quantum field they can interpenetrate it. In fact, these alternate realities can be compared to a set of Russian dolls too, one overlaying the next and interpenetrating it, the physical Universe being the outermost doll, as we shall see later. This also explains why people with incredibly sensitive extrasensory perception actually see spirits walking about; they are tuned in to another channel so to speak....

'....are you OK so far?'

'Yes, but just one question - why are the levels of the aura called subtle bodies?' inquired Vi.

'Because they're generally invisible to the naked eye. They are bodies of refined light.'

'Right, I see.'

'Good, now on with the lesson. The first three levels contain information appertaining to the physical, emotional and mental aspects of our earthly self. The fourth layer is the bridge between our earthly self and the transpersonal aspects of our Soul. The upper three levels link us to our Soul and other divine expressions of the Source.'

'What exactly is the Source?' Said G.

'The Source is the spiritual clay from which everything is moulded. In essence, it is the Holy Spirit. I intend to take a closer look at this subject tomorrow. Can it wait till then?'

'Yes, certainly.'

'OK, let's return to our subtle anatomy. It'll prepare you for the experiential session tomorrow....

'...The first layer interpenetrates and extends just beyond the physical body and is called the etheric body or etheric double. It is an energetic mirror image of the physical body and each physical organ has an etheric counterpart. Any illnesses we experience will first manifest at this level then translate to the physical body. The etheric body is said to be laid down at conception, forming a matrix onto which the physical cells manifest……..any questions?'

'Is it just like a ghostly image of our physical body?'

'That's right, G…….

'…..Next we have the emotional body which extends just beyond the etheric body and stores the feelings that connect our thoughts to our physical body. When we're in a healthy state our emotions will be fluid but this level often becomes clogged up with emotional debris from the past. If we're intent on freeing ourselves from past conditioning then this level usually needs to be worked on. There are many energies within our aura that propel our actions, some of them being unconscious and inhibiting our lives. These energies encapsulate unresolved past issues that have been hidden from our conscious awareness. I don't want to get sidetracked here, but maybe at some future date we can take a deeper look at the emotional body.'

'That sounds interesting,' said G.

'On a brighter note,' continued Phil, 'this is also the level of creativity. Emotional energy seeks expression and can be channelled and translated positively into music, art, writing and painting etcetera. When our awareness enters this realm we start to move towards group consciousness and relations with others....

'.....The next layer, the mental body, extends just beyond the emotional body and deals with conscious thought, willpower and motivation. It embraces our concepts, beliefs, ideas, notions and earthly sense of who we are, or ego.'

'What exactly is the ego, Phil?' inquired Graham.

'If I asked you the question – who are you? What would be your response?'

'I am Graham Charles, fifty one years old, six foot three, like my own company, quite shy in nature, and so on.'

'These are all labels, concepts, ideas and beliefs about yourself that you hold to be true. Collectively they constitute your ego - who you *think* you are. The ego is very fluid in nature. You can change your name, ideas and beliefs about yourself and subsequently become a new person, so in many ways it's illusionary - do you get the idea, G?'

'Yes, it's just a lot of nonsense we've clung to and said that's me.'

'Couldn't have put it better myself! Now just one more thing before we move on. These levels don't act independently of each other, they influence each other and integrate to form a complete system. For instance, thought energy often goes through a sequence of unfolding, translating into emotional energy, inducing feeling in the physical body and ultimately driving our actions. Let me give you an example...

'...I have the thought that I'd like to go on holiday which induces a feeling of happiness and excitement. Here my mental body, containing the thought, has been linked to my physical body, the feeling, through emotion, which is the simultaneous fusion of thought and feeling. This emotion then translates into action and I go down to the travel agents and book the holiday. Do you see how the initial thought undergoes a rippling effect through the various bodies to become physical reality?'

'Yes, clearly,' said Vi, 'and it shows how important thoughts are: they determine our actions.'

'Precisely, Vi: **thoughts create our reality**…..Now, these first three levels, along with our physical bodies, constitute the physical, emotional and mental aspects of our earthly nature - everyone okay so far?'

'Yes,' replied Vi. 'Our earthly self is a series of interlocking energy systems, each influencing the next and driving the vehicle we call our physical body.'

'That's right, the information in our aura can be seen as the software that animates our physical body.'

'That's a good way of putting it,' said G.

'Now, extending beyond the mental body and bridging the earthly and divine aspects of ourselves, is the Bridge or body of the Higher Self. This is an extension of our Soul that manifests in the physical body and bridges the gap between our highly conditioned ego and the boundless potential of our eternal essence. Our Higher Self brings forward the inspiration and wisdom of our true essence, the Soul, and has great awareness and understanding of our everyday reality. When our awareness reaches this level we are able to relate to others in an ambience of unconditional love, oneness and affinity. From this height we're able to observe our thoughts, emotions and ego in a detached way. This level also brings forth a handful of carefully chosen past life memories from which our current life's purpose is born.'

'Is this the level of my Uniqueness?'

'Yes it is, Vi.'

'What's your Uniqueness?' inquired G.'

'I'll tell you about it some other time, it's a long story.'

'Sounds interesting.'

'The next three layers link us to the world of spirit and collectively constitute the Soul body. The first of these is called the etheric template and its functions are truth and communication. The second is the Celestial body which deals with higher spiritual love, spiritual ecstasy, inspiration, spiritual experience and vision. The third is the Ketheric layer, our gateway to the divine mind and spiritual enlightenment. This layer often signifies the presence of a spirit guide................

'.......Well that concludes our briefing of the auric layers – has anyone got any questions?'

'Yes,' said Vi. 'Can I go to the toilet? I'm bursting.'

'I'm afraid not, you must sit there listening to..' Phil began to emphasize his words '..the **gushing water** of the **river**, the **free flowing torrent**.....'

'I'm off.' Vi jumped up and dashed into the caravan. Phil and Graham sat chuckling as their rather desperate friend disappeared through the door.

'Make sure you use the ladies!' Phil shouted.

'As you do in restaurants!' a faint voice replied.

'Yes, but I'm only half an inch away from being a woman!' Phil retorted, with a smile from ear to ear.

'Bragging again!' replied the faint voice.

Vi returned after a few minutes looking rather relieved. Phil unexpectedly jumped to his feet and started to chase her.

'What were those comments you were making about me?'

The two engaged in playful combat like a pair of young fox cubs. Phil, temporarily forgetting Vi was a martial arts instructor, quickly found himself on his back, flat to the ground. He sprung up, swept her off her feet and carried her over to the river bank.

'Time for a swim,' he teased.

'No,' she yelled, amidst fits of laughter.

'Chuck her in!' shouted G, who was now munching his way through some fruit.

'Maybe later, G., for now we better get on with our theory - count yourself lucky, missie.'

Phil reluctantly put Vi down and the three reconvened around the table.

'Now where were we?'

'Subtle anatomy,' said G.

'Oh yes. In short, we have seen that the auric layers constitute levels of consciousness that deal with different aspects of both our earthly and transpersonal selves. These different layers don't act independently of each other; they influence each other and act as an integral whole. This means that information must ascend and descend through the various bodies, which now brings me to the final subject of today – chakras…

'..The word Chakra means "wheel" and comes from Sanskrit, the ancient religious and literary language of India. These energy centres spin just like small wheels or oscillating fans and act as selective filters drawing in, radiating, deciphering and then storing emotional, mental and spiritual energies in our aura. The seven major vortices are aligned along the etheric body fusing together the auric layers and allowing information to be passed between the various levels of consciousness that make up our being as a whole. Each one resonates to a specific colour and they are connected via a central column. Each chakra is also intimately connected to one of the major glands in the physical body. Before I move on to the specific functions has anyone got any questions?'

'Let me just get this clear,' said Vi. 'The layers of the aura are storage containers for information, memory banks for specific data. At the lower levels this consists of mental and emotional energy, whereas the upper levels store refined spiritual energy. All this information comes in and radiates out through the various chakras. The chakras also enable information to move from one layer to another as well as directing these energies to and from the physical body.'

'Excellent, Vi, so what we have is a network of energy canals routing spiritual and earthly information to various locations within our anatomy, the chakras themselves being gateways for various levels of consciousness. I tend to differentiate between the functions of the auric layers and the functions of the chakras as follows. Like you said, the auric layers are storage facilities for emotional, mental and refined spiritual energies, whereas the chakras are concentrated energy vortices that process and decipher this information then relay it to the physical body. When we experience turbulence, the chakras and aura can become clogged and unbalanced; dysfunctionality at any level will ripple through the whole system. Through practice we are able to identify and correct imbalances and disharmony within ourselves and other individuals - everyone happy?'

'Yes,' replied Vi and G.

'Good, so to finish today's lesson, I will just give you a brief overview of the function of each chakra, where it's located, the corresponding auric layer, the colour it resonates to and the gland it's associated with. You might like to get a pen and paper to make a few notes.'

Graham went into the van and returned with a couple of jotters and two pens.

'There you go, Vi, perhaps in return you'll make me a sandwich when we're finished.'

'You must be hungry. It's at least ten minutes since you last ate!' she replied, sarcastically.

'Ok, let's get this over with before G. wastes away! The information I'm about to give you is compiled from a number of sources including my own experiences and will serve as a guideline only. It's really important to develop your own intuitional understanding of the chakras and this will come with practice. When we tune into each other psychically we receive many impressions: intuitive thought, images, feelings and colours. The colours that radiate from the chakras are a great clue to the emotional, mental and spiritual well-being of the person you're reading, but their meanings are highly subjective, so I urge you to go with your own intuition. In general, if the colour of a chakra is murky rather than clear, it indicates disharmony…..anyway….here goes….pens ready….don't bother about the glands, just concentrate on the colours, locations and functions for now…

'The **base or root chakra** resonates to the colour red and is associated with the etheric body. It is situated at the bottom of the spine and associated with the adrenal glands. Its functions include self-preservation, power and vitality…

'Next we have the **sacral chakra** which resonates to the colour orange. It's associated with the emotional body and connected to the gonads. It can be found between the sexual organs and naval and relates to our emotions, creativity, relationships, enthusiasm and sensuality. In addition, this is the centre of clairsentience or clear feeling.'

'Just before you move on,' injected Vi, who was desperately trying to keep her face straight. 'What's a gonad?'

A smirk came to Phil's face. His eyes darted towards G. 'You're sitting next to one!' he exclaimed.

'It takes one to know one!' retorted G.

Phil went over to him and kissed him on his shaven head.

'I love you really big man,' he said, a huge grin on his face.

'Okay, time to move on before we lose the plot,' he continued. 'The third vortex is the **solar plexus chakra** which resonates to the colour yellow. It's associated with the mental body and connected to the pancreas. It's located between the naval and the sternum and relates to self-empowerment and mental activity.'

'Can you slow down a bit, Phil, I can't get it down fast enough.'

'Sorry, Vi, I got excited after kissing G!…Next we have the **heart chakra** which resonates to the colour green and is connected to the Bridge or body of the Higher Self. It relates to the thymus gland and immune system and is situated just above the sternum. It governs the Higher Mind but also influences emotions such as compassion, unconditional love, sympathy and empathy. It connects us with everything and denotes oneness, affinity, love and healing……..did you get that down, Vi?'

'Yes, keep it at that pace.'

'Moving on we have the **throat chakra** which is sky blue when healthy. It's associated with the etheric template and located in the hollow of the neck. It governs communication, speaking our truth, saying what we really feel, as well as our intuitive instincts. The throat chakra is also the centre of clairaudience, divine inspiration and telepathy…

'Just to diversify for a moment, recently, Theodore has urged me to speak the language of my heart which I interpreted as meaning speak my truth. It just struck me that many of us deny ourselves because we're unable to express our innermost desires. We calculate our responses according to the company we're in, or distort our truth due to fear. If we're not prepared to speak our truth we're very unlikely to attract what we truly want.'

'That's true,' said Vi. 'I never really tell people how I truly feel for fear of embarrassment, or appearing needy. I must bear that in mind and be prepared to change it.'

'That's good, Vi. These sessions often bring to light things we need to change. It's all about awareness......

'Next we have the **third-eye or brow chakra** which is indigo in colour and relates to the celestial body and pituitary gland. It's located between the eyes and is concerned with clairvoyance, spiritual intuition and spiritual will…

'Finally, the last of the seven, is the Crown chakra. Located just above the top of the head and resonating to the colour white or violet it is often depicted as the halo. It relates to the causal body and the pineal gland and connects us with the higher realms of existence. Its functions include enlightenment, divine will, certainty, the higher aspirations of the Soul, spiritual truth, divine inspiration and creativity.'

'Don't we have chakras in our feet and hands too?' inquired G.

'Yes, there are literally hundreds of minor chakras dispersed throughout the body but the feet and hand chakras are quite important. The feet chakras are situated in the soles of our feet and resonate to the colour brown. They enable us to connect to the earth and ground ourselves. In addition, they enable us to draw our planet's healing energies up into our bodies and discharge any unwanted energies. The hand chakras have no specific colour; they are connected directly to the heart chakra and used to channel healing energies.'

'Right, thanks Phil.'

'Now I have given you much to contemplate but the main thing to take from all this information is that our being is very fluid in nature. We are comprised of information and energy and are permanently exchanging information and energy with both our earthly environment and the spiritual planes. Our being is a localised bundle of energy within a huge network of energy spanning many dimensions of existence. Who we consider ourselves to be at any point in time is dependent on our level of awareness. If we are absorbed in our everyday reality then we tend to feel confined and somewhat powerless. The person we think we are is an illusion, a collection of labels, ideas concepts and beliefs that we've identified with and called 'I'. The software that programs us at this level has come from messages we've received about ourselves since we were children: the internalised scripts of our lives. At this level we are actors playing out roles from scripts that other people have written for us. However, when we raise our awareness, we realise that we're not only actors but directors and producers of our own lives. When our awareness reaches the level of our Higher Selves and Souls we tap into the boundless potential that is our rightful heritage. How does that make you feel?'

'Full of hope and anticipation,' replied Vi.

'Hungry!' replied G., who was immediately pelted with scrunched up paper.

'Right, it's three fifteen. Time to relax and do whatever you wish. I'm going to rest for an hour and listen to some music, then I'll prepare dinner. I thought we'd all follow Vi's example and have vegetable lasagne – how does that sound?'

'Sounds good to me,' said G. 'What time will it be?'

'Say about six.'

'Think I'll go for a walk.'

'I'll stay here and relax,' said Vi.

Chapter 8

A Prophecy

The sky had cleared and the warm September sun beat down. The surrounding mountains took on exceptional beauty in the new light. Vi watched as a kestrel hovered over the adjacent field eyeing its unsuspecting prey. Phil went to the garden shed and retrieved a comfortable sun lounger for her to relax on.

'There you go, settle yourself down and enjoy the sun.'

'Thanks, Phil. I think I'll read for a while. Have you got any books that'll help my understanding of the things we've learnt today?'

Phil smiled. 'I guess you haven't opened the door next to your bed. Go and take a look.'

Vi went inside, opened the cupboard next to the bed and found it stacked high with books on every conceivable subject concerning mind, body, and spirit. As she searched through and perused them, she noticed a plastic wallet containing a document headed 'Prologue'. She removed it from the wallet and began to read.

PROLOGUE

From the epicentre of creation surged an infinite resource of pure potentiality, a divine energy imbued with the highest form of creative intelligence, subsequently known as God and the Source of all life. A vast void was filled as this omnipotent force moulded itself into a spectrum of realities, a landscape through which its ultimate expression, the Soul, would journey.

The Soul, a differentiated aspect of the source, is nature's privileged child; the vehicle through which the universal mind experiences and expands. Endowed with a sense of individuality and free will, each Soul has risen from a divine ocean of consciousness and set out on an eternal journey spanning many dimensions of existence.

To experience life at various levels of existence the Soul has to be encapsulated in a body of light that vibrates at the same frequency as the dimension in which it is incarnate. The function of this body is to absorb, transform and express information from that dimension. As the Soul travels from one dimension to another it accumulates these bodies or layers of experience which encompass the totality of its existence. In essence, the Soul is a multidimensional being having an energetical expanse that permeates every level of being.

At the uppermost levels the Soul is aware of unification with all that is. It is immersed in a sea of consciousness in which there is no sense of separation or divide. This 'synergenistic' state, we term love. As the Soul travels down into denser realms of existence it starts to feel a sense of separation from its roots. From this divided state the devil known as fear is born.

The densest level of experience consists of each Soul being clad in a body of matter. At this level Souls manifest themselves as planets, mountains, seas, lakes, animals and humans which comprise the physical world as we know it. One such Soul is the planet Earth which allows mankind, as well as many other kingdoms and species to have their being there.

On earth people have been endowed with a sense of self through an extension of their being known as the ego. This sense of 'I' is highly susceptible to the hypnosis of social conditioning and the accumulation of mental and emotional debris obstructs communication with its eternal essence, the Soul.

Earth has reached a critical era; the illusion of mortality has become the catalyst from which all conflict has arisen. People have entered a somnambulistic state, confused, frustrated and lacking purpose. Narcissism has prevailed and large swathes of society have become fragmented. Demarcation is at its zenith and fear is wreaking havoc. The sense of estrangement from others has resulted in complete dissonance. The battle for power is spiralling out of control and fear gathering momentum. People are inflicting punishment on themselves, parents are abusing their children, gangs fight openly on the streets and countries threaten nuclear war on each other in the name of peace. Many people are seeking refuge in mind-altering drugs and reverting to crime to fuel their addictions. This is leading to an ever deepening pit of social malaise. The human race is in danger of self destruction and time is of the essence in its liberation.

In an attempt to dissolve the conflict and combat fear, beings from higher dimensions have orchestrated a grand symphony. Many are choosing to incarnate and subject themselves to the same rites of passage as their predecessors. They are choosing to experience trauma on earth enabling them to empathize with human beings in an attempt to re-unify them with their Soul and re-perpetuate the meaning of their existence.

Two such Souls are about to embark on such a quest and in the process of preparation. They are part of a nine entity collective consciousness known as Ellissia. Seven of the nine beings have experienced many lifetimes on earth and accumulated great wisdom. These seven will remain disincarnate and act as spirit guides to the two initiates who are about to set out on a adventure. This is to be no easy quest. Many who have previously tried have fallen victim to the harsh reality of life on earth, becoming detached from their eternal essence, and finding themselves abandoned in a desolate wasteland of despair.

*

Just as Vi finished reading, the door opened and in walked Phil.

'Find anything interesting?'

'Well there's plenty to choose from; there's more books here than in the local library!' she commented, with a smile. 'This caught my attention – What is it?'

'Oh you found that – come through and I'll explain.'

They went through to the lounge and Phil began to tell the story behind the document.

'When I had my first experiences with Theodore, my guide, he told me that I'd one day pen a bestselling novel. The money generated from the book was to be used to found a holistic healing centre somewhere out in the country. He hinted that I'd be *given* the book, so, naturally, I thought I'd just sit down and channel the information directly from him. That didn't happen and the inspiration for the story-line still eludes me. That document was an attempt to put into story form some of the teachings of Theodore and it holds a lot of truth, but after I'd completed it, I couldn't move on. I couldn't put it into a practical earthly context without over dramatizing. There are millions of people out there, Vi, searching for answers and I want to write a book that combines spirituality and psychology to provide the answers they're looking for, something that will help them at a very practical level. I've gained a wealth of knowledge and experience since my initial encounters with Theodore. I got a degree in psychology, trained as a hypnotherapist, become a Reiki master and I'm now training to be a psychodynamic counsellor. It's the practical application of these different things, along with my spiritual experiences that have transformed my life and I want to relay this knowledge to the public in the form of a novel. The only time I'm truly happy is when I'm involved in this work. It's a vocation.'

Vi could feel the conviction in Phil's voice.

'I just can't see where the money is going to come from for my centre, yet I trust Theodore; he has never let me down. In actual fact, there are two major things that haven't come to fruition: the book and a child. Theodore said I'd have a child, a very special child, a prodigy who would carry my work into forthcoming generations. I've never really given any thought to having children. It seems highly unlikely now. I'm 43 years of age and have more or less resigned myself to never having any – and so, that's the story behind the story, so to speak.'

'You mustn't give up hope, Phil, there's plenty of time. This prologue is excellent. I'm sure you'll succeed, and as for the child, who knows, some people have children quite late on in life nowadays.'

'You're absolutely right. I mustn't let go of my vision - and Vi,' he paused and smiled at her warmly, 'you mustn't let go of yours either. You will find your true home, that very special place where you belong. The flower you're supposed to choose, the one in your dream, will reveal itself and you will blossom, I'm sure.'

She reciprocated his smile and they engaged in a warm embrace.

'Right, I'm off outside to read this book, and the next book I'm going to read will be your bestseller,' said Vi, cheerfully.

'Thanks, sweetie. Suppose I best prepare dinner or Graham will eat the furniture when he returns!'

'He can eat for Britain!' laughed Vi. 'See you later.'

81

On her way out she came to a sudden halt. 'Phil!'

'Yes, Vi.'

'I noticed your guitar in the bedroom. Will you play it for us later?'

'Your wish is my command, princess. I certainly will. See you later.'

After reading for a while Vi ambled over to the river's edge and become deeply immersed in herself, the hypnotic effects of the fast flowing water sending her into light trance. She thought how the river was symbolic of her life, a fast flowing current sweeping her in a direction she didn't want to go, the small eddies representing those stages where she constantly went around in circles, apparently going nowhere.

As she stood and contemplated her life, all her senses appeared to heighten, colours became vivid and her hearing acute. A white-letter hairstreak butterfly flitted by and began to encircle her as though trying to attract her attention. Eventually it came to rest on a nearby Elm tree. She stared at it fixatedly: it seemed to take on a luminescent appearance, everything else fading into insignificance. Her mind stilled, a presence embraced her and a familiar voice returned.

Transformation, dear child; the butterfly's essence is that of transformation. It has four stages in its life cycle: the egg, a beginning, an awareness that change is needed and that your old way of life no longer works; the caterpillar, the stage of identifying which areas of your life warrant change; the chrysalis, contemplation, introspection, going within and deciding how you will manifest the needed changes; and finally the birth of the butterfly, action and the spreading of your wings...

…Many humans recognize a need for change in their lives but are too frightened to put their feelings and thoughts into action. They get caught up in the chrysalis stage, cocooned in a rigid shell of fear. When this happens, learn from the courage of the butterfly. The world awaiting the butterfly outside the cocoon is totally different from anything it has ever known during other stages of its life cycle, yet it sheds its shell and takes to the skies without fear or hesitation – your transformation begins now, dear child, **be prepared to follow the full life cycle.***'*

Vi slowly returned to her ordinary state of awareness and watched as the butterfly took to the skies. At that moment Phil came out of the caravan and glanced across to where she stood. He was fascinated by what he saw. The stress and tension that usually dominated her features had completely vanished. There was no trace of the anger that constantly dogged. A light mist seemed to envelope her and she exuded an air of innocence and purity, looking almost angelic. Phil was magnetized by this apparent transformation: she looked exactly how she had in his vision. Time appeared to stand still. He felt a memory being unlocked within, sensing he'd known her for ever. He stood for a while and appreciated her beauty, then slowly strolled across and stood beside her.

'Happy?' he inquired.

'Extremely, Phil. I haven't felt like this for a long time. Thanks for inviting me.'

'The pleasure's all mine. It's amazing to think that just a short time ago the three of us were going through hell, and look at us today, completely different people: relaxed, happy and contented. I didn't know G. had such a sense of humour. He's normally so quiet and withdrawn and has difficulty mingling with people, but not today. He really seems at home. And you, Vi, I don't ever remember seeing you this way. You look about ten years younger and if you don't mind me saying so….'

He paused for a moment and gazed at her.

'You look quite beautiful.'

She gave a nervous little laugh and began to blush, a child-like smile lighting up her face. The two stared at each other for a moment, then the silence was broken by another familiar voice.

'Is dinner ready yet?' roared G., whose figure emerged from beyond some trees.

Phil and Vi looked at each other and burst into fits of laughter.

'The stomach has returned,' said Phil. 'Better get inside and serve dinner.'

'I'll give you a hand.'

'Did you enjoy your walk, G?' Phil inquired, as G. caught up with them.

'Yes, I went up that big hillside overlooking the caravan site.'

'Oh, that'll be Southern Fell, the views are spectacular up there.'

After dinner Phil lit some candles, doused the lights and the trio made themselves comfortable in the lounge. They chatted about the day, discussing the spiritual concepts in further detail. G. and Vi had many more questions and Phil happily gave them the answers. Later on in the evening Phil got out his guitar and sang some soothing ballads; the others joined in. Towards the end of the night he sang the Irish ballad 'Danny Boy' which brought a tear to everyone's eyes. Around midnight they all decided to retire.

Vi went into the bedroom, took out her notebook and started to record her latest encounter with her Uniqueness.

I'm at the egg stage, she thought. *I know I need to make changes in my life but I'm just unclear as to what changes to make. I suppose I'm in a lot of fear. I know my life isn't working but it's the only life I've ever known and I'm scared of making major changes. I guess it's time to move on to the caterpillar stage and become clear as to what changes I need to make.*

She placed her notebook back in her bag, switched off the bedside lamp and fell asleep.

Phil made up his bed in the dining area, propped up his pillows and lay back relaxing. A few minutes passed by when the stillness of his mind was broken by a melodious verse.

> *Hush little baby don't say a word*
> *Daddy's gonna a buy you a mocking bird*
> *And if that mocking bird don't sing*
> *Daddy's gonna buy...............*

Strange, why is that tune going around my mind?

The longer it persisted the more he felt it resonating with something deep within. Wisps of emotion began to fleet through his body as his feelings intensified. The melody continued to echo through his mind for a while and then slowly began to fade. As it did, he started to sense a very familiar presence enveloping him. The vivid image of an Indian squaw materialized in his mind's eye, her piercing hazel eyes, deep olive skin, high cheekbones and jet black shoulder length hair threaded into two rows of plaits revealing her astounding beauty. Phil felt his heart chakra opening like a lotus flower and an emerald green shaft of light projecting out and coalescing with her spirit, unifying them like an umbilical cord. Every cell of his body danced with a vibrancy as he bathed in her healing energy, her intense love permeating the very core of his being.

Esba, what is it? He asked mentally.

There was no reply but he noticed a shimmering form beginning to materialize in Esba's arms. As it became clearer, he could see it was a baby. Esba stood in silence smiling, rocking and cradling the child in her arms. The image stayed imprinted in Phil's mind for a few minutes then slowly faded away as he felt Esba's energy withdrawing from his body.

What was that all about? He thought. *Esba can be quite abstract and elusive at times. What was she trying to tell me? Was she indicating that the child Theodore once spoke about will manifest? Or is it a rebirth of some other kind?*

He tussled and mused over these questions for a while, his wary mind unable to make much sense of them, then, still feeling the effects of Esba's warmth, he drifted into a deep sleep.

Chapter 9

The Universal Mind:
an Infinite Expanse of Consciousness.

Phil arose early the next morning and decided to take a walk. The air was crisp and fresh and imbued with the invigorating scent of wild flowers. A shallow mist rose from the dewy ground weaving its way through trees and hedgerows adding an air of mysticism to the scenery. He followed the contours of the meandering river through several fields and into some woodland where he found a spot to rest and contemplate. This morning his mind was filled with only one thing – Vi.

What happened yesterday when I saw her beside the river? There was a graciousness and purity about her that seemed so familiar yet I've only ever seen her looking that way in a vision...... It felt as though a long lost memory had returned and I was being reunited with someone I'd known for eternity... I felt an inexplicable bond, a oneness that surpassed anything I've ever felt before...

...Today I'm filled with this intense feeling of love for her - what's happening?......Is she my Soul mate? It appears that we've spent at least one previous lifetime together... or is it simply that I'm falling in love with her? ...Surely not. I've known her for seven years and I've never seen her in that light before.

His thoughts began to drift to his recent encounter with Theodore.

The surface is about to become tempestuous, he said. What was that all about? At the time I intuitively linked it with Vi...... He also spoke about fighting fear with love and speaking the language of the heart - speaking the truth.... It feels like I'm being prepared for some sort of battle involving Vi

- What could it possibly be?... I guess I'll just have remain vigilant and see what materializes.

As he ambled back through the woods, the silence broken only by the interference of his thoughts, he heard a faint rustling sound behind him. He slowly turned around and could barely make out the outline of a large animal peering at him through the mist. As he moved closer, he was able to discern that the curious creature was a deer. Well versed in the teachings of Native American Indian medicine by guide, Esba, he began to contemplate the meaning of this encounter.

Gentleness - the deer teaches us to use the power of gentleness to fight our battles. Am I being given another weapon to add to my artillery for this elusive battle?...Love and gentleness are not about fighting; they're about surrendering.

His intuition began to kick in.

Paradoxically, I feel this war is to be won by surrendering,...I'm being told to drop my defences and let my true essence overwhelm the enemy... my opponent is already wounded... dropping my defences is about letting go of pride and speaking the language of the heart... this is the strategy that will bring victory.

His thoughts began to slowly dissipate as the deer became enveloped in mist and vanished.

Vi had arisen not long after Phil and had also decided to take an early morning walk. As she strolled along the river bank she thought about a dream she had had during the night.

Violent waves rolled in from the ocean crashing against the cliff causing it to fracture and crumble. She had tumbled over the edge and was clinging on for dear life. Her partner, Tom, gripped her hand tightly and tried to pull her back up to

safety. As she struggled, she became tired and weak. Part of her just wanted to let go but she was terrified of what lay below. She felt her hand slipping, then awoke.

These dreams really are meaningful, she thought. *This one appears to be about my crumbling relationship with Tom… I know it's a great source of unhappiness but the thought of letting go fills me with fear… On the positive side I can trust him, he's loyal, reliable, honest and provides security… From a negative perspective, he doesn't like to participate in any of the leisure activities I enjoy. He'd sooner stay in and mope around the house. He's very insecure where money is concerned and tends to watch every penny. When I go out with other people and enjoy myself he puts an immediate damper on it, seemingly not wanting my happiness. In fact, one statement he often makes is that 'you shouldn't get too happy or you're in for a downfall'… what a terrible grey outlook to have on life… I've tried so many times to change him but it's like flogging a dead horse. In many ways he's an old man in a young man's body… I know I'm not the easiest person to live with. I have this great propensity towards anger which causes me to explode and he often gets the brunt of it…I don't know why I'm like that, I just get so frustrated… Most of the time I feel like his mother. I've played that role all my life and I don't want it anymore… I'm really scared of leaving him and being left on my own. It takes me so long to gain trust in men. I'd really like someone who'll love and care for me. I've done it for others all my life. Someone to have fun and adventure with, someone who'll nurture me and treat me like a lady… This dream really does reflect my situation, not wanting to be where I am but terrified to let go. In other words, I still don't know which flower to choose… At least the signposts are beginning to emerge.*

The events of the previous day came to mind.

I guess I'm at the caterpillar stage, identifying areas of my life that need changing. Maybe if I have the courage to go through the full life cycle and let go of that crumbling cliff then, instead of falling into the stormy ocean, I will take to the skies, just like the butterfly, and fly to that special place where I belong.

Phil and Vi returned within a few seconds of each other to find G. chasing a hen around the caravan.

'There's food in the fridge, G. You don't have to hunt for your breakfast!'

Vi glanced at Phil and bit her bottom lip.

'I made some breakfast for us all and decided to have mine outside…,' panted G., continuing to give the unsuspecting bird a run for its money. 'I put it on the table, went to make a cup of coffee and when I came back she was on the table helping herself - typical of women you can't turn your back on them for a minute!'

'Excuse me!' retorted Vi. 'Less of the sexist remarks, please.'

'All creatures bring us wisdom, G.,' Phil continued, antagonistically. 'Learn from the Native American Indians and discern the messages that the animals bring you. That hen is telling you that you're going to start your day in a "foul" mood.'

'Oh sod off!' retorted an exhausted G., who had now abandoned his pursuit of the terrified hen.

'See, it's taught you another thing, too.'

'What's that?'

'**Foul** language!'

Vi and Phil burst into fits of laughter. G. glared at them and tried to cover his smile with a grimace.

'Oh look,' said Vi. 'A horse.'

A smirk came to Phil's face, 'would you believe it, another animal message for G.'

'Oh what now?'

'He's saying what's with the long face, big fella!'

Vi and Phil began to roll about laughing.

G. rushed into the caravan, grabbed an egg from the fridge and went to launch it at Phil. As he did, his heavy hands clamped the egg so hard that it smashed. The other two were now in hysterics.

'Glad you're up for the crack,' Phil said mockingly, his face now stained with tears of laughter.

'Only yoking,' taunted Vi.

When the pantomime ended they all settled down and converged around the table for breakfast.

'Did you enjoy your walk, Phil?'

'Yes - I did, Vi.' He replied, without elaborating. 'And you?'

'It was really interesting.'

'So what are we doing today?' injected G.

'Would you like to know the "pecking" order?'

'Oh don't start all that again.'

'Yesterday I gave you a lot of information. The reason I did so was to show how science is converging with spirituality and beginning to slowly prove what many of our wise elders have known for centuries. In addition, if you decide to pursue this path you'll hear people speaking of energies, auras, chakras etcetera and I thought this info would give you an idea of what all this esoteric language is about.'

'It's certainly helped. It was quite difficult to grasp, but it gave much food for thought.'

'That's good, G. As you meditate and channel you'll experience the truth in it all.'

'Phil.'

'Yes, Vi?'

'Could you type up a document containing all this information? Something we can study?'

'Yes I ……….'

Phil's mind began to wander as he became distracted by the image of a rainbow coloured folder in his mind's eye. It slowly rotated through 180 degrees to reveal the ghostly outline of a wolf on the front cover. He began to realise that by compiling documents now, he was actually preparing course material that he would teach in the future, hence the wolf - the teacher. This weekend was a signpost in itself.

He regained his composure, saying nothing to the others, and carried on with the conversation.

'Sorry - where was I… Oh yes, certainly, Vi, I'll do it next weekend when I'm up here alone.'

The three laughed, joked and talked about a variety of subjects over breakfast, then began to settle down for the day's lesson.

'First of all, let's see what you remember from yesterday – What are chakras?'

'Energy vortices that receive, transmit and decipher various information from both our earthly environment and the world of spirit.'

'Well done, Vi – where is this information stored?'

'In the corresponding layers of the aura.'

'Excellent, G. - why are the auric layers referred to as levels of consciousness?'

'Because they're layers of our mind, each dealing with different types of information. The lower three are connected to the physical, emotional and mental faculties of our everyday reality; the middle one is a bridge to our transpersonal selves and the upper three are connected with the divine aspect of ourselves and the spirit world.'

'Right, now what lies in the space around us?'

'A spectrum of other realities.'

'In simple terms these other planes of existence can be collectively referred to as…?'

'The spirit world.'

'Correct…. Now today I want to take a look at these other planes of existence and keep things as simple as possible. You've had the scientific explanations, let's now look at the spiritual side and make these abstract concepts tangible…

'…Yesterday, G., you asked about the Source and I said it was the spiritual clay from which everything is moulded. Today I'm going to elaborate on this….

'The Source is the ultimate in creative intelligence, a limitless resource of divine light that exists as both pure potential and moulded experience. Many of the ancient Rishis and Gurus were in agreement about one thing – **we are all from the one body of consciousness.** Let me read you a passage from the prologue I wrote in order to expand on this…

'From the epicentre of creation surged an infinite resource of pure potentiality, a divine energy imbued with the highest form of creative intelligence, subsequently known as God and the source of all life. A vast void was filled as this omnipotent force moulded itself into a spectrum of realities, a landscape through which its ultimate expression, the Soul, would journey.

'What this is saying is that the Source is the ultimate mind or the Universal mind as it is often called. This is the one body of experience of which we're all expressions. Put simply, the Source, or the Divine Mind, once existed as pure potential and wanted to experience, expand and evolve. As sunlight divides into the seven colours of the rainbow, so the divine light of the Source moulded itself into various levels of experience. These are the dimensions we're going to talk about shortly, each plane being a level of consciousness within the Divine Mind. Can you envisage this?'

'Yes, just like our own being is divided into different levels of consciousness.'

'That's right, Vi. In many ways our own personal Universe replicates the bigger picture. As the microcosm so the macrocosm so they say.... So to continue, the spiritual landscape is now in place but the Source needed explorers to traverse these worlds and expand and evolve its experience. So the divine energy further differentiated into localised bundles of intelligence known as Souls.'

'Let me get this straight,' said Vi. 'I see this as being like a tree. The trunk is the Source from which everything else stems. The branches are the different levels of experience or dimensions, and the leaves are the individual Souls experiencing these various realities.'

'That's an excellent analogy, Vi: everything is an extension of the Source. The leaf is not separate from the tree but it does have its own individuality, so to speak. One point I might make is that the leaves on the branches nearest the trunk are closer to their roots, just as the Souls in the higher dimensions are much closer to their spiritual roots.'

'Right.'

'Now to experience life at these various levels of existence, the soul has to be encapsulated in a body of light that vibrates at the same frequency as the dimension in which it's residing. The function of this body is to absorb, transform and express information from that dimension. As the soul travels from one dimension to another it accumulates these bodies or layers of experience which encompass the totality of its existence.'

'Just like the Russian Dolls.'

'Yes, Vi - exactly. Now yesterday we spoke about information being passed up and down the chakras and the Soul level of our being encompassing the totality of our eternal experiences, remember?'

'Yes,' they both replied.

'Let's now have a look at what happens at our time of transition. When we die our physical body goes back to the earth. The accumulation of emotional and mental energy containing our whole life's experience ascends from the lower bodies, via the chakras, to the level of our Soul. This means that the emotional, or Astral Body as it is often called, is freed up and available for use. During transition our awareness enters the emotional body and this becomes the primary vehicle through which we explore the Astral planes. All that happens at death is that we exchange one cloak for another of finer fabric and, in Vi's terminology, put on a different virtual reality headset – do you follow?'

'Yes, energy is neither created nor destroyed; it just changes form,' said Vi.

'Exactly…OK let's move on and look at these various worlds. The earthly dimension is the lowest in terms of frequency. Here the energy is more dense than the subsequent levels which are known as the Soul planes…

'…The lower Astral plane is closest in frequency to the material plane and hopefully we'll give this dimension a miss when we leave here. The reason being is that this is the level often referred to as Hell or purgatory. It is where our awareness goes when we've been extremely self indulgent on earth. People who have committed horrific crimes: murderers, rapists, drug dealers, terrorists and so on, who haven't owned their actions stay at this level until they're able to acknowledge their misdeeds and repent. These entities often fail to acknowledge their death and roam around on this plane lost and confused. When we channel or do psychic work we have to protect ourselves from these lower entities because they can leech onto us and cause problems. An example of a lower Astral entity is the poltergeist.'

'I notice you say *entity* rather than Soul. In some books I've read it says the *Soul* becomes lost.'

'There are differences of opinion about this. Theodore says no Soul is evil and remains at the level of enlightenment. It is the ego or personality complex of energy that becomes lost. Simply put, what he's saying is that the ego becomes severed and goes astray, failing to reunite with the eternal, loving essence of the Soul.'

'What happens to this part on the lower astral level?'

'Well there is no punishing God as such. This aspect becomes its own judge and jury. Still ensnared in greed and narcissism, it is unable to ascend to the harmonious planes and suffers dearly as a result of its wrong-doings. Its own Soul, in conjunction with other Souls, will work with it and try to disperse the dark elements with light until it repents and is able to move on.'

'So where do most of us go after transition?'

'The higher Astral plane is where most who have lived a fairly decent life on earth go after transition. This is the level that mediums reach through clairvoyance, clairaudience and clairsentience. Such people have brought through much valuable information from this plane and most say it is similar to ours except its harmonious and serene. Here our sense of individuality is still in tact and we still experience emotion in some form. Colours are said to be much more vivid and the energy much more refined. Here we review our lives, acknowledge our mistakes and successes, and continue to evolve. Animals are said to reside here also.'

'I often wondered what happened to animals,' commented Vi. 'It's nice to know that my cats will go to a nice place when they pass over...... so what comes after the astral plane?'

'The next in vibrational frequency to the Astral plane is the Mental plane. This is commonly referred to as Heaven. As its name suggests, our primary vehicle for exploring this dimension is the mental body. Here form starts to disintegrate and everything is composed of shimmering light; we exist on this plane as pure intelligence only. Spiritual leaders, great teachers and spirit guides reside at this level. My guide, Esba, exists primarily at this level. She is a being of pure light.'

'But you said Esba was an Indian squaw?'

'Good point, Vi. When spirit guides communicate with us they often send images of themselves as they were in a past incarnation. This is so we can personify them and perceive them in a form that is tangible. In reality they are neither male nor female; they are pure consciousness or spirit.'

'Oh, I see. What level does Theodore exist at?'

'Fundamentally, the next level, the Celestial plane. But these entities can traverse the different realities at will.'

'Actually, Phil, I thought you'd just made these invisible friends of yours up because you haven't got any other friends!'

Phil picked a pen up off the table and flung it at Vi. 'Did I tell you that witches also end up on the lower Astral plane?'

Laughter.

'So where to next, Phil?' said G.

'As we ascend further we enter the Celestial plane. Here our sense of individuality starts to disperse and we enter unity consciousness. We still have a sense of self but we recognise everything is a mere extension of everything else. This is the level of the angels, extremely enlightened guides, Jesus, Buddha and so on –

I wouldn't worry about this place too much if I were you, G., you'll never be an angel - greed is one of the seven deadly sins!'

Laughter.

'Next is the causal plane. Here all sense of individuality disperses and everything merges as one. This is the level that holds the records of every Soul's eternal experiences, often referred to as the Akashic records.'

'So are the Akashic records like a giant library containing the experiences of every lifetime of every Soul?'

'That's right, Vi. Every thought and every emotion are said to be recorded here along with the accumulation of our ancestral wisdom.'

'So is this the highest plane?'

'No there's one more. The seventh dimension is literally pure potentiality waiting to be moulded into experience. It's the epicentre, if you like, of that limitless reservoir of divine intelligence in its purest form.'

'Just to get this straight in my mind,' said G., 'we have emerged from the pure potential of the Source, travelled through each of these dimensions to the Material plane. At each level we've been given a body of light through which we experience that particular layer…'

He paused to think for a moment.

'Something just occurred to me - are the layers of the aura the accumulation of these bodies?'

'Well spotted, G. Yes they are, and through our subtle anatomy we are connected to every level of existence, just like radios receiving many different broadcasts – everyone happy?'

'Yes the pieces of the jigsaw are really coming together now,' said Vi.

'Good, just before we have a break I'll show you a diagram that should make things a little clearer.'

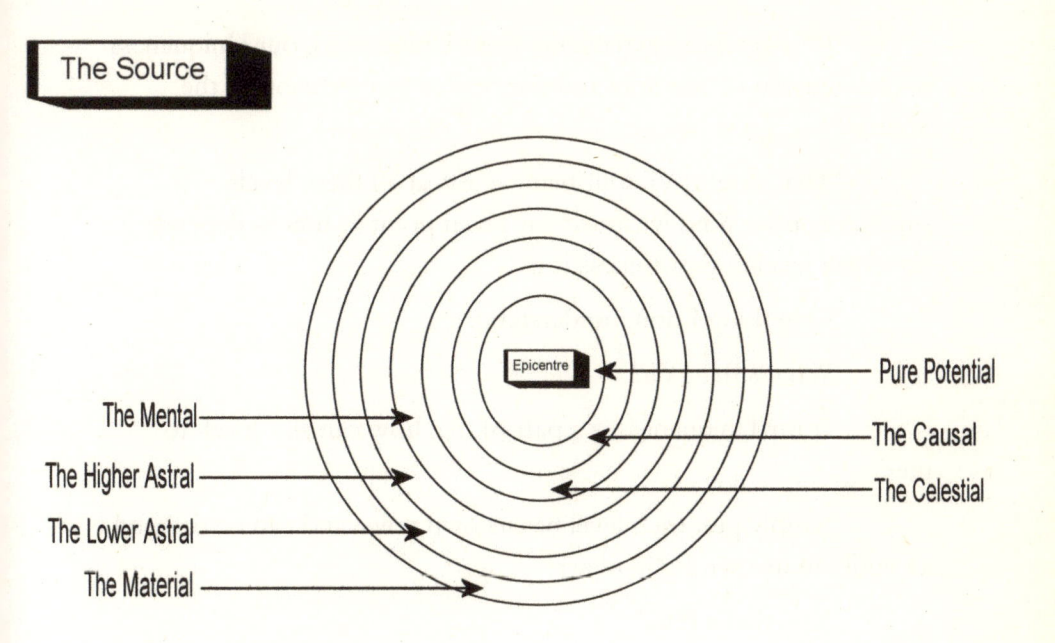

The Source

- Epicentre — Pure Potential
- The Mental
- The Higher Astral
- The Lower Astral
- The Material
- The Causal
- The Celestial

'There you go, seven movies showing in the one multiscreen cinema of the Source. The cinema is the one body of consciousness in which everything is housed. Each movie represents life on a single layer or level of the divine consciousness. The actors, scenery, directors and producers are all moulded from the same fabric: the divine light of the Source. We are currently playing a role in the movie of the material world but throughout the course of our eternal journey we jump from one movie to another. I must add, this is a simplistic overview of the bigger picture; I feel certain there's much more to it than this. Maybe we'll gain further insight as our journey progresses. But, for now, I hope it helps.'

'It certainly does, it explains a lot of things. My Uniqueness said we're all extensions of the one body and let me look…..'

She removed her notebook from her bag.

'Our ego is an extension of our Uniqueness, our Uniqueness is an extension of our Soul and our Soul is an extension of the Source.'

'That's right, Vi. Our being exists at all these levels simultaneously. Who we are at any given point in time is dependent on which level our awareness is at.'

'One thing I don't understand.'

'What's that, Vi?'

'If my Uniqueness is a part of me, how can she speak to me?'

'Simply put, each level has its own voice and can be deemed an entity in its own right, okay?'

'Yes, that's fine.'

'Shall we break for lunch and this afternoon we'll move on to channelling in preparation for tonight?'

G. decided to go for a stroll along the river while Phil and Vi prepared a salad for lunch. After they'd finished and plated the food, they sat outside in the warm September sun.

'You look so well, Vi.'

'I feel it, Phil; I don't want this break to end.'

'Well, you're welcome here anytime.'

'Thank you,' she replied, with a smile that touched Phil's heart.

'Hi John, how you doin?' said Phil, as a friend from a neighbouring caravan walked by.

'Not too bad.'

'How's Ann?' Phil inquired.

'Oh, that's over, we split up last week.'

'Oh, I'm really sorry to hear that - are you OK?'

'Naturally, I'm up and down, but I know it was the right thing to do. We'd been very unhappy for some time. It was a tearful but amicable parting. Some people are just not meant to be together. We'll both be much happier in the long run.'

The last sentence rang through Vi's mind like a wake-up call. She felt that someone had just staged the whole event solely for her benefit - a signpost. She went quiet and deep into thought:

I suppose when two people aren't meant for each other they're better off parted. It's not about blame, it's purely about differences. If two people stifle and thwart each other's growth then it's time to let go. This is not an act of selfishness, it's an act of love. If I can't fulfil Tom's needs and he can't fulfil mine then, if we love each other in the truest sense, we should set each other free to pursue our individual needs elsewhere.

'Are you OK, Vi?' inquired Phil, noticing she had become distant.

'What, oh yes, I was just thinking.'

She quickly snapped back to the present. 'Will you play your guitar for me?'

'Certainly.'

Phil went inside and got his guitar. After playing a few lively songs he found himself inadvertently slowing down the pace and reverting to the verse that continued to haunt him, his humorous mood turning somber.

'Hush little baby don't say a word, daddy's gonna buy you a mocking bird.......' he sang in a soft voice.

Vi felt a rush of emotion, her stomach turning upside down. Within seconds the tears started to trickle.

'What's the matter, Vi?' Phil inquired.

'That song, it seemed to trigger something within me – what made you play it?'

'I don't really know, it just keeps flitting in and out of my mind. It gets me emotionally too – every single time.'

'The last time I heard it was at our Val's. She had a heart shaped musical box in the nursery.'

'How come you've never had children, Vi? I've always sensed that you'd like a child.'

'Sometimes I do feel that way, but Tom and I have been having difficulties for some time now. I wouldn't like to bring a child into that atmosphere. I know what damage it can do.'

'Oh, I am sorry......Anyway, maybe when you find your true home you'll meet Prince Charming, have two lots of triplets and a pet chicken especially for when G. visits!'

The sunshine came back to Vi's face; they both began laughing. 'You always have the knack of cheering me up.'

As G. walked up the winding path that led up to the fell he was in deep thought.

I've always been a bit of a loner and convinced myself that I don't need anybody. Accept for my marriage of course, but that's been a total sham. Most people don't even know I'm married. (G. still lived with his wife of fifteen years but they had been emotionally estranged for most of that period. They now lived their everyday lives on an individual basis.) *I've never felt as happy as I do right now. Friendship is really important. We're not meant to spend our life in isolation. In the past day and a half I have laughed more than in all my previous years put together. And last night, when we all sat in the candle light singing songs, it was so intimate. I could feel the comradeship and a real sense of concern for each other. I really do feel something's changing.*

He continued his walk with a warm smile in his heart and a spring in his step.

*

G. returned from his walk looking radiant and refreshed and the trio tucked into their salads and a large array of fruit. After a short rest they all took their seats around the table and began to discuss the process of channelling.

'Can you tell me what it involves again, Phil?'

'Certainly, Vi. Channelling is the process of using your body as a conduit for spirit guides. These wise and loving entities have no physical form and rely on us to bring their teachings and healing energies through our physical body to the earthly plane.'

'Can they take control of us?'

'No, Vi, they never try to take control, they merely encourage us to rely on our own inner wisdom.'

'Is there anything to be scared of?' she continued, determined to disperse her apprehensions.

'Not when we follow the correct procedure. As we've seen, there are entities that are lost and can cause problems if we don't take precautionary measures. Tonight I will use symbols, prayer and light to put protection around us all so that we're not vulnerable to these lower entities. The best form of protection is the guides themselves. When we make a strong connection with a spirit guide we are totally shielded from these negative energies. To put your mind at ease, Vi, I have never experienced anything detrimental during a session.'

'Thanks, Phil; that makes me feel a lot better.'

'Is channelling the same as mediumship?'

'Not exactly, G., but saying this, I do feel that channelling enhances our mediumistic capabilities. On a number of occasions I have brought through personal messages from deceased friends and relatives of people. Both processes involve expanding our awareness and becoming sensitive to subtle levels of consciousness. Incidentally, this is why a person who channels is often referred to as a *sensitive*. A medium transmits and receives messages from Souls who have recently departed from earth. These communications are often directed at relatives and friends who seek reassurance and proof of Soul survival. The messages mediums bring through are of a personal nature and offer comfort to those friends and relatives left behind on earth. When we channel we use ourselves as vessels for information imparted by non-physical entities that may or may not have been incarnate on earth. Often these are highly evolved Souls who act as teachers and healers to those of us on this plane. Although their messages can be of a personal nature, quite often, they are concerned with global, planetary and universal issues.'

'I see, so what are the benefits of channelling from an earthly perspective?'

'For me, channelling is a journey of self discovery which involves radical change. When we absorb the wisdom and love of spirit guides their light has an uncanny way of illuminating the darker side of our nature known as the shadow: parts of ourselves that we've disowned, truth that we're in denial of, traumatic events that have been repressed, inner conflicts and blockages, all tend to surface. This may sound a little daunting but it's a very necessary part of the process of awakening. People tend to think that what's outside of their conscious awareness no longer influences them, when in reality, these are the forces that predispose them to destructive patterns of behaviour - inhibiting and constricting them. So the process of awakening can be quite rocky involving an intense period of self-examination.'

'It all sounds a bit daunting.'

'Maybe G., but let me assure you the rewards far outweigh the deficits. When I first started channeling I had a honeymoon period of about two or three years, feeling like nothing could touch me, then my issues started to resurface. I set about sifting through the wreckage of my past and that was a very difficult period. The tough people of this world aren't the bullies and oppressors, they're the people who can turn and face themselves. My period of self examination turned out to be a real turning point. I developed a healthy thirst for knowledge of a spiritual and psychological nature. I studied psychology, trained as a hypnotherapist, trained in holistic healing techniques, meditated, channelled, attended many workshops and, more recently, started training in psychodynamic counselling. Inadvertently, I was developing the tools to become a competent therapist and teacher which I now believe to be part of my destiny. So can you see how my misfortune, all the trauma in my life, actually turned out to be beneficial? If I hadn't have experienced my grey days, I'd never have found the path to my destiny.'

'Alchemy,' said G.

'Exactly. I slowly started to turn my shadow into light, my trauma into riches.'

'Alchemy - you said alchemy,' injected Vi, as though something had just struck a chord.

'Yes, Vi.'

'My Uniqueness spoke about spiritual alchemy, turning my traumas into my wealth. She said we *choose* some of our experiences and I got really annoyed thinking who in their right mind would choose what I've been through, but listening to you talk just now has made me think.'

'It's very difficult from an earthly perspective to think that we've actually *chosen* a difficult path. However, as our awareness rises and we look at the bigger picture, we begin to see how it's possible. If we experience trauma and then heal ourselves, we're in an ideal position to reach other suffering people. We can empathize with them and give them the tools we've gathered to help them transform their lives too.'

'I can see exactly what you mean.'

'That's good, Vi. It's very difficult, but if we can turn our way of thinking, it helps us see things in a different light - now has anyone got any further questions?'

Vi and G. shook their heads.

'Okay, I thought we'd all participate in an experiential session later and see what happens, then tomorrow night, I thought I'd verbally channel Theodore and allow you both to ask questions – how does that sound?'

'Exciting,' said Vi

'Really looking forward to it,' said G.

Chapter 10

Unveiling the Hidden Realms

The lounge area had been transformed into a sanctuary, the intimate glow of a pair of gas mantles complementing the comforting flicker of an octet of votives. Incense sticks sent wisps of smoke percolating toward the ceiling, permeating the air with Eastern fragrances. The soothing sound of the rushing river pervading the silence added a further dimension to the peaceful ambience. A vase of freshly cut carnations surrounded by a spread of angel cards lay on a small circular table.

The trio settled down and relaxed, removing their shoes and loosening their clothing. Phil suggested a short period of silence to allow their internal dialogue to settle. During this period he asked them to focus on the spread of angel cards and allow their intuition to guide them to choose one. Graham picked *Brotherhood and Sisterhood*, Vi picked *Love* and Phil chose *Unity*. The next few minutes were spent contemplating the personal meaning of these cards.

Phil started the session with a script for releasing tension and anxiety then instructed everyone to concentrate on their breath and become one with its rhythm and flow. He then asked them to shift their focus to the soles of their feet and envisage two golden tubes extending down and penetrating deep into the earth's core. After discharging any unwanted energies via the golden tubes, they allowed the planet's healing energies to rise up and enter their bodies, permeating every cell, bone and tissue. Using visualisation techniques, Phil coaxed the seven major chakras to open and become receptive and sensitive to emotional, mental and spiritual energies.

'Envisage a seedling of vibrant white light embedded deep within your heart centre,' he continued, in a low, gentle tone. 'Focus your attention on this seedling and watch it expand and envelope your heart as it is fertilized by your loving thoughts….as you exhale see this ellipse further expand and envelope the whole of your body….bathe yourselves in this light…..notice our individual energy fields beginning to meld and unify as one embryo of divine white light in which we're all encapsulated. …envisage an emerald green shaft of light emanating from your heart centre and penetrating deep into the heart of the person to your left, unifying and binding us together in a circuit of love. Now see the Star of David materializing from the ether and coming to rest gently on your forehead, protecting you from negative energies.'

He continued with an adapted version of the prayer of Saint Francis Assisi, asking the Universe to make them channels of its peace and then started to release three simple heart sutras. As the words 'peace', 'harmony' and 'love' rippled through the air, the atmosphere became imbued with a peace that penetrated their very core, each of them feeling the ordinary world drifting further and further away.

As they basked in the peaceful ambience, Phil's concentration was suddenly broken by a voice that vied desperately for his attention. Mary… Mary… Mary…Mary.

He paused for a moment to acknowledge the voice.

What is it, Mary? He asked mentally.

You must help her, you must love her. The voice whispered.

A number of disturbing scenes suddenly filled his mind.

A bedraggled little girl, clad in tattered clothes, stood in a school yard encircled by other children who chanted 'TRAMP', 'TRAMP', 'TRAMP'. The little lady stared sorrowfully at the ground. The scene faded and another emerged. A man violently beat up a woman; the little girl crouched in a corner, bruised and rigid with fear. Again the scene faded and another appeared. The little girl lay on her bed clutching a doll and crying herself to sleep.

Phil struggled to hold back tears: he felt his insides being ripped apart.

What have you been through, Vi? He thought.

Opening his eyes slightly, he saw the others still in a deep state of relaxation.

A wave of love rippled through him as he set eyes on Vi. He sent her a thought.

Be peaceful little lady, you're safe now, I love you.

She gave a little smile as though acknowledging his intention and then broke the silence.

'Phil,' she whispered.

'Yes, Vi.'

'I feel as though someone is stroking my hair.'

Phil smiled. 'I believe you have a visitor from the higher Astral plane - your grandmother, Mary. How does it feel, sweetheart?'

'Warm and comforting,' she replied.

'Enjoy her love; she seems intent on helping you.'

Phil started to feel a gentle breeze oscillating between the palms of his hands. Esba's form appeared in his mind's eye. He smiled as her warmth embraced him.

'Thank you for joining us, Esba.' he whispered.

'Phil,' said G. 'I can see colours swishing everywhere before my eyes.'

Phil smiled, 'I think you've just encountered Esba. Her energy's vibrant and colourful. Relax and enjoy it.'

Pressure started to build between Phil's eyes as his third-eye chakra opened wide. His inner vision became crystal clear and immediately locked into G's sacral vortex - images began flash through his mind.

A young boy stood in a garden looking dejected. He could hear all the other children playing outside but his parents wouldn't allow him to participate – the scene faded and another emerged. The little boy was now in the schoolyard. The other children played in groups but he played alone. The scene faded – another emerged. The boy was now a teenager, a hermit, absorbing himself in books.

Sisterhood and brotherhood, my friend. Esba whispered through Phil's mind.

As he continued to scan G's chakras, he noticed that his solar plexus was so large it was smothering his sacral gateway. This intuitively told him that G's intellect was acting as a defence mechanism, preventing him from acknowledging his emotions and hindering him from forming meaningful bonds. Phil began to transmit a thought to him.

You have a family now big man. Welcome home.

Phil opened his eyes slightly and noticed that G emanated a radiance, looking like a happy little boy. At this point he noticed that his solar plexus chakra began to retreat and allow his sacral chakra to breathe once again.

'How are you feeling big guy?' he said, in a mellow tone.

'Mmm,' G. smiled, 'Terrific.'

Phil's awareness then locked into a ball of orangey-brown sludge that lay in the area of Vi's sacral chakra. The image of the bedraggled little girl emerged once again. He immediately felt a wave of sadness sweep over him.

'Vi,' he whispered, 'I'd like you to concentrate on the area of your sacral chakra and tell me how you feel.'

110

Pause.

Vi focused herself.

'I feel sad…so very, very sad,' she replied, her voice beginning to break up.

'Do you see anything?'

'Yes, a little girl,' she sniffled.

'What's she doing?'

'She's crying and has her arms outstretched toward me.'

'Vi, this little girl is your inner child and you're her mother now. She needs you to listen to her needs….. See yourself walking towards this lovable little lady.'

Phil continued, his voice oozing tenderness.

'Kneel down and caress her hair…….wipe the tears from her eyes.'

He gave a pause, allowing Vi to follow his instructions.

'Now promise her you're never going to leave her and from this moment on, you'll give her anything she wants…..embrace her tightly and tell her how much you love her.'

Tears welled up in Vi's eyes as she re-united with her inner child; she began to sob.

'Let them flow, honey,' Phil whispered. 'These are the tears that have been eroding your insides for years.. let them all out.'

He paused for a while allowing the cathartic process to take its course.

'How do you feel now, sweetheart?'

'Better thanks,' she shuddered, 'I feel as though I've just let go of a lead weight.'

'That's wonderful little lady. Now don't forget, be kind to yourself.'

Phil now began to scan her chakra system. The muddy orange of her sacral chakra also appeared in her throat vortex suggesting there were ingrained emotional issues she desperately needed to communicate. Her solar plexus gateway was overloaded and spinning sluggishly as her intellect tried to shut out her emotions. Her energies were totally divided: she was following her head rather than her heart. Her fear pushed down the emotions that so desperately sought expression and this was sapping her energy. A fiery red blaze encircled the clear emerald green of her heart chakra, indicating that her anger inhibited her capacity to love.

Phil's attention was suddenly diverted; he noticed Esba's energy swishing and spiralling around G. His attention locked back on to his sacral chakra. From the swarthy mist that enveloped it, a little boy emerged looking lost and lonely.

'G., I want you to envisage your inner child too. Can you do that?'

'Yes,' came a faint reply.

'Can you see him?'

'Yes.'

'How do you feel?'

'Terribly sad.'

'Is he saying anything to you?'

The atmosphere became subdued. G's sacral vortex erupted spewing out dark clouds of contaminated emotional energy. The big man began to lose control. 'Love me…love me…..please love me,' he cried.

'Let them flow big man.' said Phil, his voice oozing compassion, 'It's time to give your emotions a voice. Those pent-up tears have formed a reservoir inside. It's time to release the pressure and allow them to break down the damn of your rational mind….let them all go.'

G. continued to let out woeful cries. The others remained silent, allowing the much needed catharsis to run its course.

When the tears subsided, Phil reunited G. with his inner child. After the reunification process, he took both G. and Vi on a therapeutic journey of healing.

'Now let this soothing picture come to mind……….'

The following guided meditation took them through meadows and fields and utilized the colours they saw to balance their chakra systems. During this journey they walked hand in hand with their inner children in an atmosphere of love and fun. The ambience of the room quickly transformed from sadness to joy.

Phil was about to bring the session to a close when he sensed a vibrant energy hovering around G. The atmosphere in the room became light and joyous.

'G., I see a man…he's laughing and showing me what looks like a wheelbarrow. He says he's sorry for leaving in such a hurry – does this make any sense to you?'

G. felt a lump in his throat. 'Yes it does,' he murmured, 'Tony was the only real friend I ever had. I met him while working on a building site just after I left school. We'd have a few drinks at lunch hour and then spend the afternoon pushing each other about in a wheelbarrow. He was killed in a car crash.'

'He's just letting you know he's fine and watching over you.'

'Thanks Phil - thanks Tony.' G. said, appreciatively.

The time had come to end the session. Phil thanked Esba, Mary, and Tony then began closing down the chakras. He instructed everyone to call their awareness back behind the windows of their eyes and centre themselves. Finally, he grounded them by getting them to envisage roots growing from the soles of their feet deep into the earth below.

'Now, in your own time, open your eyes and familiarize yourself with the surroundings.'

Phil opened his eyes followed shortly by Vi and finally G. They sat in silence for a while readjusting themselves to the environment. G and Vi looked raw and vulnerable as all their protective veneer had been stripped away.

'Wow!' said G. 'What just happened? I've never experienced anything like that in my life. I could see colours swirling all around me and I went through a million and one emotions.'

'I must admit, G., I've never been involved in such an intense session. You just never know what to expect. I felt Tony came through to remind you of joys of friendship. It must have really set you back when you lost him.'

'Yes, it did; it was devastating….but at least I know he's happy now.'

'How are you feeling, Vi?' Phil inquired.

'I don't know,' she replied. 'I haven't quite come back to earth yet. Like G., I could see all sorts of different colours and I saw some images too….a dove and…..what do you call those white horses with wings?'

'The Pegasus,' replied Phil. 'The spirit world often uses the language of symbols to communicate. The Pegasus is a symbol of transformation and the dove a symbol of purity and love.'

Vi still looked quite dazed so Phil carried out some further grounding work with her. The trio then formed a circle around the table, held hands, and blew out the candles, dedicating the light to their forthcoming journeys.

Later that evening, as they sat relaxing and enjoying a hot drink, Phil spoke about the things he'd seen during the session. They both acknowledged the truth of his findings. Consequently, Vi opened up about her past and G. spoke about his isolation. Phil informed them that these early relationships are still active within the emotional body. He went on to say that they are often *unconsciously* re-enacted in the present, severely inhibiting and constricting current relationships. He told them that psychodynamic counselling was all about these internalised relationships and suggested they might like to do some work on the emotional body in the future.

Around 11.30pm G. and Vi retired. G. lay on his bed thinking about how his childhood maybe influencing his present behaviour.

> *My parents wouldn't let me play with the other kids, and they didn't have much time for me either, they were always too busy. I never really received any tender loving care; everything had to be rational and clinical. Doing well academically was all that mattered to them. I even qualified as a teacher but never pursued it. I suppose I became rebellious. At school I found it really difficult to make friends. I didn't have any social skills. When I lost Tony I just convinced myself I didn't need anyone and that's the way it's been up until now. I suppose this is all that illusionary ego stuff, those ideas and beliefs about ourselves that we cling on to. What a load of old cobblers. I do need meaningful companionship. Two years ago I felt so lonely and abandoned that I attempted suicide. If it hadn't have been for the next door neighbour I wouldn't be here now. This weekend has been a wonderful experience. We've worked, laughed, and cried together and there's been a real sense of......* he suddenly remembered his angel card......*Sisterhood and Brotherhood.*

Vi also lay on her bed thinking.

> *Mary died before I was born. I never knew her but I got a wonderful feeling tonight when she stroked my hair. I guess she really does want to help -*

thank you, Mary. And Phil - there's certainly a lot more to him than meets the eye. I know he's a clown and I know how caring he can be but I never knew he was so heavily involved in this kind of thing. He really is dedicated. He asked me to promise my inner child that I'd listen to her needs. I guess this is part of the caterpillar stage. All my life I've attended to the needs of others and not given a thought for myself. If I'm going to make changes then I have to identify my needs and see which ones aren't being met. Up until now I've had a great need for safety and security but these are not enough anymore. For the past few years I've felt dead inside, feeling as though I'm existing rather than living. I must spend time with myself, listen to my inner child and get in touch with my needs.

Phil thought about G.

No wonder he finds it so difficult to mingle. The past really does have a tremendous influence on the present. He wasn't allowed to play with other children as a child and when he did finally befriend someone they were snatched away. That must've been the final straw. My heart really went out to him tonight but sometimes we have to be broken down in order to be rebuilt. And Vi, my God, she's really been through the mill. Her life has been a real battleground.

His thoughts turned to Mary.

I will love her, Mary...I promise you. It appears I've been gifted with an abundance of love for her and she'll have the full benefit.

He began to think about the affectionate terms he'd used during the session.

'Honey', 'sweetheart', 'little lady' - I've never spoken to anyone like that before but it felt so good. I just wanted to hold and comfort her but I know I must be careful. She's not normally a tactile person. I'm one of the privileged few who she lets near. In general she shies away from any sort of affection. I'm not surprised after what she's been through, poor little sweetheart. She must be terrified of love. Anyway she's on the right path now; she'll find her way home.

Unable to sleep, he picked up his guitar and began to play. Thinking of Vi and that special place were she belongs, the song 'Somewhere Over the Rainbow' came to mind. He started delicately finger picking the strings and, in a soft voice, began to sing the melody.

Vi lay on top of her bed relaxing as the dulcet tones filtered through. The sound began to resonate with her heart chakra and it opened up like a blossoming rose bud, the emerald green vortex spiralling effervescently, dispersing the fiery red of her anger and sending the energy of love careering through the mental defences of her solar plexus straight down into her emotional vortex. Her sacral chakra ignited like a catherine wheel on the fifth of November, lighting up her insides and sending sparks of emotion fleeting throughout her body. She got up, quietly opened the bedroom door and peered out to find Phil totally absorbed in the music. She tip-toed through to the lounge and took a seat opposite him. He looked up to see her beauty in all its splendour, her innocence and purity piercing the core of his heart. He glanced at her adoringly, then closed his eyes and absorbed himself back in the music. As he did, the lucid image of a deer appeared in his mind's eye. Tears trickled down Vi's face as the melody reached something deep within her. On singing the last note, Phil placed his guitar to one side, took a seat next to her and began stroking her hair with the gentleness of a fawn. They engaged in an affectionate embrace and he whispered softly into her ear.

'I'm going to take every tear you've ever cried, little lady, and turn them into the most beautiful rainbow….. at the end of that rainbow lies a magical place, that very special place where you truly belong.'

Chapter 11

Unconscious Dynamics of Relationships:
The Past is Buried Alive.

As the weekend had been quite intense, the trio decided to declare Sunday a day of leisure. Graham arose at 6.30am, put on his hiking gear, made himself a packed lunch and set off to pursue one of his favourite pastimes – fell walking. Phil and Vi surfaced about an hour later, had a light breakfast, then set off to explore the Lake District.

The twisting incline wound its way through fields and woods which were littered with wildlife. A small stone bridge arced across an effervescent river which splashed playfully against boulders and rocks as it weaved its way down to the lake below. The surrounding mountains reached up into the clear blue sky which was tarnished only by one or two rain clouds. Occasionally Vi broke into fits of laughter as Phil exaggerated the effects of driving over a cattle grid, shuddering violently and springing up and down in his seat like a jack-in-the-box. Half way up he pulled the car off the narrow road onto a gravelled area situated amidst some trees.

'Let's go, there's something I want to show you.'

Phil asked Vi to close her eyes and guided her across the road into a clearing.

'Now open them.'

'Wow.. Phil.. that's fantastic!' she gasped as she found herself high on a ledge above a magnificent lake, the surface reflecting the mountain range that stood guard on its banks.

'What's this lake called?' she inquired.

'Derwent Water.'

The visibility was good and they were able to make out clusters of yachts sailing gracefully in formation choreographed by the gentle breeze that filled their sails. Vi stood hypnotized by the breathtaking scene while Phil perched himself on a nearby rock and observed her.

She looks so happy and contented, he thought. *I hope she enjoys every minute of it; she deserves it. After last night, I can't help seeing her as a little girl. I feel just like a doting father. Perhaps that's what all this love is about. Maybe I've been gifted it to nurture her, just as I'd nurture my own daughter.*

After a few minutes he got to his feet, took a few short paces to where she stood, and put his arm around her shoulder.

'I love you,' he said, with an adoring smile.

She immediately froze, becoming rigid and uncomfortable.

Phil was taken aback - startled by her reaction. He suddenly realised she may have misinterpreted his show of affection. He removed his arm in a manner that hid his own discomfort and silence fell. After a few minutes they walked back to the car, the atmosphere slightly tense, neither of them knowing what to say. As Phil went to turn the ignition key a voice whispered through Vi's mind.

Be prepared to go to the edges of fear, a ship anchored in a safe harbour cannot explore the oceans.

She broke the silence.

'Phil,' she said, nervously.

'Yes, Vi?'

'Last night, after the session, I told you lots of things about my life.'

'Yes and it took an awful lot of courage,' he replied, empathetically.

'Well there's something I left out, something I've never told anybody…'

Phil looked into her sad eyes and waited for her to elaborate. There was no response, she looked fragile and vulnerable.

'Do you want to share it with me?' he asked in a gentle tone.

'I trust you, Phil; I've always known that I could trust you.'

'Then I'll listen if you want to talk.'

Vi fidgeted, nervously curling strands of her hair around her finger.

'I told you that I'd been adopted and my foster-parents died a few years ago…'

'Yes.'

'Well there's something else…'

She paused. Her head fell into her hands and the tears started to fall.

Phil reached over and took hold of her hand, delicately caressing it with his thumb. 'In your own time, sweetheart,' he said compassionately.

You must restore her faith, be gentle. *A voice whispered through his mind accompanied by the vision of a fawn.*

She started to sob and uttered a few broken words.

'…..I was sexually abused by my foster-father.'

She turned to Phil and he embraced her, rocking and cradling her until all of her tears had subsided.

'Listen to me,' he said, staring directly into her eyes. 'You're a remarkable person. A caring, sensitive, beautiful little lady and I love you. Despite your life's experience you have a wonderful sense of humour and I have every admiration for you. You're unique and special. Whenever you need a friend I'm here for you, seven days a week, twenty four hours a day.'

'Thanks, Phil,' she sniffled.

'Vi - would you consider going for psychodynamic counselling? I feel it would be of great help.'

'No, Phil. I won't go to a counsellor,' she retorted, 'I don't trust them - can you help me?'

Phil had acquired some of the tools necessary to deal with such situations but he was now faced with a dilemma. He was becoming very close to Vi and this wasn't an ideal situation for counselling. However, if he refused, she may feel rejected and he couldn't afford for this to happen. He quickly sent out an impulse of intent to the Universe - *Do I help her?*

You must help her, you must nurture her, came the reply. Without hesitation he offered his help. He suggested they have some informal chats in which he would endeavour to bring to her awareness some of the hidden forces that may be inhibiting her. She felt a sense of relief. At last she had someone she could trust, someone to talk to. A trace of a smile returned to her face.

'Now, I'm going to take you to the top of the hill and introduce you to a few friends of mine - Ok?' said Phil, injecting a sense of lightness back into the conversation.

They continued up the incline, the car weaving its way past hikers and several sheep that had escaped from the bordering fields, occasionally halting at passing points to allow other vehicles through. As they skirted the perimeter of a hill, the trees began to disperse and the tiny hamlet of Watendlath came into view.

Vi felt as if she'd travelled back in time a few centuries. Eight hundred and forty seven feet above sea level and set in the fold of the mountains, the isolated hamlet consisted of a handful of whitewashed houses, a couple of slated barns, a farm, a waterfall and a pebbly tarn. Central, stood a packhorse bridge under which an aerated beck flowed, its banks sprayed with red Herb Willow and red Loose-strife.

Phil escorted Vi to one of the old slated barns where they were confronted by a huge pot-bellied pig.

'Meet Oscar,' he smiled. 'The only living creature that can eat more than G!'

'He's lovely,' said Vi, patting the pig on the head.

Phil removed some apples and carrots from his bag. Oscar shuffled towards him grunting and drooling in anticipation of the feast. The beast devoured the food with the elegance of wart-hog then idly sauntered off and lay down in the corner of the barn.

'Look you've bored it to death,' laughed Vi. 'You have this uncanny way of making things sleepy!'

Phil spotted a pile of dung on the floor and pointed to it.

'And you have an uncanny way of making that stuff come out of your mouth!' he countered.

Vi picked up a sizeable mound of hay and threw it all over him. By the time she'd finished he resembled a scarecrow, covered in hay from head to toe.

'Aahh Aunt Sally,' said Phil, doing a feeble impression of Worzel Gummidge.

'I guess you never done impressions on stage!' mocked Vi.

The two left the barn chuckling to themselves and made their way across the packhorse bridge.

'Look, Phil,' said Vi, spotting two Shetland ponies.

'Let me introduce you to Yin and Yang.'

'Yin and Yang. I know about them through my martial arts.'

'Yes, you would. The Source is said to be comprised of two polarised energies, Yin and Yang. Yin is feminine, receptive, in-flowing energy. This is the polarity used when channelling, and Yang is masculine, expressive, out-flowing energy, used for healing and physically manifesting our creative ideas. As we're all moulded from the energy of the Source, we have both feminine and masculine properties. To function to our full potential we need to balance these energies within us; we need to be open to incoming energies and able to express them in a productive way.'

'Yes, that's a similar explanation to what I've been given,' said Vi.

They fed the remainder of the apples and carrots to the ponies but it seemed that Yang's appetite had failed to be satisfied. He took hold of Phil's coat, started gnawing at it, then dragged him forward.

'Don't eat him all,' chuckled Vi. 'You'll get indigestion!'

'I can feel some expressive energy flowing through me,' said Phil, 'sod off!'

They said goodbye to the ponies then ambled over to the picturesque tarn which nestled amidst the surrounding fells. A few anglers waded in the calm waters fishing for trout, whilst others cast their lines from small rowing boats. Phil dipped into his bag once again pulling out a loaf and handing half of it to Vi. She laughed heartily as a gaggle of Geese and a couple of dozen ducks merrily waddled towards them. She broke off some bread and threw it to the ground while Phil beckoned the birds to take the food from his hands. He urged her to do the same thing, telling her to place the bread on the flat of her hand. She looked apprehensive as the large white geese began to encircle her, hissing and flapping.

'Look they won't hurt you,' he said, reassuringly, as a goose snatched a piece of bread from his hand. 'See, they're harmless.'

The goose suddenly took hold of his middle finger and started to yank at it, causing him to jump with fright.

'Oops!' he exclaimed. 'Maybe it's not such a good idea after all!'

'You've got a real way with animals,' chuckled Vi.

Next stop was the National Trust tea room. They ordered some sandwiches and drinks and then took a seat outside on a wooden bench. A robin and a great tit perched cheekily on the edge of the table. Vi broke off a piece of her sandwich, grated it, and sprinkled the crumbs on the table, then watched as the hungry birds pecked away.

Phil's eyes became fixated on a flower that swayed gently in the breeze: he began to drift off, his physical senses becoming subservient to his extrasensory perception.

'Vi,' he said, still hypnotized by the flower.

'Yes, Phil?'

'Has your sister recently lost a baby?'

'Yes,' she replied, astonished.. 'Her chances of having another are virtually nil.'

'No, she'll have a baby boy next year, around summer time. Remember that she lost a shell, a cloak of matter. The life essence is still very much alive and existing at another level. Sometimes disincarnate entities choose to incarnate only as far as the foetus to leave the expectant parents with a lesson. It may be to experience loss and undergo the grieving process or it may be to enable them to turn their attention to their spiritual nature and realise there is no loss, only change of form. Anyway, this entity is going to reincarnate and will emerge next summer.'

Phil snapped back to his ordinary state of awareness and stared at Vi compassionately.

'She's very depressed isn't she?' He said.

'I don't believe this,' she replied. 'Val's been really down since she lost the baby and has lost all faith in having another.'

'Please give her this message, Vi. She needs to hear it. Tell her to take care of herself and build up her strength. She's been drinking quite heavily hasn't she?'

'Phil, this is spooky. Yes, she's been drinking heavily, drowning her sorrows. But what if you're wrong?'

'Some messages are ambiguous and lack clarity, but this is very strong. Please tell her.' (Momentarily, he thought of the image of Esba cradling the baby and wondered if it was connected to Val.)

'I will, Phil, if you are sure - she'll be delighted.'

The two tucked into their sandwiches and sipped hot tea, the atmosphere becoming light and jovial.

'Let's have a bit of fun,' said Phil. 'If I were a genie and could grant your every wish, what would you ask for?'

'First and foremost,' replied Vi, 'I'd ask for purpose in my life. I know I have a reasonable job but it doesn't fulfil me. I feel trapped, like a gold fish in one of those small round bowls, swimming mundanely around in circles. I'd like to wake up every morning knowing I was going to do something really interesting and meaningful.'

'Well, Vi, I have a vision,' said Phil, beginning to fantasize about his dream. 'I'm going to write a book, in fact, several books. And I'm going to open a centre in the countryside. I'm going to have lots of animals, a music room and a lake in the grounds where I can write in peace. I need good therapists and teachers to work alongside me – interested?'

Vi's face lit up.

'Oh yes - what a dream! But I'm not a therapist or a teacher.'

'Not yet, but don't forget spiritual alchemy. When you dissolve your issues and rid yourself of the forces that bind you, you'll become highly creative and manifest everything you want. You'll become a shining example to others. People will flock to see you in the hope that you can help them transform their lives in the same way as you have transformed your own.'

'Can I bring my cats?' she said, becoming totally absorbed in the fantasy.

'Yes, of course, and we'll take Oscar and Yin and Yang too. However, I think we'll skip the geese!' he laughed.

'Just think, Vi, spending our days in a tranquil location, doing what fulfils us, helping others and at the same time helping to heal this planet.'

'Yes and having lots of fun,' added Vi, excitedly, 'travelling and having adventures.'

'Yes.' The fantasy began to snowball. 'I want to buy a place in Crete and spend part of the year there. I love the romantic atmosphere of the Greek islands. They breathe inspiration into me.' Phil paused for a moment. '….. I can see something else happening here.'

'What's that?' inquired Vi.

'Remember we spoke about fantasy being the gateway through which we reach other dimensions of existence?'

'Yes.'

'Well it has another extremely important function. Theodore says that fantasy and imagination are also the mechanisms through which we mould pure potential energy into our dreams. Right now we are potters moulding the spiritual clay of the Source into a possible future. Just think, if we manifest this vision, there'd be good reason to accept that we chose a difficult path. If we hadn't, this dream would never have come to light. If, or should I say *when*, this vision manifests and we realise our destiny, we'll be the happiest people on earth and everything we've been through would have been worthwhile. As we turn our own darkness into light we can serve the Universe by assisting others to do the same.'

'Yes,' said Vi as though something had just clicked into place.

'Now, can I grant you any other wishes, Princess?'

'Yes, I'd like to meet Prince Charming, someone who'll look after me, someone to love me, someone to have fun and adventure with and, maybe someday, have a family with.'

Phil drifted for a moment as Theodore's voice reeled through his mind.

Speak the language of your heart.

'Vi,' he said, a little uneasily. 'There's something I feel I must tell you. Yesterday I became aware that my feelings towards you had changed somewhat. I really don't know how to explain this but I feel I must be absolutely honest. It happened in an instant when I observed you standing by the river. After last night's session, part of me feels that it's a fatherly or brotherly love but I really can't be sure.'

Vi didn't take too much heed to what he was saying, her low self-esteem causing her to believe that he just felt sorry for her and was being kind.

'Oh,' she replied, nonchalantly.

'Anyway,' intervened Phil, 'whatever it is, it feels good and I promise you I'll utilize it for your benefit. In fact, I intend to make every day we spend together your birthday.'

She gave a little child-like smile then started to talk about her relationship with Tom. Phil listened intently as she spilled out her frustrations and doubts and expressed concern over her outbursts of anger.

'Vi,' he said, 'there's a possibility you may be viewing your relationship through distorted eyes.'

'What do you mean?'

'Yesterday we spoke about the emotional body and how it retains blocked energy resulting from unresolved childhood issues – do you remember?'

'Yes.'

'And we spoke about this being the software that unconsciously programs our responses in the present?'

'Yes.'

'Well your experience of significant males has been pretty dismal to say the least. The violence of your biological father and the sexual abuse of your foster-father may be heavily influencing you're ability to form intimate bonds with men. You said you don't know what takes over you at times and that you fly into rage. It may be that these past relationships are the cause of this rage.'

'No, they can't be, they happened such a long time ago. It's Tom, he aggravates me.'

'This may seem true on the surface and indeed it may be an area that you need to evaluate, but these traumatic experiences could well be contaminating your view. **Past relationships are not dead - they are buried alive and highly active in the unconscious realm of your mind**...

'...The mind is like an iceberg, our conscious awareness being the tip that sits above the water, our unconscious being the vast majority lying below the surface. Our unconscious is peopled with many different characters who are often in conflict with each other, making us feel fragmented.'

'How d'you mean?'

'Remember we are not solid entities. We are fluid, comprised of energy and information. When we interact with others we exchange energy with them; it flows back and forth. Via this process we internalise versions of people who have influenced us in significant ways during the course of our lives. Within us we have complexes of energy that envelope our parents, siblings, school teachers and so on. This energy is dynamic. The relationships we had with these people are still active within this hidden realm of our mind, often programming us to behave in rigid ways. These internalised relationships are often re-enacted in the present; that is, they are externalised. But most people are unaware of it; the process takes place at an unconscious level….. Tell me, Vi, how did you feel earlier, when I put my arm around you and told you that I loved you?'

'Frightened…really frightened, and guilty too. I felt frightened that you might try to take advantage of me and yet, I know you'd never do such a thing, so I felt guilty for thinking it.'

'Where do you feel this fear has come from?'

'I suppose,' she thought hard, 'those experiences I had with my foster- father.'

'Exactly. Unconsciously you regressed to that little abused girl and perceived me as the perpetrator: you recreated a past traumatic relationship in the here and now, but you were unaware of it.'

'I see,' said Vi, beginning to see the practical implications, 'no wonder we get so confused and irritated.'

'Precisely, Vi, we are being programmed by unconscious mechanisms. Do you see how this can severely hinder your ability to form close intimate bonds and limit your potential to love?'

'Yes, I most certainly do.'

'What's actually happening is that you are transferring a complex of thoughts and feelings appertaining to a past situation into a current encounter.'

'This is amazing,' said Vi, seeing the truth in what Phil was saying.

'Do you ever behave in this way with your partner?'

'Yes, sometimes when he touches me it freaks me out. I make excuses such as, my leg's sore or that tickles, so he'll remove his hand.'

'If you showed affection to him and he responded likewise how would you feel?'

'Terrible - rejected and angry.'

'Do you ever consider Tom may feel the same way?'

'Well up until now, I never have, but I'm sure he must.'

'And how do you think it must make him feel?'

'Absolutely awful. Soul destroying.'

'Exactly. It's highly likely to trigger issues in him and cause him to react in various ways. Let's say he feels rejection. His response will not only be determined by the current interaction, but by an accumulation of internalised experiences from his past. This phenomenon often leads to a distorted view: an emotionally charged response. He may revert to mechanisms he utilized in the past to elicit his needs. For instance, sulking, complaining of illness, self pity, aggression, emotional blackmail, and so on.'

'So let me get this straight. All past relationships with significant others are internalised and ongoing in our unconscious. Without being aware of it, we recreate these relationships in the present: we transfer the thoughts and feelings connected with these past events onto people in our lives today. This, in turn, causes them to react in a way that has been determined by their history.'

'Correct, Vi, and when these processes go unacknowledged they spiral out of control and lead to terrible conflicts…..Now you also said that you sometimes fly into a rage, feeling like something has taken over you.'

'Yes.'

'In what situations does this commonly occur?'

'When Tom raises his voice or is off-handed with me, my reactions are often way over the top and I feel terrible afterwards.'

'This may be due to the recreation of the violent relationship you had with your biological father. Tom raises his voice, you regress to the physically abused child of years ago, and your past behaviour jumps up to dominate your response.'

'This really would explain why I go crazy. The situation is being fuelled by my past experiences,' said an enlightened Vi.

'Precisely.'

'So am I stuck like this forever or can I dissolve these past issues?'

'The answer is to deal with the catalyst relationships, the ones with your father and foster-father.'

'In general, if you speak to your friends about these people they're likely to say things like "what a bastard" and with some justification I might add. However, such comments will only serve to make your inner conflict worse, fuelling your anger and further restricting and inhibiting your life.'

'So what can be done?'

'Well you don't have to forgive, although it does help. These people have to take responsibility for their actions, but that alone won't relieve your inner turmoil and this is about *you* not them. The answer is to try to understand how they've been programmed to behave in such barbaric ways. I feel I can give you an understanding of your biological father's behaviour……

'…..No one drinks like your father because they enjoy it. It's generally because they're trying to obliterate stuff from their minds. You said some of your family had recently visited him in hospital where he was detoxifying and he'd looked like a man at death's door?'

'Yes, that's right.'

'This is not the sign of a happy, contented human being; it's the sign of a person who wants to self destruct, a man serving a self imposed penance. I can almost guarantee that he's drowning in his own guilt. Being an alcoholic myself, I know what this feels like: it's horrendous. I'm not condoning his behaviour; I'm saying that there are reasons why he acted in such a violent way. Many people who act out violence have been subjected to the same rites of passage themselves; they too have been the target of such abuse. This pattern can be handed down from generation to generation.'

'But why do some people turn out like that while others grow up to be decent human beings?'

'Because the latter have not identified with their conditioning. They've identified with their Uniqueness and grown in a different direction. They are biased towards their Higher Selves rather than being programmed by life's conditioning.'

'I see.'

'When I was destroying myself with drink I was incapable of owning my turbulent feelings, they were far too distressing. So what I did, again unconsciously   (I was totally unaware I was doing it) was to see these feelings situated in other people. This way I didn't have to look at myself. I could apportion blame to others; it was *they* who were the cause of my problems. The feelings we are unable to cope with, the shadow side of ourselves, we project onto others and they become the scapegoats. This phenomenon is called "shadow projection", and it was first discovered by eminent psychiatrist Carl Jung…

'…I dearly love my parents, Vi, but in drink, I blamed them for everything. On one or two occasions I nearly came to blows with my father. Afterwards, as I sobered up, I couldn't cope with the guilt so I drank myself back into oblivion and a vicious circle ensued. The message I'm trying to relay is that I'm sure your father loves you and he's now punishing himself for his chronic behaviour. When we're caught up in these horrendous cycles we often project all our crap onto the ones we love most.'

Vi felt a pulse of emotion sweep through her. For a moment, she empathized with her father. She began to realise that she could have easily turned out the same way. After her angry outbursts, Tom had often said she was just like her father. She had always maintained she had no love for her dad but, if she was totally honest, she was heartbroken and really did love him. The image of him pushing her around the garden on his motorcycle suddenly came to mind.

'So you see, Vi, human relationships are quite a complex subject. There are so many unconscious forces that propel us to behave in the ways that we do. Nothing is ever as it seems on the surface. Some of these unconscious forces even determine the partners we choose.'

'How do you mean?' Inquired Vi.

'Well, tell me what initially attracted you to Tom?'

'He was gentle. He never got angry. In fact, none of his family appeared to get angry. I felt safe with him.'

'You say none of his family appeared to get angry?'

'Well, certainly his parents didn't.'

'Mmm..' said Phil, thoughtfully. 'This may be a clue as to why they were attracted to each other - have you ever heard of relationship fits?'

'No,' exclaimed Vi, 'what are they?'

'Relationship fits are unconscious mechanisms that draw people together – "chemistry" as it is often called. There are five fits in all: positive mirror image, negative mirror image, opposites, unresolved childhood issues and insecure with insecure. Every couple fits into one of these categories to some degree. The relationship between Tom's parents seems to fall into the category of "positive mirror image". Here both partners have never been taught how to handle so called "negative emotions" so they avoid them; gloss over them or completely dismiss them. You have learnt that the messages we receive throughout childhood, both verbally or through modelling, exert a strong influence upon us.'

'Yes.' Replied Vi.

'Well these messages often result in rigid ingrained beliefs. With the positive mirror image couple the belief that binds them together will be something like "I must not get angry". Their inability to cope with anger results in them bonding. Choosing a partner of the same disposition means that their beliefs are not challenged. They're safe, and together they can perpetuate their beliefs.'

'Mm... that's makes sense,' said Vi, 'it's scary trying to express emotions you're not used to, so it would make sense to choose a partner who avoids them too…..but where do Tom and I fit into all this? This scenario doesn't explain our relationship.'

'I was just coming to that…Do you think it's viable that Tom may have inherited the belief "I must not get angry" or "I must not show negative emotion"?'

'Yes, definitely.'

'And how about you?'

'Well in a sense, I was brought up the total opposite. It felt unsafe for me to show positive emotion; love and kindness etcetera. They left me feeling exposed and vulnerable.'

'So could it be that one of your ingrained beliefs is "I must not show positive emotion"?'

'Yes, without a doubt.'

'Okay, but being human we will inevitably feel both positive and negative emotions. Maybe you've disowned the positive emotions because you deem them to be a liability but you still feel them. And Tom will feel negative emotions despite discarding them. Where do you think these redundant feelings go? They're energy; they can't just disappear.'

'I don't know.' Replied Vi.

'Then let me ask you another question….. with this additional information, do you have any inclination as to why you were attracted to Tom?'

Vi thought for a moment.

'Because we're opposites - they say opposites attract, don't they? But using this philosophy wouldn't we have chosen partners of a similar disposition to ourselves?'

'Not necessarily, some people do go for a mirror image. Others, as you have quite rightly identified, go for the complete opposite. But there are reasons for it. Have you any idea what these reasons might be?'

'I haven't got a clue.'

'Which proves a point – they are unconscious choices- covert transference of feelings is in operation again here. The relationship fit you seem to fall into has been quite rightly described as opposites. The transference phenomenon is a little less obvious to spot. With opposite fit couples, one partner will express the emotions that the other has disowned.'

'Are you saying that Tom expresses positive emotions for me and I express negative emotions for him?'

'Exactly. You act as a conduit for his anger and he acts as a vessel for your passivity - two halves come together to give a sense of wholeness.'

'Wow!' exclaimed Vi, 'that really sits right.'

'Opposite fits come in a variety of guises: controlling - submissive, introvert - extravert, aggressive - passive, parent - child and so on. But the same mechanism is in operation.'

'Parent – child?' Inquired Vi. 'That's how our relationship feels at times. I feel like his mother, forever having to keep him in line.'

'So what's your investment in adopting that role? Why do you *choose* to play mother?'

'What do you mean? It's a bind. I don't enjoy it.' she retorted.

'There's always a pay off, Vi. We may think we do things because we have to, but, in reality, we do them because they fulfil a need in us….Let's look at this a little closer…

'Independent of age, we all have a parent and a child complex within us. They are learned patterns of behaviour that we have internalised. We revert to them as coping mechanisms or strategies to get our needs met. In counselling we use these modes of operation to gain insight into the dynamics of relationships. The parent, I divide into two contrasting complexes. The first I call the *caretaker*, the complex concerned with caring, loving, nurturing and helping. The second I call the *oppressor*, the punishing, critical, censoring part of ourselves. Both have negative and positive aspects. For example, in addition to being a tyrant, the oppressor can have the positive attribute of instilling discipline. And, whilst being loving and caring, the caretaker can be smothering and controlling, not allowing the child to grow up. ….. are you with me so far?'

'Yes, I think so.'

'OK let's move on to the inner child complex. This too is divided into two distinct categories. Firstly, the *wonder child*: spontaneous, energetic, curious, loving and uninhibited – it's the part of us that feels free and loves pleasure. I prefer to call this the *soul child*, as it's very close to it's spiritual roots. Secondly, the *programmed child*, which is highly conditioned. This complex develops as we learn to change our feelings and behaviour in response to the world around us. When operating from this position we often revert to complying, sulking, aggression, aloofness and avoidance in reaction to external demands. The programmed child can also be divided into two sub-categories: the *manipulator* and the *wounded child*.'

'That sounds like Tom, he manipulates; he sulks when he doesn't get his own way. But then I suppose I do tend to give him a hard time.'

'If you tend to operate from the oppressive parent complex there is probably good reason for it. The oppressor thrives on control. As your boundaries were violated frequently during childhood, you probably felt disempowered and out of control. Stepping into this mode enables you to take back control - but it can lead to problems in relationships. If your partner is happy to be the programmed, yielding child, then he won't confront you and the relationship will work fine. However, if he steps out of role, all hell can break loose. When such relationships go wrong, this is exactly what tends to happen. The partner in child mode rebels and steps out of role. The oppressor then becomes insecure as he or she is no longer in control.'

'So what is the answer, how should a good relationship operate?'

'Well, my idea of a healthy relationship is one in which both partners are fluid and able to shift through these complexes when appropriate. We all need nurturing at times and we all need discipline. In addition, we all need to act rationally and dispassionately at times, which brings me to the final complex – *the analyst*.......This is the part of us that is concerned with collecting information, organising and analysing. It operates free from emotion. When we enter analyst mode we respond to situations logically and rationally; free from the emotionally charged responses typical of the other complexes. When operating from this mode we are dealing with the situation as it is. We are not viewing it through the lens of our memory, distorting it, and adding our baggage to it – we are in the present moment.'

'Mm...I see,' said Vi, 'I suppose when I first met Tom, he was the caretaker and I was the child. Paradoxically, my childhood never really allowed me to be a child. Tom was very caring and sensitive when we first met and I thrived on his nurturance for a while. But then it all started to get a bit too much. I felt smothered... Is this why you say the caretaker can be controlling?'

'Yes, exactly. The person acting in this role, as a result of their own insecurities, has an investment in keeping the child down and not allowing them to grow up. They have a need to be in control. Like I said, it's normally the child that gets fed up and rebels.'

'That's what happened to me. I told him not to be treating me like a child. I started to widen my circles and make new friends and he appeared to change. He started to sulk and revert to emotional blackmail. It was at this point that things started to go wrong, arguments, lot's of them. I suppose it was then that I became the oppressor – I changed roles.'

'You learn quickly, Vi.' said Phil. 'like I said, these relationships work fine until one partner steps out of role and the other is unable to cope….What do you think was going on within Tom at the time?'

'I suppose he started to feel insecure at the prospect of me growing up and so reverted to the programmed, manipulative, child: sulking and using emotional blackmail to get my attention. But then

I rebelled, wondering where the person I'd met had gone. I found his new role quite pathetic and didn't hold back in letting him know. I became very critical, it was almost as though a tape was running in my mind and I was saying things to him that my father had said to me.'

'Bingo!' exclaimed Phil. 'This is exactly what the caretaker complex is - past tape recordings of our parents re-playing themselves in the present.'

'I see, this is amazing stuff…. will you just run through the others again and I'll make a note of them - I'll make a therapist yet!'

'Certainly. The **wonder child** is the energetic, spontaneous, uninhibited, unconditioned, curious, fun-loving part of ourselves. I prefer to call this the **Soul child**, very close to its spiritual roots. The **programmed child** is that part which has learned to change its feelings and behaviour in accordance with external demands. It often reverts to compliance, sulking, and avoidance in order to get its needs met. This is the highly conditioned part of us. The **caretaker** is concerned with caring, loving and helping. While the **oppressor** critisizes, censors and punishes. Finally, the **analyst** is the part of us that's concerned with collecting information, organising and analysing. It operates dispassionately - free from emotional charge………. Got all that?'

'Yes, thanks Phil.'

'The thing about all these complexes or sub-personalities is that when we have an awareness of them we can identify them in ourselves and in others. This can give us a much better insight into our relationships. Just observe couples and see if you can identify the fit………find it helpful?'

'Very.' Replied Vi. 'One last favour. Would you mind just running through the relationship fits again so I can write them down too.'

'No problem, I will also elaborate on the two I haven't mentioned: the negative mirror image and insecure with insecure – ready?'

'Yes.'

'Okay, here goes. Relationship fits are unconscious mechanisms that draw people together – "chemistry" as it is often called. There are five fits in all. The **positive mirror image** emerges as a result of neither partner being taught how to handle negative emotions, in particular anger. Choosing a partner of the same disposition means that their ingrained beliefs are not challenged. They're safe and together they can perpetuate their ingrained beliefs...

'The **negative mirror image** is the direct opposite. People in these relationships have never been taught how to handle positive emotions and can be likened to two naughty school children, always fighting and squabbling. They choose each other because of their inability to handle positive emotions....

'**Opposites** are drawn together because one expresses the emotions that the other has disowned - two halves coming together to form a whole...

'The **insecure with insecure** fit involves what might be perceived as the perfect couple: good standing in the community, nice house, nice clothes, nice car, large circle of friends and good jobs. They are initially attracted to each other because of their perceived strengths - able to cope with anything. This can be very similar to the positive mirror image fit. However, when one partner dips the other doesn't know how to handle it and usually becomes very angry. Arguments and fights ensue and the relationship goes from heaven to hell. These couples find it very difficult to separate and even when they do they often get back together because they tend to remember what heaven was like...... have you managed to get all that written down?'

'Yes, Phil, but one thing is still bothering me. I can't understand why some people continuously attract violent partners - I'm thinking of my mum.'

'Maybe the last relationship fit, **unresolved childhood issues,** will shed some light on the matter.......do you know if your mother had an abusive parent?'

'Yes, her father.'

'Well, it's been found that some people choose partners in order to resolve issues they had with a parent. The feelings they had towards the parent are transferred onto a partner. Usually the partner will have some similarities to the parent: looks, mannerisms, traits etcetera. The relationship is set up, unconsciously of course, to try to get the original relationship right. Should this relationship break down, it's not unusual for such people to attract someone else of a very similar disposition and try again.'

'So how can they break this pattern?'

'By working on the catalyst relationship; the one with the parent. If they resolve the issues they had with the parent then the pattern appears to subside; it no longer serves a purpose.'

'That's unbelievable, but it explains so much. Phil, this conversation has been so enlightening and helpful - thank you.'

'Thank *you* Vi...something else just struck me.'

'What's that?' inquired Vi.

'Remember a couple of weeks ago I suggested that the signposts may be ushering us together for a reason?'

'Yes.'

'Well this weekend you and G. have enabled me to put my teaching skills into action which I feel is preparing me for the future. At the same time, by helping you, I'm been given an opportunity to put my counselling skills and psychological knowledge into action, taking me one step closer to my goal. My mediumistic and intuitive faculties have been stronger and clearer than ever. Earlier on we were fantasising about a future, moulding a vision and thinking we may be heading for the same destiny. You pointed out that you were not a therapist or a teacher but over the last couple of days you have absorbed an awful lot of information and gained several insights into the dark forces that lurk within you and impede your growth. If you dissolve the wreckage of your past you'll be in a prime position to help others and become an excellent therapist. In addition, your connection with your Uniqueness will accelerate your growth and enable you to facilitate channelling groups – do you see the connotations of all this?'

He paused and went into deep thought.

'Let's ask the Universe a question.'

He looked up to the sky.

'Am I, Phil Harrison, and this beautiful lady, Violet Rowan, heading for the same destiny?'

Just as the last word left his mouth the sunlight hit the density of a rain cloud and it dispersed into a beautiful rainbow. Phil felt a tingling sensation right throughout his body. This time he couldn't hold back the tears.

'Look behind you, Vi.'

She turned around and her eyes began to moisten.

'A rainbow, at the end of which lies that special place where, it seems, we may both belong.'

As they stared in disbelief of what was happening, a second rainbow arced across the sky - a mirror image.

'I do believe the heavens are sending us a message, Vi,' uttered a highly emotional Phil, 'the signpost home.'

He slid his hand across the table and locked their fingers together. A blissful energy flowed between them and all sense of separation ceased. A voice began to whisper through Vi's mind.

As twins emerge from the one embryo, so Soul Mates emerge from the Source as one.

Chapter 12

Coalescing with Spirit Guide – Theodore

During dinner the trio chatted about the verbal channeling session that would take place later that evening. Phil told the others that he would enter a trance state and invite Theodore's energy into his body. He reminded them to think of any questions they wished to ask. When they'd finished, G. and Vi went and found a place of seclusion to ponder their questions while Phil prepared the caravan for the session.

*

The lounge had once again been transformed into a haven, recreating the serene ambience of the previous evening. A tape recorder lay on the table in readiness to record the night's events. Graham and Vi sat in anticipation poised to ask their questions. Phil sat upright, his hands resting on his knees and palms facing upwards in a gesture of openness. He closed his eyes becoming one with the rhythm and flow of his breath and steadily entered a trance-like state. A gentle breeze oscillated between the palms of his hands. The atmosphere became absolutely still, the energy in the room almost tangible. Phil mentally invited Theodore to take residence in his body and immediately felt an all-pervading essence seeping in through his crown chakra. An almost imperceptible alertness swept over him and a new personality emerged.

Thank you, dear ones. Thank you for creating a bridge between our two worlds, a channel through which I can bring my vibration and join your earthly processes in such an intimate way. Though I am known to the sensitive as Theodore and perceived in the form of a monk, in truth, I have no cloak of matter. My being is composed of pure light. My evolution has involved many incarnations on your planet. I have existed in many forms and played many roles. Now I seek to assist in the liberation of humanity...

'...You are on a journey my friends, a journey that will ultimately take you home to the oneness from where you came. As you have travelled away from this oneness you have experienced segregation from your roots and an illusionary sense of separation from each other. It is from this divided state that the devil known as fear is born. The direct opposite of the love vibration is fear: fear that constrains, stops growth, keeps you rigid; fear that says you must not explore or change direction; fear that demands you must stay where you are and not take risks; fear that promotes stasis. Fear, dear ones, is the root of all conflict. Love enables, fear constricts and inhibits. I urge you to become warriors of light and explore your darkness with the light of love. Evolution is not just about bringing in the light, it is about exploring the shadow, as within the shadow there is a great well of creativity and knowledge...

'...I am here this evening to invite you to look at your choices, to look at areas of stuckness, difficult patterns in which you are enmeshed, and to urge you to create a space for a new loving energy to enter. In order to fulfil your potential you need to create a space to release your stuckness and connect with that impulse of spiritual flow that will carry you home. This can be an opportunity for you to bring with you all of your being, your confusions, your joys, your uncertainties, your grievance. Let all be present now, the being that is you, and let us be together and expand in this cradle of love...

'...Now my dear friends, would any of you like to create the first strand of energy between our two planes and pose the first question?'

'Theodore,' Vi said a little nervously, 'what exactly is the shadow and how does it affect our lives?'

This is a very good question, dear one, and it provides an opportunity for me to explain how the human psyche splinters and becomes fragmented...

'...You were born whole and your journey home is a quest to reclaim that wholeness. Throughout the course of your earthly journey, opposing energies

from the secular realm have infiltrated your being and your psyche has become fragmented. Your psyche can be likened to a house that becomes inhabited by many uninvited guests, each guest a bundle of beliefs and attitudes that fuse together and take on an independent life-form. These bundles of energy, or sub-personalities as they are often called, vie for supremacy and are often in opposition to each other. One such sub-personality I shall call the "Mask". This is the face that you put on public display, the face that opens the door so to speak. Another, the "Shadow", is quite elusive, hidden from public view. The Shadow is a very powerful force that lurks in the dark cellar and is capable of destroying the foundations…

'*…Shortly after incarnation, during early childhood, you are introduced to a world of duality, a world of opposite polarities. Your cultural heritage impresses upon you an acceptable way of operating in the world. You are taught right from wrong, good from bad, love from hate, and so on. A sorting process begins: everything perceived as negative has to be discarded whilst your virtuous traits are harnessed and outwardly displayed. The internalised ideals of society form a cluster of energy and information from which your first inhabitant or sub-personality, the Mask, is born. The Mask parades your noblest traits in order to be socially accepted. It is a pretence - an unrealistic interface between you and the outside world - a mechanism devised solely to gain the approval of others. Conversely, the unacceptable traits, those that have been discarded, form another sub-personality. This unacceptable segment of your being is relegated to the realms of your unconscious, hidden in the cellar so to speak. However, the Shadow is an integral part of your earthly nature and contains intrinsic remnants of the primitive and instinctual ancestral heritage of your forefathers. At some stage in the evolution of human consciousness, these so-called negative traits have been useful. For example, anger and aggression enabled early man to survive attacks from predators in hostile environments; it was a means of survival. Through genetics and natural selection, you have inherited these traits. They are a natural part of your being and cannot be ignored. However, used unwisely, they can cause great destruction. The Shadow complex may be forced beneath the threshold of consciousness, shoved in the cellar and seemingly forgotten, but it is not dead and buried - **it is buried alive**. This abandoned complex of thoughts and feelings remains highly active* *within the realms of your unconscious, accumulating energy and gathering momentum…*

'… So, in answer to your first question, the Shadow is the culmination of all your unacceptable traits that have been bound together and taken on a dark destructive life-form that lurks beneath the threshold of your consciousness. Left unattended it has the power to reduce your psychic house to a heap of rubble - do you understand dear one?'

'Yes,' said Vi.

'Then let me introduce you to another inhabitant. The intermediary between the opposing forces of the Mask and the Shadow is the "Ego", the third inhabitant of your psychic house. The Ego is the personality that emerges as a result of the battle between the perceived negative traits of the Shadow and the idealism of the Mask. It is your centre of consciousness and it tries to maintain equilibrium… Do you understand?'

'Yes, but I thought the ego was all the ideas, beliefs and concepts about ourselves that we had identified with?'

'This is true, my friend. The Ego is born of the conflict between the Shadow and the Mask and then evolves as a result of assimilating many messages. From childhood onwards, you receive many messages from significant others in your life, parents, school teachers, clergymen, friends and so on. When you identify with these messages, they imprint into your centre of consciousness and determine who you believe yourself to be. Whereas the Shadow is unconscious, the Ego is your conscious centre: it is the part of yourself that you refer to as 'I' or in simpler terms, your personality… So now we have your personality and two sub-personalities residing in your psyche and you can see that your initial wholeness is becoming fragmented…

'…To own one's Shadow would mean social suicide so to preserve one's standing in the community, the Ego reverts to defensive mechanisms and disassociates itself from this dark complex. The number one defensive mechanism is known as "projection". Here, one's hostile and persecutory feelings are seen as being situated in others who are then experienced as adversaries. For example, an angry person may experience others as being angry and

intimidating, a jealous person may accuse others of being envious, a dishonest person may see others as liars and so on. In effect, the external world becomes a mirror. A person living this delusion is susceptible to paranoia as he experiences the world, and the people in it, as hostile and threatening. Shadow projection is also a serious threat to social and international peace for it enables people to turn those whom they perceive as enemies into vermin and legitimately hate, attack or, in extreme cases, exterminate them. For example, the serial killer projects his own inner evil onto others and sees his murderous actions as virtuous, cleansing the evils of society. Whole groups are infected by these delusions; like minded people congregate and project their collective Shadow onto other groups. This delusion can result in extremities such as ethnic cleansing and international conflict. Shadow projection leads to scapegoating which occurs at the individual and collective levels: it is a powerful force that causes major imbalance in the collective consciousness of humankind ......Does this answer your question, dear one?'

'Yes,' replied Vi, somewhat agitated, 'but the shadow scares me, it sounds like a demon that's out of control, what can we do to contain it?'

'Unquestionably, control of the Shadow is a very necessary part of human evolution as without it civilized behaviour would cease to exist. However, to project it onto others only exacerbates the problem. The first step is to become aware that it exists. As it operates at an unconscious level, most people are unaware. It may show itself as a sudden outburst of rage or a constant feeling of persecution, but, as you have seen, unaware people will apportion blame to others. So people must be educated and their awareness brought to the concept of projection. The next step my friend is not to alienate this energy, it is to integrate it into your conscious awareness, allow it out of the cellar and into the light and then befriend it and work with it. The Shadow is not all bad, it has many positive attributes. For instance, the Ego can, at times, become inflated. When this occurs, the shadow will form an alliance with your Higher Self and aid the deflation process, bring you back down to earth so to speak...

'...Confronting one's own shadow can be daunting, inducing feelings of guilt, unworthiness, and embarrassment. Fear of rejection can arise should the

Shadow's true nature be exposed. Nobody wants to own anger, jealousy, dishonesty, immorality and so on because they are perceived as undesirable, yet they can be useful tools when perceived in the right way. Anger can be a great agent for change. Most of the positive major changes on earth have resulted from anger and rebellion. Jealousy can help you identify your insecurities and enable you to work on them. Dishonesty can reveal your belief that you are incapable of attaining the things you want purely on personal merit. Therefore it is disempowering. Confronting your shadow can be liberating, releasing much self potential and instinctive energy and making it available to the personality as a whole. Reclaiming this energy results in a sense of greater vitality. You will feel more effervescent, creative and whole...

'...In addition, the Shadow encompasses some of your noblest traits. Many cultures and religions nurture you away from claiming your own divinity, urging you to seek God or the divine in external forms, when, in truth, God is everything my dear child. **God is not an entity from which you are separate: God is a body of consciousness of which you are a part. God is a divine ocean of consciousness that expresses itself in myriad ways. You are a unique expression of this omnipotent being, a wave in the divine ocean, a spark from the eternal flame. Godliness is the very fabric from which you are made.** *If your Godliness cannot be owned for fear of reprisals from society then it too is cast into the shadow. I urge you my dear one, seek the gold in your shadow - reclaim your Godliness. This Universal Intelligence created everything in existence without any effort whatsoever. You are part of this intelligence.* **You cannot be different from that which you are a part. You are both the created and creator. You have invested within you the power to create your every desire. There are no exceptions to this truth: your creative power is limitless.'**

'But how do I embrace this creativity? How do I create my desired life?' Vi intervened.

Whilst you "slept", whilst you were unaware of the internal forces that programmed you, you habituated a way of thinking that bred scarcity. Let go of the preoccupation with "can't", "impossible", "don't deserve", "that happens to other people – not me", *and replace it with* **"I create whatever I desire"**. *Whether it be loving relationships, improved finances, a new home, a new car, a new career – whatever - hold a vision of it in your mind. Let this image grow out of all proportion. Imagine you already have it. Let the wonderful feelings induced surge through your being. Let this vibration pulsate out into the infinite expanse of the Universal Mind. Finally, "know" your desire is on its way…*

'…As you practice this procedure you will become a magnetic beacon, attracting everything you desire. The Universe is omniscient – all seeing. It will honour your request without question. **Know** *this - there is no room for doubt. Doubt will change your vibration and impede the process. Habituate a way of thinking that says* **"I am therefore I can"** *and remember the following procedure:* **imagine your desire has already actualized – feel the feelings this evokes – radiate these feelings towards the Universe - "know" your wish has been granted. You will be astounded at the results……..** *Thank you for your question, dear one - do we have another?'*

'Yes,' said G. 'Something is puzzling me - who am I? If *I* was born whole and became divided into ego, mask and shadow yet none of these are my true self, who is the *"I"* that was born whole? Who is the *I* that identifies with the ideas, concepts and beliefs about *myself* that constitutes the ego? I'm confused.'

'I sense your frustration, dear one, and this is indeed an area of great confusion…… please let me explain…

'…The "I" that identifies with the messages that you have received about yourself throughout your current lifetime can be regarded as your attention. **Attention, is the "eye" through which your sense of "I" is derived.** *As you are now aware, your being is comprised of many different levels of energy and information. At the lower end of the spectrum is your Ego or earthly self. The Ego can be likened to the sun in that it is your conscious centre around which everything else orbits. Orbiting your centre, in the realms of your personal universe, are many other complexes of energy and information that drive your actions from an unconscious level. In addition to the Shadow and the Mask, you have learnt that there are versions of whole people which you have*

internalised during the course of your current life: parents, school teachers, clergymen, friends. In fact, anyone who has had a significant impact on your life. So you can see that your psychic house is heavily populated by many different characters that propel you to think, act and feel in predisposed ways. If your awareness is encapsulated in your personal universe, entrenched in all its limiting beliefs, then your sense of self will derive from this eclectic amalgam of limited information. You will feel confined, powerless and insignificant...

Now, when your attention is raised to a higher vibration and takes residence in the complex of energy known as your Higher Self or Uniqueness, you are able to observe your earthly thoughts and emotions in a detached way. They no longer have any power over you because you are not identifying with them: you have transcended them. Here the complex of energy known as your Higher Self is watching the complex of energy known as your earthly self because your attention is embedded in the former. **Consciousness has become aware of itself.** *Expanding this phenomena will give you an idea of how vast your being is and how it traverses many different realities. You can raise your attention to the level of your Soul or Monad, the Soul's Soul. When your attention fuses with the Soul complex you become your Soul. When it melds with the Monad complex you become your Monad. Whatever your attention is immersed in, you become. Each stage of ascension gives a further sense of freedom and limitless potential as you realise your true essence and move closer to the field of pure creative potential known as the Source...... Does this answer your question my dear friend.'*

'It certainly does,' gasped G.

'Then do we have another question, my friends?'

'Yes,' said G. 'Earth can be a hostile place to live. I now realise that by owning our own shadow we can help restore harmony. How else can we combat planetary conflict?'

'Conflict arises from fear my dear friend and fear arises from an illusionary sense of separation. The antidote for fear is love; for love is unity and where there is unity there can be no separation. A new world view will arise when people re-experience the "oneness" from which they emerged. It may appear beyond your control to restore harmony to your planet for fear has spread by

contagion spiralling out of control and resulting in war. But if you understand that each incarnate being on your planet is part of the one consciousness - the collective consciousness of the earth - you begin to realise that, as you develop yourselves and unify with like-minded people, you can positively affect the balance of the earth consciousness as a whole. Like a sponge absorbs water, the collective consciousness of earth will eventually saturate with love, leaving no space for fear......Human liberation, the second coming of the Christ consciousness or whatever you wish to call it, will occur as a result of people just like yourself peeling back the layers of consciousness until they reach the God within......Do you understand my friend?'

'Yes, thank you.' Said G.

'Theodore,' Vi said in a nervous voice. 'My Uniqueness said that the foundation of my true home is true love. What is true love?'

True love is the highest state of consciousness, dear one. Your natural state of being is that of true love, for true love is simply unity - unity with all that is. To consciously experience this oneness is the true meaning of being "in love", being in divine oneness. When your awareness is rooted in the ground of all being – divine oneness - then you have attained enlightenment and will receive the gift of freedom...Does this help?'

'Yes, but how do we access this oneness?' Vi asked.

'By transcending the duality of your mind. True love lies beyond good and evil, right and wrong. It lies beyond attachment to form. To access this oneness, start by observing your mind. Watch your thoughts arise from an apparent nothingness and dissolve back into this nothingness. If you should become attached to a thought, that is, if your attention is consumed by a thought and it carries you away from your focus, simply become aware of it and regain the position of observer. With perseverance your thoughts will eventually dissipate opening a gateway to a peace that will consume your whole being. When you attain this peace you are "being" in "true love", you are re-experiencing the oneness from where you came. All happiness stems from this state. People are under the great illusion that their happiness is dependent on the attainment of external things, relationships, jobs etcetera. Happiness is always something they

are striving for, something that will happen in the future. However, if they should get the right job or find the right relationship, their happiness is normally short-lived and they are left disillusioned once again. This is because what they truly seek is their true home, the oneness from where they came. This unified state lies within them right **now**...

'...*Your lower earthly mind is a seductress filled with conditioned ideas of happiness. It will try to entice you into its web of delusion, filling you with the idea that external things will bring you happiness. Don't be fooled by its ploy.* **Control your mind; don't let your mind control you.** *Humans often speak of people with great minds when, in reality, the lower mind of which they speak is often a source of impedance determined to shepherd you into herd thinking. It is what lies beyond this mind that is the great source of creativity. Watch your mind vigilantly and become aware of its seductive tactics then be prepared to transcend it. Practice the art of transcending your thoughts my dear one. Enter the field that lies beyond the realm of thought for in this field you will find your home. When you return from this state the peace and creativity you will have attained will flow out into your earthly environment and create circumstances that will bring you ultimate happiness. Only then will external events provide sustained happiness......Does this answer suffice, my child?'*

'Partly,' said Vi, 'but can true love occur between two human beings?'

Yes, but we must remember that two halves do not always make a whole. Human relationships are quite a complex subject and attraction is often based an unconscious processes. This type of bonding is based on the fulfillment of needs which stem from each partner's childhood experiences. True love is experienced when two human beings retain their individuality even when unified. Partnership is not about owning another human being or typecasting them; it is about accepting their uniqueness and respecting their individuality. By its very nature, true love is unconditional. When two humans collapse themselves into a relationship they lose their sense of identity and individuality, putting demands on one another and trying to mould their partners' into what they think they should be. True love is about acceptance and respect and from it, once again, stems the gift of freedom...Does this answer your question, dear one?'

'Yes, thank you, Theodore.'

'Time for one more question, my friends.'

'My Uniqueness has suggested that I've chosen a difficult path, which I now accept. Yet there's something I find very disturbing about this. The idea seems to suggest that perpetrators of abuse have a license to carry out terrible acts in order to present circumstances for others to learn. Quite frankly this appalls me.'

'And so it should, dear one. No one is instructed to violate another human being's rights. This runs totally contrary to Universal Law. Anyone who carries out such acts will be subject to the law of karma. If they fail to redeem themselves, they will inevitably pay for their actions... Let me expand on the bigger picture; I feel it may deepen your understanding...

*'...At this stage in the evolution of human consciousness, beings from the higher dimensions are choosing to reincarnate with the specific purpose of breaking destructive family patterns - patterns that have been handed down from generation to generation. As there are no preordained futures, these beings monitor families where the probability of dysfunctionality is extremely high. When they incarnate into such environments, the abuse occurs as a result of the perpetrators being self indulgent, misguided, lost, frightened or confused. Their actions are most definitely **not** orchestrated from the higher realms for the good of your growth...*

'...You have learnt that people who administer physical abuse, in many cases, have experienced trauma themselves. This is also the case with perpetrators of sexual abuse. It is most unusual to find a perpetrator of sexual abuse who hasn't been sexually abused themselves. Saying this, I must point out that only a small percentage of victims become perpetrators. So whether the abuse be sexual or physical there is actually a catalyst; this is often a destructive pattern stemming many generations. This heritage does not excuse the actions of perpetrators, however, it may invoke an element of understanding and possibly compassion...may I ask you, dear child, how do you feel about your foster-father?'

Vi fidgeted nervously, glancing subduedly at G.

'I hated him for what he did to me,' she answered angrily, 'it was wrong and he shouldn't have done it.'

Her eyes began to moisten.

'But in all other areas of life he was a good man – he had many virtues.' She sniffled. 'He worked hard, bought me nice clothes and there was always food on the table. This is why I find it so difficult. I feel guilty for loving him and guilty for hating him. When he died I knew that I'd loved him. I mourned his death for quite some time. I just wish he could've explained to me why he did what he did.'

'As I have explained my dear one, almost without exception, perpetrators of sexual abuse have been abused themselves.'

Vi felt a shiver run down her spine as a disconcerting thought occurred to her.

'Does this make me a liability?' she asked, worriedly.

'No, my child, it certainly does not. As I stated earlier, only a very small percentage of victims become perpetrators. The reason that statistics for sexual abuse are so high is that those who do go on to abuse, do so many times.

'Oh – I see,' said Vi, relieved.

'I am concerned with your healing now, my child. If you can dissolve the conflict that lies within you, you will free up space for love to enter. Whatever you feel about your foster-father is valid for you. But to live with this conflict inside of you can only lead to deep confusion and unhappiness. To help reconcile the warring parts of yourself, perhaps you can separate your foster-father from the wrong action he performed. His actions were undoubtedly wrong, but they were not his whole identity. People, at times, can be likened to computers. If you program them wrongly then they can malfunction. Your foster-father was indeed sexually abused as a child and he carried on the legacy. You put an end to that heritage by identifying with your Uniqueness, as most victims do. Now it's time to enhance your quality of life and enrich your relationships. People who have suffered sexual abuse often have great difficulty in forming intimate relationships as a result of their experiences. If you can separate your foster-father from the

155

wrong action he performed then maybe you can concentrate on his virtues. This will have the effect of freeing you from the bondage of your past and enable you to begin to love without fear. The alchemical effect of this process will greatly enrich your life and enable you to reap the fruits that you so rightfully deserve. I offer you this explanation my child…

'…You are one of those beings who has chosen to experience dysfunctionality. The nature of the trauma was uncertain before incarnation and would only be determined in the physical realm. However, as you monitored your potential family from the higher realms, the probability of physical abuse was high. The next set of circumstances materialized as a result of your domestic situation on Earth. You were fostered and became the target of sexual abuse. Your primary purpose was to break these destructive patterns which meant you would need great strength. The success of your mission was highly dependent on you being able to heal yourself. You cannot change the traumatic events of your past but you can change the way you **feel** about them. This is not for the benefit of the perpetrator; it is purely to reconcile the warring parts of yourself and enable you to find a level of peace. Earlier you asked about choice, and today you have a choice. Remember you co-create your own reality. **Today is the first day of the rest of your life**; you can "choose" to be bound by your past and allow the cancer of victimisation to erode you, or you can "choose" to assimilate the invaluable insights that such trauma can behold and use it to recognise your destiny. You are awakening now my dear one and you are gaining understanding. With your newfound knowledge and experience you can heal yourself and then reach out to the collective and help others heal their wounds too……Does this help your understanding, my friend?'

'Yes, it does. Thank you, Theodore. I've never wanted to believe that either my father or foster-father were inherently evil. I've always sought some explanation and you've just provided me with one. Thank you again.'

'Thank you for your question, my friend. Now walk with faith and follow the remaining signposts home……. It is with love and light that I must now leave you.'

The ambience of the room remained serene as Theodore withdrew his energy. Phil slowly came back to his ordinary state of consciousness and opened his eyes, unable to recall most of the information that had passed through him. He sipped at a glass of water and remained silent for a while, mentally grounding himself. He then stood up and beckoned the others to join him. They formed a circle, clasping hands, and offered thanks to Theodore. After which they blew out the candles and dedicated the light to all the suffering people of the world.

'That was incredible,' said G. 'I could've never imagined the complex forces that drive us as human beings…. Are you okay, Vi?'

'Yes. That was very emotional for me but so liberating. What Theodore said made so much sense. What my foster-father did was disgusting and I hated him for it. I was a child and he violated my boundaries. Yet this was only one aspect of his personality, he had many virtues. He could be caring, kind and sensitive. Living with this confusion was the most difficult thing of all. I know I'll never forget what happened, but I can change the way I feel. I want a better quality of life and to achieve it I have to find a way to reconcile the warring parts of myself. Knowing that my foster-father was sexually abused does help, but I'll never understand why someone who's been through such atrocities could inflict them on another human being.'

'As ludicrous as it might sound,' interjected Phil, 'sexual abuse is not always a traumatic experience. I once counselled a girl who, like you, was sexually abused by her step-father; the abuse started when she was aged six. Aged thirteen, she overheard some girls talking about sex at school. She couldn't understand why these girls hadn't had sex with their father's too: she thought it was normal up until that point. Other survivors actually found the experience pleasurable and some associate it with love. When such people go on to become perpetrators, they may fail to see the harm they're doing: they *know* it's wrong, but they don't *feel* it's wrong. In other cases, the survivor may have experienced orgasm during the abuse. If these people go on to become perpetrators it's common to find that they try to re-create the circumstances that gave them this sexual gratification. This is the case with many serial rapists.'

'My God,' said G. 'This subject is complicated.'

'It certainly is,' replied Phil.

'I've just thought of something that might help me,' said Vi. 'If my foster-father experienced his abuse as loving and couldn't see the harm in what he was doing, then he never meant to harm me.'

'Possibly, Vi, and if this way of thinking helps you then use it. Like you said, you can't change the events of the past, but you can change the way you feel about them. Our concern is not for your foster-father, it's for you. His actions cannot be excused: he has to take responsibility for them no matter what the circumstances. But the most important thing now is that you find a way to free yourself of his legacy. Grasp hold of whatever helps you to resolve your inner conflict.'

' I was terrified to admit I loved him. I thought that, in light of what he'd done, I must be weird. On the other hand, taking into consideration his goodness, I felt guilty for hating him – I felt I was betraying him. I shouldn't feel guilty for hating his actions, they were wrong – very wrong. On the other hand, I shouldn't feel guilty for loving the rest of his identity.'

'No, you shouldn't,' said Phil. 'Whatever you feel is okay, with the exception of guilt of course. Survivors of sexual abuse can experience a range of emotions: guilt, shame, confusion, disgust, rage and self hatred. These can lead to behaviours such as: depression, self mutilation, suicide, sleep disorders, sexual disorders, aggression, the list goes on and on. The effects can be devastating. In order to help such people, we must authenticate their feelings, tell them that whatever they feel is okay. We have no right to impress our feelings onto them. This could exacerbate the problem and have grave consequences. The most important thing is that they don't transfer their feelings onto others, that is, they don't generalize and adopt the attitude that "all men" or "all women" are abusers. This can only serve to inhibit their chances of forming intimate relationships.'

'You're right, Phil. I was very wary and suspicious of all men. Tom was the only one I really trusted and that took quite some time to develop. I feel that, in time, I'll be able to let go of some of the ghosts of the past and begin living.'

'How do you feel, Phil?' inquired G. 'I couldn't believe the transformation in you; it was almost as though someone else was sitting there tonight.'

'They were, G.' Phil replied, with an endearing smile.

*

Later that evening the trio decided to review the tape. During the course of the conversation that ensued, Phil brought G. up to date with the phenomena of relationship fits. As the night progressed the conversation centred around the proposal that 'true love' was unity consciousness. They came to the conclusion that there was a vast difference between love based on needs and true love.

The experience of love based on needs was due to the 'chemistry' or unconscious forces that attracted couples together. It was highly conditional and only worked within given boundaries. However, everyone agreed that there were many lessons to be learnt through such relationships: past issues could be highlighted and resolved; opposites could learn to assimilate the attributes of their partners and work towards balance; people could realise they were placing unrealistic demands on their partners; avoidance of certain emotions could be challenged and couples learn to integrate both *good* and *bad* aspects (in reality, all emotions have negative and positive qualities – interpretation is the key to positive transformation). Relationships based on unconscious forces also provide opportunities for people to discover the various complexes that dwell within them. They offer the chance for people to expose their vulnerabilities and face their innermost fears, presenting circumstances through which they can grow and evolve.

True love, conversely, is totally unconditional, independent of internal forces. True love is our natural state of being. It is a state in which we re-experience the oneness from which we came. From the perspective of relationships, when two people are in 'true love', they both have their being grounded in this oneness. When this happens, all demands subside, the love is without condition, and total freedom prevails. People who experience true love, have worked through the debris of their emotional and mental bodies and their awareness is firmly embedded in their heart chakra - the centre of unconditional love which bridges the earthly and transpersonal aspects of ourselves.

The evening came to a conclusion with a conversation pertaining to the belief that we co-create our reality.

'So there is an element of choice,' said G. 'We decide on some things before incarnation; other things materialize during the course of our lives?'

'That's right, G. We decide upon our life's purpose and that will play a role in the situations we experience on Earth. The path we choose may be difficult during certain stages of the journey, but if we sift through the silt that clouds our minds and determine our purpose, then we'll experience a joy that transcends anything.'

'Phil,' inquired Vi, 'If we make choices before we incarnate, and beings from the higher realms orchestrate some of our experiences, does it mean that we don't have any influence over our lives at an earthly level?'

'Far from it, Vi, we have a tremendous influence. As Theodore said, we can create our every desire. I think you've just brought up an excellent topic on which to finish the evening – something I intended to talk about tomorrow before we leave…...it's been a long night - do you both feel up to it?'

'Yes,' came the reply, G. and Vi enthusiastic to learn more.

'Remember how when we break down the various stages of physical structures we are left with sub-atomic particles?'

'Yes.'

'Well, Albert Einstein found that these particles behave in singular ways. What he meant was that each particle has a mind of its own. He also found that they respond to thought. This has enormous implications as to the power of thought. Let this next part sink in real deeply:

If each sub-atomic particle responds to thought and the quantum field is a mass of these particles, then the very fabric from which our physical world is comprised is able to respond to our expectations. If we permanently think negative then we will influence these particles in a way that creates negative circumstance – our negativity will become a self fulfilling prophecy. If we are able to dissolve our impedances, the rigid patterns that cause our negative thinking, then we can influence the field in a way that will create joy, fulfillment, happiness and contentment. Our greatest sense of fulfillment will manifest when our thoughts coincide with our life's purpose and we create circumstances that lead to our destiny – we have every tool at our disposal, we just have to recognise our true potential.'

*

Vi lay in bed, pleasantly tired after the evening's events. Her eyes began to feel leaden. She turned on her side to face the wall, making herself comfortable and started slipping from the conscious to the unconscious. Her lids closed but there was still a prism clear image of the room behind her shuttered eyes. The ambience of the room gradually began to change. An uneasy calm passed through her. She became listless and edgy, sensing she wasn't alone. Suddenly, an arm wrapped around her neck gripping her in a stranglehold. She froze. Her anger erupted fuelled by fear. She struggled and fought, striking out wildly but could not free herself. Her body began to convulse with panic. She thrust her elbow backwards one more time but her arm appeared to pass straight through her assailant. Her mind became chaotic. Her entire life flashed before her. In a last ditch attempt to save herself she called out to Theodore and Esba. Nothing happened. She called out again. This time, a short phrase echoed through her mind.

Love it, don't fight it.

Immediately, her body began to relax. She composed herself and sent loving thoughts to the dark entity. The atmosphere began to soften. She sensed the intruder had departed but couldn't be sure; she was still facing the wall. Terrified to turn around, she lay rigid for a while and started tremble. Eventually, she plucked up the courage to look behind her. She was alone, the figure had disappeared. She lay on the bed perplexed and trembling.

Was that a bad dream? She thought. *It couldn't have been - everything in the room was just as it is now.*

She quickly got out of bed and scurried through to the lounge.

'Phil, wake up.' She said, prodding him.

Phil opened his bleary eyes to see that Vi was obviously in a state of shock.

'What is it?' he asked.

She began to relay her experience.

'I didn't know what to do. Somehow, I remembered you saying that the best form of protection are the guides themselves, so I called for help of Theodore and Esba. They appeared to say "love it don't fight it" and a calmness came over me. I sent some loving thoughts to the figure and it disappeared...... Phil, did this really happen? Or was it my mind playing tricks?'

Phil appeared unphased by Vi's encounter which gave her a sense of reassurance. 'I've had similar experiences to this, Vi. Remember me telling you of my experience here when I became suspended between two worlds?'

'Yes, I do Phil.'

'Well, like you, I was aware that my physical body lay on the bed, but *I* was elsewhere. My consciousness had wandered into a non-ordinary reality. It seems like you had also entered a non-ordinary state, a reality that had superimposed itself over your material world. Such expeditions are the basis of all mythology. The shamans utilized such journeys to great advantage. We must remember there are many realities that co-exist. The ancients often used to travel into these alternate worlds to converse with the Gods or fight their inner demons which would take on form in these realities…. Did you see your assailant?'

'No, not physically, but I was aware it was a dark shadowy figure, like a silhouette.'

'Think about it, Vi. This encounter makes so much sense. It has a real powerful message. I feel this figure was your shadow that had taken on form in a non-ordinary reality. Your past traumatic experiences form a large part of your shadow complex and they, as we have seen over this weekend, are severely inhibiting your life. In other words they have a stranglehold on you. To transform our shadow we have to bring it into the light of our consciousness, befriend it and work with it as Theodore said. The guides responded to your call for help with the light of love and, as a shadow cannot exist where there is light, it dispersed. The message here for you is to fight your fears with love, transform your shadow into light, change your way of thinking and create your dream reality - spiritual alchemy, Vi......Does this feel right to you?'

'Yes, it does, Phil. Absolutely. It was another signpost.'

'Exactly, Vi, remember signposts come in all shapes and forms.'

Chapter 13

Uni-Verse: One-Song

Splintering particles of consciousness came dancing out of the nothingness illuminating the darkness like a swarm of radiant glow flies. They spiralled and twirled and, as though choreographed by an invisible intelligence, formed themselves into a shimmering embryo of resplendent light. Entwined images flashed within its lens, blinking in and out of existence at the speed of light. The face of a wise old monk transposed into that of an Indian squaw which fluidly changed into a young woman, then a middle aged man. A further blizzard of particles sprayed from the void enveloping the ellipse and translating into an entrancing structure: a crystal temple. A landscape appeared: fields, trees, streams, fountains and waterfalls. The embryo segregated leaving two bubbles of light which hovered just above the marble floor of the central hall. Sparks arced from one to the other in a display of divine interaction. With one enormous surge, light sprayed in every direction dispersing the bubbles and the forms of an aged monk and a young Indian squaw were projected into being.

Theodore had lowered his vibration and entered the Mental plane to rendezvous with a highly evolved aspect of his *own* being - Esba. At this level of experience they existed as pure intelligence, shimmers of refined light, yet form and surroundings could be projected at will, sculptured by the power of thought.

Esba stared into Theodore's saintly grey-blue eyes as he began to initiate communication - without words. Together they sent out a telepathic invitation to another aspect of their being.

*

The majestic mountain range rose up from the midst of the monsoon sodden rain forest. Rain drops danced on the palm trees that littered the undulating landscape. Waterfalls cascaded down from the backdrop of mountains feeding an effervescent river.

Phil strolled through the breathtaking scenery, allowing nature to impart its wisdom. He watched the white water rapids powering their way past obstacles, determined to reach their destination, intuiting that nature was telling him to do likewise. Sheer determination and single mindedness was her message.

A Boa slithered from beneath a rock. Phil cast an enquiring eye on it, contemplating how he had to shed the layers of illusion to reveal the truth. He was co-creator of his own reality. Belief was the key to manifestation. The energy and information of the quantum field was intelligent. Einstein said, *'atoms behave in singular ways and respond to thought.'* What he meant was that every atom has its own intelligence and can be influenced telepathically. As atoms are the building blocks of everything we deem to be physical, we can effect positive change purely through the power of thought. We can heal and manifest anything we desire through the power of thought. We have boundless potential. We just have to believe it. People believe they think positive when, in actuality, they have a light coating of positivity which covers a mass of negativity. Their negativity affects the quantum field in a detrimental way. On a mass scale this brings chaos and disharmony to our planet. We must nurture our thoughts, release the conditioning of society, and recognise our potential. Whatever we desire must reign supreme in our mind. We must believe we can manifest our every desire with every rudiment of our being. Belief is the precursor of manifestation; it's the midwife that births reality from thought.....

...I will have my centre.... I will teach and heal.... I will write my books. I will live my dream. Phil proclaimed, zealously.

A tide of inspiration began to flow through him. His whole being began to dance to the rhythm of the Universe. He glowed with a passion for life. Up ahead he spotted a wooden bridge arching across the river. He almost floated to its centre where he stopped to commune with nature. The wonder child within had stepped forward to preside over his thinking:

Jesus said, '***to enter the kingdom of heaven we had to see life through the eyes of a child.***' William Wordsworth, the English poet laureate, proclaimed '***the child is father of the man.***'

Of course! Phil thought, an ever increasing sense of excitement building. *To penetrate the veil that separates us from the higher dimensions we have to see life through the pure, unconditioned, eyes of the wonder child – the Soul child. Imagination and fantasy are a core part of that child's natural state of being. These attributes have been discredited by the manipulative powers that be, to disempower us.*

'Wake up world!' he shouted at the top of his voice.

'Take back your power and let's unite. We're all one and when we realise it, we'll bring about a new world view.'

His voice echoed through the wilderness, bouncing off the mountains. His sense of excitement rocketed and he began to enter a fourth dimension of existence. Nature sprites emerged from the trees and surrounded him on the bridge.

'Come and join me,' he bellowed, laughing with sheer delight.

Rabbits, birds, and animals emerged from the nothingness and encircled him on the bridge. Pegasus flew in from the unseen. Unicorns descended from the cosmos. His awareness was entrenched in his heart chakra and he felt an affinity with everything.

He witnessed the dawn of all creation. Mother Earth broke away from Father Sun and began to cool down. The first inhabitants of our planet, the stone people, absorbed the intelligence of the sun and cultivated the land in preparation for the plant people. The plants provided the twenty-one percent oxygen needed for other forms of life. The animals emerged and consciousness became mobile. Next came human beings, nature's privileged children. Nature was in collusion with her many aspects and together they orchestrated a divine plan.

The stones, trees and plants that surrounded Phil now began to take on a human element and joined him too. A bolt of inspiration hit him from the heavens and a song started to emerge in his mind, the words coming effortlessly. He began to sing:

'There was a time, I knew, that everything was one
A time before all conflict had begun
A world so pure and filled with harmony
Lay within that child I used to be.

'But then the tide of turbulence rolled in
To flood my world with its conditioning
It washed away my link to the divine
Immersing me in fears of humankind.'

His gentle tone now shifted to one of purpose.

'The clouds of discontentment blocked the light
My universal home went out of sight
Drowning in humanity's contaminated views
Pollution filled that child's mind and he began to lose
The magic that connected him with worlds no one could see
For they've been blinded by the wrath of rationality
Enmeshed within a system of delusion and denial

The teachings of enlightened ones condemned without a trial
It's time to find the wisdom of that child within again
And let his light shine forth and be the father of all men
So step out of the darkness of your plight
Step into the ocean of the light.'

The song now raised to a crescendo and the anthem-like chorus rang out. The animals, trees, plants and nature sprites joined in and sang out 'we are one.' Monkeys shook the trees with delight, wolves danced with sheep, predators danced with their prey for as far as the eye could see. There was complete harmony.

'We are one
We are unified - sparks from the divine flame
We are one
When we remember then we'll all be home again
Jettison the debris you've collected through your life
Throw away the guilt, the shame, your troubles and your strife
Step out of the armour of your fear
Bring our liberation one step nearer.'

The song took on a gentle ambience again.

'The time has come for our planet to evolve
Let down our guard and into oneness all dissolve
I'll cradle you and you will cradle me

This love will suffuse and the whole world then will see…'

A sense of excitement began to build

'A new world view, a shift in collective consciousness
Explore our minds and step into the cosmic dance
Peel back the layers of illusion that disguise the truth
And there you'll find the fountain of eternal youth.

'Let's wake up to a world that's so supreme
Where each of us can live our ideal dream
Separation can't exist where unity prevails
Conflict will be obsolete as wisdom fills our sails
We shall all be vessels for the universal light
Co-creating a new world with magical insight
So sit behind that child's eyes and see what he can see
Other worlds that co-exist in perfect harmony
Let's listen to the messages that whisper through our minds
Subtle words of wisdom comes from spirit so refined
So on that journey we shall now embark
And let the signposts lead us through the dark.'

Processions of children from every conceivable background came to join in, singing at the tops of their voices.

'We are one

We are unified, for all eternity

We are one

The essence of true love is simply unity

Ground your being in oneness and commence a new journey

Hand in hand with everyone we'll reach our destiny

The plants, the trees and animals, the planets and the stars

Are all extensions of ourselves, they're relatives of ours

Cradled in a living womb of loving energy

The nothing that births everything and yearns to set us free

Don't stand alone, a solo voice, apart from everything

Join the cosmic choir and together we will sing...

We are one'

The chorus continued repeatedly, echoing throughout the land, ricocheting off the mountains, sending out a potent message: HARMONY AND UNITY. All sense of demarcation vanished. Phil knew that everything was part of himself: Uni-Verse, One-Song; each of us a unique note, collectively composing a divine overture.

Phil's euphoric experience finally began to dissipate; the people, creatures and sprites fading back into the nothingness. Phil stood alone once again on the bridge. *Music is to be part of my life again*, he thought. *I will write songs to awaken people.*

He pulled a scrunched up notebook from his back pocket and began to write the words of the song. After he'd finished, he looked up and noticed that one of the animals had remained - a wolf. His thoughts drifted to the Native American teachings of Esba. She had taught him that, unlike traditional medicine, Native

American medicine encompassed anything that improved a person's connection to the hidden realms: The Great Mystery as the Indians called it. Medicine, in this sense, meant anything that brought balance, harmony, strength and understanding to Mother Earth and her inhabitants. Each animal species exhibited a pattern of behaviour that imparted a unique lesson - a medicine. The wolf was a pack animal with a strong sense of individualism, a pathfinder who explored uncharted territory in pursuit of knowledge then returned to share its findings with the rest of the pack.

Phil heard a voice urging him to follow the wolf. He began to sense he was about to discover new truths that could be shared with others. His purpose involved teaching and wolf medicine empowered the teacher within. He watched the creature intently as he followed it up the mountainside, observing how its keen senses and instinct were its guiding force.

As they reached a height of about a thousand feet, landslides and thickening mist made conditions treacherous, yet wolf negotiated the hazardous terrain with great precision. The journey was long and arduous. Night began to fall when they reached the entrance of a cave. A maze of dark cavernous tunnels lay before them. Wolf waited at the entrance, baying at the moon, the symbol for psychic energy. A hazy luminescent mist emerged from the cave and enveloped Phil. His body began to vaporize and suffuse into the luminescent haze. The mist swished back into the cave as though sucked by a powerful vacuum and Phil felt himself being thrust forward at the speed of light.

*

Theodore and Esba watched as a blizzard of particles sprayed from the void and Phil materialized in the main hall of the crystal temple. They smiled at each other, knowing their call had been answered.

'Welcome, dear one,' said Theodore, without words.

'Where am I?' Phil replied, confused.

'The halls of learning,' answered Esba, mentally. *'It is time for you to learn the origins of your being and see how consciousness has cascaded through the various levels of existence – please join us.'*

Phil felt his body begin to vaporize again and noticed the same thing was happening to Theodore and Esba. Each of them took the form of a shimmering ellipse of light and hovered above the marble floor. Then the bubbles began to fuse together and become one. Phil's awareness rocketed. He felt as though he had been plugged into a spiritual internet and a vast amount of information was available to him.

A scene began to materialize on their collective screen of consciousness. The womb of all creation appeared, yet didn't appear for it was a nothingness; a void from which everything was birthed: the *nothing* that contained *everything*. A shimmering ellipse of multi-coloured light emerged from the void and started to divide just like the cells of our bodies, each one taking on an independent life of its own.

Monads, thought Phil, *the first individualized sparks from the eternal flame, beings of super consciousness; our primordial source of intelligence.*

He watched as the Monads multiplied and took residence in the highest realms of existence. These super-beings were endowed with free will and wished to expand their knowledge and explore the denser realms. So, born in the image of the creator and capable of giving life, they each gave birth to a number of children. Phil watched as each Monad projected several Souls into being; each Soul an appendage of its creator. As Phil continued to observe, these Souls further differentiated, projecting several more appendages of consciousness into an even denser realm of existence. These entities included ourselves - earthly beings.

The scene faded and the bubble of light began to segregate into three. Phil, Esba and Theodore took on individual form once again.

So you can see, dear one, said Theodore, *the Source is the ground of all being, the highest state of consciousness where everything exists as pure potential. The Monad is an appendage of the Source and encompasses the experiences of a number of Souls. The Soul, in turn, is an appendage of the Monad and embodies the experiences of a number of personalities. So every entity is intertwined and interdependent in a network of consciousness that cascades down through the various dimensions of existence.*

'The ground of being for *several* earthly personalities is one Soul?' inquired Phil.

Not exactly, Phil, interjected Esba. *These others could be incarnate on Earth or on some other planet in the infinite expanse of the Universal Mind. Members of our Soul family could also be incarnate on one of the other spiritual planes.*

'Oh - I see,' said Phil, who now realised he too was communicating non- verbally. 'So each of us on Earth has a Soul family who are all appendages of consciousness emanating from the one ground of being – our soul?'

Precisely, said Esba, an air of mysticism in her tone. Phil immediately began to sense he was about to be entrusted with a great revelation. Then, suddenly, he was assaulted by barrage of light from which emerged a holographic image. Theodore stood central, encircled by twelve points of light. The seedlings of light began to expand and Phil noticed that each one contained a form that appeared to blink in and out of existence. Beams of light radiated out from Theodore's heart chakra fusing with each cell and forming a celestial wheel. Slowly, the features of each form became more pronounced. Phil was filled with an overwhelming sense of unbounded love.

The nature of revelation finally started to emerge. He could not only see himself encapsulated in one of the embryos, but three of the other cells enveloped images of Vi, G. and Esba. Each personality now began to introduce themselves.

'Roma, currently incarnate in the twenty-first century - Psychic medium and healer.'

'Robert, twenty-first century - quantum physicist.'

'Ann-Marie, twenty-first century – school teacher.'

'Emily, nurse during the Crimean war - nineteenth century.'

'Esba, disincarnate guide and healer.'

'Graham, twenty-first century - accountant.'

'Violet, twenty-first century - accountant.'

'Sanji, currently fourteenth century - seer.'

'Angelique, currently disincarnate - guide.'

'Ramone, sixth centrury Greece - philosopher and teacher.'

'Ellissia, disincarnate - guide and healer.'

'Phil, twenty-first century – author, composer, healer, teacher and founder of the Synergy School of Holistic Development.'

'What!' exclaimed Phil, staring at his own holographic image.

'I exist in your future....seek me out,' the image replied, somewhat cryptically.

Phil thought he was experiencing delirium tremens again, yet there was one last revelation to come. An explosion of light erupted from the cell containing Esba's image and from it emerged the holographic image of a little girl.

'I from your future too, daddy,' she gurgled, her eyes radiating wisdom beyond her years.

Phil felt the child's penetrating smile melting his heart.

The sheaths of light radiating from Theodore now began to retract, drawing each of the personalities closer to him. One by one the identities were absorbed into his being and the twelve became united as one.

Phil felt intoxicated by something he had never ingested via a bottle. He was totally astounded by the enigmatic experience. 'You are my Soul,' he said, gawping at Theodore in total disbelief, 'and these others are my Soul brothers and sisters.'

Yes, dear one. I am your guide and your Soul. Though I am partially comprised of the experiences of my personalities, I have a core identity which is grounded in my Monad, just as your earth personalities are comprised of parts of other human beings, sub-personalities, yet maintain the core identity of your Uniqueness.

'And Esba is my spiritual sister and also my guide?'

Yes, replied Esba. *Some members of your Soul family remain in the higher realms and act as spirit guides to their Soul brothers and sisters. It is quite possible that, should I incarnate again, you will act as spirit guide for me. You must remember that you are not the sum total of your Earthly experiences. Your being is wise and boundless, spanning every level of existence.*

'But I'm confused. Some of my Soul family claimed to be *currently* incarnate in eras long since past - this can't possibly be!'

*This **is** true, dear one. Past, present and future co-exist in the continuum of the eternal present.*

Phil looked highly confused but didn't bother to pursue the question. His mind was at saturation point. Yet, he was determined to ask one final question.

'Who was that little girl?' he inquired.

Esba smiled. The scene faded.

Phil awoke from his deep sleep, unable to remember most of his dream. Amidst the sheets on his bed, he noticed a scrunched up notebook. He opened it to find it filled with writing that was hardly legible. After studying it for a while, he realised that the words seemed to take on the form of a song?

Chapter 14

Reflections

Vi retreated to her favourite spot by the river and G. found a secluded place in the nearby woods, each of them seeking solitude to assimilate their newly acquired information.

Everything is information and energy, thought Vi. *Our personal energy field encompasses many different complexes of energy. Each complex, or sub-personality, is a group of narratives and experiences that have a common theme. They're like audio and video recordings that have infiltrated our inner world and form the basis of our conditioning, inner people that demand us to think, feel and behave in rigid ways. All these bundles of energy are orbiting around our ego, our conscious centre, and impacting on our sense of self. A mind that's filled with all these preconceptions cannot be free. We must release these shackles and move into the present moment – after all, the present is all we ever have. If we let the thoughts of these internal saboteurs dominate our thinking then the quantum field will respond by creating circumstances that reflect them.*

So we don't pick our partners because of their large breasts, pert bums or vivacious bodies, thought G. *If so I'd have never chosen Joan!* (A smug, self-satisfying, grin spread across his face, his contempt for women emerging as a result of the turbulent relationship he had with his oppressive, manipulative, mother).

These relationship fits are very interesting, he pondered. *I can see myself in the 'unresolved childhood' issues fit. Joan has many of my mother's characteristics: control freak, domineering, over-assertive, over-sensitive, inflated ego leading to delusions of grandeur. In fact, she's just a god damn bitch!.... Saying this, I've never attempted to leave her. I rarely even get angry with her –*

an ingrained belief I suppose. I was brought up to regard anger as inappropriate and unacceptable. But, as Phil said, it's needed at times to effect change. Aristotle summed this up when he said - **there is nothing wrong with anger. The trick is to get angry with the right person, at the right time, for the right reasons'.** *Through defence systems, mechanisms our ego uses to protect its identity, we are apt to displace, project or transfer our anger. We direct it at the* **wrong** *person, for the* **wrong** *reasons, at the* **wrong** *times. This is inappropriate but most of the time we don't even realise that we're doing it – it's totally unconscious. Perhaps this sheds some light on my disastrous marriage and reveals the reasons why I chose Joan as my partner. I didn't confront my mother. I didn't challenge her rigid views and I don't do it with my wife either. I just conform and accept. My God, my self-esteem must be low. I must have a low sense of worth otherwise I would vent my anger when appropriate – stand up for myself. Sometimes we have to confront and challenge people to provide them with an opportunity to look at themselves. I must be prepared to challenge Joan next time I feel she's being tyrannical and unjust. I must take back my power and build up my self-esteem. In fairness, I must also acknowledge my own stuff. I'm apt to think she's forever scheming against me, hatching plots to make me unhappy. I'm often suspicious and mistrusting of her - almost paranoid. With insight, I can see that these are issues I had with my mother. I'm recreating the relationship I had with my mother in the present - with Joan. Why? - To resolve the issues I had with my mother.*

So, thought Vi, *we can displace our forbidden emotions by choosing a partner who will express them for us. In my case, love is a liability so I disown it. Unconsciously I attracted a partner who would express it for me. Conversely, his background prohibited anger, so I acted as a vessel for his anger. Two halves coming together to form a whole - opposites. In addition, I now know why I'm apt to operate from the oppressor complex - it gives me power. I might moan and groan about Tom but unconsciously the relationship suits me just fine. My life's experience has taught me to stay in control and the oppressor is very controlling - control is the weapon I use to defend myself. Tom operates from the submissive, manipulating, programmed child state, so he doesn't threaten me. He doesn't get angry very often but he is apt to revert to sulking and emotional blackmail -*

manipulation. Outsiders often wonder why we stay together. Yet, with my new-found awareness, the reasons are very obvious.

G. started to think about thoughts themselves, and how they cascade down through the subtle bodies to become experience.

I've always felt oppressed and disempowered. My life experience has impressed upon me that women are the dominant sex. I spoke to Phil a while ago about a tendency I've developed to dress up in women's clothing - cross dressing. Unlike transvestism where a man feels like a woman trapped in a man's body, cross dressers are quite happy to remain male but enjoy dressing up and assuming the persona of a woman. Now my awareness is heightened, I can see how my thoughts have influenced my actions. I associate power with femininity and when I dress as a woman, I feel powerful and superior. Here my internalised scripts and preconceptions are rippling down through the various subtle bodies to become actual experience.

He began to laugh, thinking of the first meeting he had with Phil. When he told Phil about this facet of his personality he expressed concern about people finding out and asked Phil to keep this information confidential. They both ended up in pleats of laughter when Phil replied 'there's no point in hanging your dirty frocks out in public.' Phil's humour had an air of acceptance, alleviating any tension. G. felt totally reassured.

Phil glanced over at Vi. *Relationships,* he thought; *in my case, numerous, various but always transient.* He'd always felt unsettled and unable to commit himself. After the heartache of ending his last relationship, he swore he wouldn't get involved for at least a couple of years - that was nine years ago. Presently, with insight, he could see that he operated fundamentally from the caretaker complex. He thrived in relationships were his partner took the role of the needy, submissive child. He loved to nurture. He knew this fulfilled a need in him - a need to be needed. He was also very aware that the caretaker could be very controlling, not allowing the child to grow up.

He looked at Vi again and thought how she exuded childlike qualities: purity and innocence. He knew that if he was to nurture her for a while, he must allow her to grow up and move on. However, there was something distinctly different about his attraction to her - something that seemed to run very deep?

Vi's thoughts drifted to her past relationships with significant males. Naturally, she still had mixed feelings but her awareness had given her strength and understanding.

I wonder what my father has experienced to cause him to act in such distasteful ways? I don't suppose I'll ever be the kind of daughter who flings my arms around him and tells him how much I love him, but I do feel some sort of reconciliation is needed. And my foster-father.. well.. I despised him for what he done to me. I hated him. It disgusted me. My feelings have been so mixed up. I felt guilty for hating him and guilty for loving him. The important thing now is that I reconcile the warring parts of myself. This is not about him, it's about me. He's dead now but his legacy still lives on inside of me. I know he was sexually abused too and this does give me an element of compassion, but in my eyes, it's no excuse, I have every right to be angry. But if I continue to think like a victim, then I'll attract circumstances that will reinforce my belief; I'll never be able to give fully of myself. I'll never be able to experience the richness of meaningful love. I'll probably never forget what happened but I can change the way I feel about things. What he did wasn't his whole identity it was only a part of him. I'll bear this in mind and try to remember his virtues. This way I can dissolve my inner conflict and lay the past to rest. I don't want to have to choose a partner who expresses love for me, I want to do it myself. I feel love, it just scares me to express it. I want to be free to explore the unknown, let go of the old and bring in the new. Confront my fears and fly into a new life, just like the butterfly. If I want to learn to love then I must be prepared to become a little vulnerable, let down my guard and experience the unknown. This is the lesson I will take from all this.

Since his night time excursion, Phil felt that his awareness had shot through the roof. His whole being seemed to be alive and vibrant. He felt blissful; overflowing with inspiration and creativity, feeling that he could achieve anything. He had heard of people having similar experiences, crossing the threshold into the Great Mystery and returning full of inspiration and creativity. He also began to reflect on how thoughts cascade down through the various subtle bodies to create experience.

Real inspiration emerges when our Mental bodies become clear enough to absorb the subtle, inspirational thought of spirit, he thought.

He had spent years untangling the mess that impeded his connection to the divine. Now it was beginning to pay off. He felt as though the inspirational thought of spirit was flowing straight through him. Although he remembered nothing of his dream, he was sure he'd been somewhere. The automatic writing in his notebook provided unquestionable evidence. He felt as though his Soul body had been imprinted with a message that was desperately trying to seek expression. Music began to sail through his mind. He picked up the notebook in which he had painstakingly re-written the almost illegible words of the song, then rushed into the van and retrieved his guitar.

Later that afternoon the trio packed up their belongings and decided to spend the last hour of their weekend out in the sun. Phil picked up his guitar and started to perform the song. The others listened to the words intently becoming totally absorbed. When he came to the chorus, they started to join in. Phil got an uncanny sense of déjà vu: this had all happened before – some place else? They all started to sway and break into dance, singing 'we are one' at the tops of their voices. Curtains twitched in neighbouring caravans as curious campers looked on intrigued. An infectious joy began to grip the trio and radiated out to touch other people.

Friends from neighbouring caravans came over and joined in too. Almost before he knew it, Phil found himself encircled by a small gathering of joyous people who had their arms around each other swaying to the anthem-like chorus, the intoxicating atmosphere relieving the group of all their inhibitions. The chorus rolled on and on, more and more people came to join in, emotions became heightened, and a wonderful sense of unity transpired. As the curtain descended on what had been a wonderful weekend, this small gathering of people set an example for humanity – LET GO OF FEAR, LET GO OF PRIDE, LET GO OF DEMARCATION, LET GO OF CONFLICT. LET'S ALL COME TOGETHER AS ONE AND SET THE STAGE FOR A NEW PARADIGM – A NEW WORLD VIEW. UNITED AS ONE WE CAN WALK HAND-IN-HAND TO A DESTINY THAT IS JOYOUS AND HARMONIOUS. A LAND OF INFINITE POTENTIAL WHERE EVERYTHING IS POSSIBLE. A PLACE WHERE YOU, I, AND ALL THAT IS, CONVERGE AS ONE – THIS PLACE IS OUR TRUE HOME. **WE ARE IN THIS WORLD *BUT NOT OF IT.***

Chapter 15

Past-Life Influences

Vi pushed her shopping trolley around the supermarket trying to disown the embarrassing figure who accompanied her – Phil. He took off up the aisle clutching a bunch of bananas doing an impression of an ape! She turned up an adjacent aisle in an attempt to shake him off, but he came hurtling around the corner doing an impression of Mr Bean!

'You're mad!' she exclaimed, chuckling merrily away to herself.

'It's good to let the wonder child loose now and again!' he replied, now donning a bright yellow shower cap fashioned in the style of a duck, complete with bright orange inflatable beak!

The shopping took twice as long as it should have. Vi spent most of her time replacing items she didn't need. These extraneous goods that Phil had kindly thrown into her trolley included: a three foot cuddly lion, a wooden Pinocchio puppet and a child's tricycle which he embarrassingly pedalled all the way from the toy department!

After the weekend they had become almost inseparable, taking every opportunity to get away from the office and chat. They fantasized daily about the future: the book, the centre, travelling and writing music emerged as the main topics of conversation. On a couple of occasions they were able to spend the day together. Phil adhered to the promise that he would make each of these days her birthday and presented her with a gift wrapped parcel and a card.

After a few weeks, his feelings intensified. He was now certain he was falling in love with her. Something quite unexplainable had happened on that weekend and his feelings towards her had radically changed. Deciding honesty was the best policy, he told her of his feelings. His disclosure was met with both delight and apprehension. Her soft demeanour, the glint in her eyes and her coy smile, provided unquestionable evidence of her enchantment. Yet, she was entering the unknown and fear was arising. Secretly, she too had been feeling the emotional effects of their bond and this brought with it a sense of vulnerability. Feelings were emerging that she hadn't felt for years. Her emotional fortress was being threatened. She was far from ready to relinquish control. Then there was Tom to consider. They had been together for years and she felt indebted to him. Maybe things could have been better but she felt sure she loved him in some way – or was she just trying to convince herself? Being an extremely loyal person, her emotional propensity towards Phil instilled her with guilt. She felt she was betraying Tom, so she denied her feelings. There were times, however, when she dropped her guard and Phil felt the intensity of her love. One weekend whilst at the caravan he received a text that read:

> **A young girl is on the TV singing**
>
> **'Somewhere over the Rainbow'**
>
> **I'm sitting here crying my**
>
> **eyes out thinking of you**

On receiving this, a tide of love washed over him and just wanted to be by her side.

At other times she would describe having identical feelings to him but never attributed them to anything in particular. Phil had become accustomed to her incongruence. One day she'd be extremely close and intimate, the next, guarded and fragile. He understood. She was in a very difficult position. He constantly reassured her that his love was unconditional.

Their bond became increasingly visible to others. Colleagues started to talk but Phil and Vi appeared unconcerned. Their relationship had an air of innocence; a kiss on the cheek and a hug was as far as things went. Something extremely special had developed between them and people couldn't help but notice.

Once a week the trio would meet at Phil's place. One week they would have an experiential session, the next a support group in which they would discuss their personal affairs. G. looked like a new man, his self esteem was rising at an incredible rate. On a couple of occasions, Phil used hypnotherapy and regressed him back to childhood. They were highly emotional experiences but had started to pay dividends. G. began to move out of the programmed child role and stand up for himself.

Vi's anger had lessoned over the weeks. Although she was still prone to the occasional irrational outburst, she was improving. When she felt a rage emerging, she would quickly remove herself from the situation. After screaming into a pillow, pounding her punch bag, or writing a letter to release the emotional charge, she would sit down and take stock of the facts. On many occasions she recognised that past relationships were being recreated and so didn't pursue the argument. On other occasions, when she felt her anger was warranted, she moved into analyst mode, stating her case without the emotional charge of the oppressor or programmed child complexes. As a consequence, her home situation had started to improve. She could see the situation through a much clearer lens. However, this had added to her confusion. She longed to be with Phil, yet, she could not envisage life without Tom. Her energies were totally divided.

Despite his personal feelings, Phil was very supportive and urged her not to make any rash decisions; it was far too early. He suggested she give it time and see what happened. He also used childhood regression with her. Again, the experience was highly emotional as hidden truths emerged from the depths of her unconscious. However, a great deal of healing had taken place as a consequence. The main insight gained was the extent to which she loved her biological father. She had subsequently sent out impulses of intent to the Universe, asking that they be re-united. They hadn't gone unheard: help was on its way from the higher realms.

Tonight was their meeting night. The activity – past life regression. The subject – Vi. She just hoped that Phil would move out of the 'zany child' state before the session commenced!

*

'You are now standing at the top of a long, spiral staircase which seems to twist down and around forever. On one side of the staircase is an ornate banister on which you place your hand as you begin to walk, gently down. As you twist and spiral, deeper and deeper, you feel a sense of lightness and notice that you are floating…. On reaching the bottom of the stairs you feel you are leaving the ordinary world far behind….

'…Standing before you is a heavy oak panel door…you make your way toward it. Push open the door, push with your mind……now walk through…… you find there are five more steps leading down into the archives……down the five steps now, down, deeper and deeper. Five, four, three, two, one - zero. Relaxing more and more, as you go deep, deep down inside yourself….

'…You now find yourself surrounded by thousands of books….old ones, new ones, large books, small books, thin ones and thick ones. Some of the books look as though they could be hundreds or thousands of years old…looking up you notice that each section is dated by century, the 1900's, the 1800's and so on. The deeper you go into the archive, you see there are no dates, you notice pictures instead of words, some ancient symbols that you don't quite understand……

' …Now walk along the rows and rows of books until you find one that seems to call your name…'

The room fell into complete silence. Vi's breath became deeper. Her eyelids fluttered rapidly. A couple of minutes passed by.

'I see it….high on one of the shelves…….it's glowing,' she murmured, her voice a whisper and her words drawn.

'Good….reach up and retrieve it……now open it up……notice what the pages are made from.'

'Parchment,' she replied.

'What do you see?'

'Photographs - hundreds of them.'

'Good, now feel yourself being drawn into the book….until you're totally immersed…this is a magical book…….the characters are coming alive and animated…now tell me what you see...'

'I'm in a courtyard full of people……the people are calling me Emily………the year is 1245.'

'Good..now tell me what you are wearing?'

'…. I'm wearing an embroidered garment – a gown… It's cold and I have a fur lined cloak to keep me warm……. It's fastened by a jewelled clasp around my shoulders…… I have a conical hat, wooden shoes, and lots of jewellery.'

Her face suddenly contorted.

'What is it, Emily?' Phil continued.

'The man with me… he makes me cringe.'

'Do you know who he is?'

'Yes… he's a knight… I'm betrothed to him but I hate everything he stands for.'

'Then why are you marrying him?'

'My father…. he's a powerful man…….he's this man's superior…….he's forcing me to marry him……I feel imprisoned……they're both corrupt.'

'Why… what are they up to?'

'They're exploiting the poor people…..they're oppressive….**I hate them!….I hate them!**'

She started to get a little distressed but Phil saw no cause for concern.

'Okay, relax. He isn't going to harm you.' He continued.

She calmed down.

'…..I won't marry him……I'm going to escape ….. ..Galfridus is going to help me.'

'Who is Galfridus?'

'The court jester….' Her face broke out into a faint smile.

'He's my dearest friend…he's here too.'

'What's he doing?' inquired Phil.

'….. he's playing a lute and singing to a crowd of people….. they're laughing……but he's clever.. very clever……the words of his ditties have a subtle meaning….. the crowd understand them…..he's exploiting my father and his men - the hierarchy….but it goes unnoticed because of his idiot-like persona….

' ……He's just spotted me…he's looking towards us and smiling….he's coming over…making his way towards me…..weaving his way through the crowd…he's really close now…..very close…he's here, encircling us…….he's starting to sing a ditty… he's singing it over and over again…it has a hidden meaning ...I sense it....but I don't know what it is.......he's singing:

> **See with owl's eyes**
>
> **for in darkness you roam**
>
> **Move 'further to wolf'**
>
> **and you'll find your true home.**

'... it holds the key to my freedom...I know it does......the man with me, the knight, he's getting agitated...telling Galfridus to go away.....He won't go, he just keeps singing the ditty....the knight is ordering some men to restrain him .....they're coming to get him...they're getting closer....he's trying to hand me something... it's a flower...I can't reach it... I can't reach it!......they're dragging him away..... he's still singing the ditty......oh no! everything's fading ...going dark..... ..'

'Ok... that's fine.... Let it go...let it fade back into your unconscious....and relax. .... Feel you're awareness coming slowly back to the present...feel it taking residence behind the windows of your eyes...back to this time and this place and normal conscious awareness. In a moment, I'm going to count backwards from five to one...when I reach one you will be wide awake and pleasantly relaxed. 5....4.....3.....2.....1....wide awake.'

Vi's eyes opened, her eyelids flickering as she readjusted her focus. She sat in quietness for a few more moments.

'Are you okay?' Phil inquired, passing her a glass of water.

'Yes,' she replied, somewhat torpidly. 'That jester Phil.... I felt a real affinity with him.....something that ran very deep.....I didn't recognise him physically, but there was a real sense of familiarity about him.'

Phil and G. listened intently.

'.. and when he sang that ditty,' she continued, 'he was trying to tell me something…it had some sort of hidden meaning - a message. It was a signpost, Phil; I'm sure of it. I know it was a past life, but that verse had something to do with the present – I just know it. ..G. would you pass my bag please, I want to write the words down before I forget them.'

As she scribed the words into her notebook she entered a ruminative state, as though trying to decipher the meaning:

See with owl's eyes

for in darkness you roam

move 'further to wolf'

and you'll find your true home.

'Do you think it's got something to do with a teaching, Phil? The wolf is the teacher – right. And Galfridus seemed to be stressing the phrase "further to wolf", as though it was a conundrum.'

'I really don't know, Vi, you'll have to work that one out for yourself. Your inclination about it having connections to this life is very credible though. Some therapists refuse to believe in past lives but use past-life regression as a tool to gain insight into their client's present state. Past lives can often mirror circumstances that are happening in the here and now.'

*

Later that night, Vi lay in bed thinking about the night's events.

Past lives can reflect circumstances in our current life......mm.... I felt imprisoned in that life just as I have done in this one. Although I didn't see the end of that life, I have a strong feeling that I didn't find my freedom. I always wanted it, but when it came to the crunch, I was terrified to lose what I had. I was wealthy and had status, but really, that was meaningless. I was deeply unhappy. I was totally bankrupt both spiritually and emotionally. I failed to recognise my purpose in that lifetime. I'm sure - and that is having an impact on this lifetime. If we fail to learn our lessons in one lifetime, then they re-emerge in another. A handful of our past lives are accessible to us during our current lifetime and from them emerges our current purpose. I wanted to help the poor in that lifetime..the people my father exploited...I had a real sense that I wanted to be a nurse and aid in the healing process of these people....Galfridus was trying to help me recognise my destiny in that lifetime and...it's weird...but I'm sure he's trying to help me in this one, too. That ditty holds a key. I know it – it's a signpost. And the flower he was trying to hand me... I wonder could it be the one I'm suppose to choose in this lifetime..the one in my dream?

She began to slowly drift off to sleep with the sound of Galfridus still echoing through her mind. She smiled. In many ways Galfridus reminded her of Phil...

See with owl's eyes

for in darkness you roam

move 'further to wolf'

and you'll find your true home.

Chapter 16

Light Dispels Darkness

Vi was in her bedroom preparing herself for the family gathering. It was Val's thirty-second birthday and the surprise party was to be held at the home of her mother – Vera. Tom had been feeling a bit under the weather and had decided not to go. His attempts to persuade Vi to stay in with him had failed dismally. She towelled her hair dry, put on a light layer of make-up and hurriedly dressed herself. Ten minutes later she arrived at her mother's house.

Vera informed everyone that Val was coming on the pretence that she was being taken out to a restaurant - she had no idea about the party. She was expected to arrive any time now. No sooner had she finished addressing her guests when the sound of a car engine was heard purring outside. She peered through the window.

'Quick, they're here,' she said, ushering everyone into the kitchen and dousing the lights.

As she led Val and her family through the door, Vi hit the lights and the crowd re-emerged, singing 'happy birthday'. Val was overwhelmed as her brothers presented her with a huge cake and a bottle of champagne. She blew out the candles to cheers of hip- hip hooray, then asked everyone if she could have their attention.

'Unfortunately, I'm not going to be able to drink this.' She announced, her face solemn.

The room fell into silence.

'I'm having to refrain from alcohol for a while.'

An air of apprehension fell.

'What's up, Val?' inquired Vera, concerned.

Val's solemn demeanor suddenly translated into a warm glow. She paused again, determined to leave everyone in suspense for a while longer… Finally, she broke her news.

'I'm pregnant!' she roared with delight, 'against all the odds, I'm pregnant again.'

She was immediately swamped by well wishes, some of them shedding tears of joy.

Vi stood in the corner observing the joyous celebration; in particular, Charlie, who danced around in circles. She was totally stunned, unable to comprehend the news. Memories of Watendlath came flooding back. Phil had prophesied this event. She rushed over to congratulate her delighted sister and asked when the baby was due.

'June,' replied Val.

'The summer of next year,' Vi murmured, ruminatively. 'Exactly when Phil predicted!' In a flash, she'd disappeared, leaving Val with a look of idle curiosity on her face.

Vi leapt up the stairs two at a time, adrenaline pumping through her veins. In her mad scramble, she missed a step completely, stumbled backwards and just managed to grab the rail. Her heart pulsated. She dashed into the bedroom, retrieved her phone, sifted through her address book, and found Phil's number.

'Come on..pick up…pick up.'

'Hello.'

'Phil, you won't believe it!' she spluttered. 'She's pregnant again.. just as you predicted….. the baby's due next June.'

Phil decided to play dumb, his voice laced with mischief. 'Who is?'

'Val…..remember?.. you predicted it.'

'Val who?'

'Oh come off it. You're just winding me up. Phil she's pregnant…and you predicted it…despite the odds..that's amazing!' Her voice began to calm and take on an air of sincerity. 'I'm so sorry, I never did give her your message. I didn't want to build up her hopes unnecessarily.'

'Oh ye of little faith,' quipped Phil, before dropping his clown's mask. 'I'm delighted for her. And for you too, Vi. Your family deserve every happiness.'

'You should see little Charlie, Phil. She's a darling. She's bouncing around everywhere, so excited….I wish you were here right now so I could give you a great big hug.'

'Mm…' pondered Phil, somewhat promiscuously, 'where are you?'

'In Val's bedroom.'

'I'll be there in two minutes!… Maybe you'd like another addition to the family!'

'Stop it..,' she giggled. 'Thought we might celebrate on Monday, over coffee - somewhere quiet.' Her tone suddenly softened, becoming spiked with affection. 'There's something else I want to talk to you about.'

'Certainly, Vi. I'll look forward to it.'

After putting down the phone, Phil remained emblazoned in her mind. A firework display erupted in her sacral chakra and dispersed throughout the whole of her body. She felt like she was walking on air. Floating. She rushed downstairs, picked up Charlie, and swung her around in circles.

An hour passed by in which time she danced until she dropped, fuelled by a rush of furtive thoughts. Deciding it was time for a break, she took her drink and sat on the stairs.

Unkown to anyone, there were two uninvited guests at the party, two entities that had received Vi's plea for assistance. She hadn't received her last shock of the night yet. The forces that orchestrated the forthcoming synchronicity hovered just above her head, vibrating at frequencies undetectable to the physical senses.

Vi attributed her pleasant sense of lightness to the couple of brandies she'd consumed. But, in actuality, clairsentience was in effect; she was absorbing the vibrant energy of her two onlookers.

Suddenly, the shrill sound of the door bell startled her. She was just able to make out the silhouette of a man peering through the opaque glass panel. After placing her drink on the telephone table, she headed towards the door. As she did, she got a strange sense that she wasn't alone.

The door caught on the carpet as she tried to open it. She knelt down and tussled with the obstructing tuft of wool. With one mighty tug, the door swung free and bashed her on the head.

Rising to her feet, holding her forehead, she whispered several expletives under her breath. Then, unwittingly, she started to utter a few words.

'That knocked some sen…..'

Silence.

She froze.

Immobilized. Mute. Stunned by the sight of the person standing before her. Aged beyond his years, looking forlorn and remorseful, was her father. He shot her a mournful look before dropping his gaze to the floor.

Concealed in the surrounding space, Theodore and Esba radiated loving undulations into the ether in an attempt to promote harmony. To her astonishment, Vi felt a sudden urge to put her arms around her father. She stalled, not quite able to comprehend what was going on. As her dad dejectedly raised his head, she saw something she'd never witnessed before – tears trickling down his cheeks. Her demeanor softened. Her eyes reddened. Her heart opened. She stepped towards him, slowly outstretched her arms and nervously embraced him. Shudders rippled through his body as he began to sob.

When the tears dispersed, they took a seat on the wall outside, still unable to find the right words to say to each other. After what seemed like an eternity, he finally broke the ice.

'I've been a fool, Vi. And since I've packed up the drink, I've realised how big a fool I've been. I lost you completely, and the others, understandably, have very little time for me, with the exception of your mother that is. I came here tonight because something compelled me to do so. I was sifting through a drawer looking for my medication when an old black and white photograph fell out onto the floor. I picked it up and it broke my heart…. Do you remember when I used to push you around the garden on my motorbike?'

'Yes, I do……. It made me so happy.'

'It was a photograph of that… After I set eyes on it, I couldn't stop myself coming here. I just had to see you again, Vi.'

They spoke outside for a while, then Vi ushered him into the party; the rest of the family looked on in utter disbelief – oblivious to the celestial visitors, they wondered what had led to Vi's sudden change of heart.

She poured him an orange juice and they chatted for a while, catching up on the lost years. Then, the conversation centred around the forthcoming new addition to the family.

Shortly after midnight, the events of the night started to take their toll, so Vi decided it was time to go home. Before she left, she invited her father to her home for a meal. He gratefully accepted. They fixed a date in January – his birthday.

*

Phil was overjoyed by Vi's news. Unable to sleep, he decided to take a late night bath. Laying in the bubble filled tub, surrounded by candles and incense sticks, he contemplated the evening's events.

My psychic senses seem to be getting stronger. That experience at Watendlath was so powerful. There was no doubt in my mind that Val would become pregnant again. I didn't hear voices or see images - I just knew it. Claircognizance, as it's sometimes called; knowing without the logical steps normally involved. It's strange but when I have these experiences, I feel I'm connecting with someone else, someone who's a part of me, yet, has their own unique identity. It's as though their energy amplifies my psychic abilities.... I wonder who it could be?

He lay his head back on an inflatable pillow and began to soft focus on a guttering candle flame. The gentle flicker had a hypnotic effect, quieting his rational mind.

'Who are you?' he whispered, repeatedly. 'Talk to me.'

He started to enter a deep state of relaxation, his awareness drifting into a matrix of communication channels where time and space were of no consequence. His upper chakras opened and became highly receptive. The energy in the room began to change as two orbs of light entered the space around him. The image of a jester wisped through his mind and the air became imbued with the fragrance of flowers. He got a strong sense of déjà vu as the vision of the celestial wheel flitted through his mind. Then, his inner screen went dark. From the void a flickering image started to appear. A female, of Romany gypsy heritage: jet black hair, piercing wolf-like eyes and a silver Star of David draped around her neck. He felt a great affinity with her. Her voice echoed through his mind.

Soul family, my friend. A synergy of consciousness. Soul brothers and sisters are intricately interwoven and can share their strengths and attributes with each other. We often merge without even recognising it. We do this at a level where we exist as one... You must pursue your destiny, my friend. And pursue your loved one too because she is part of your destiny. Don't be deceived, see with owl's eyes. See through the veil of fear. Galfridus and I are here to assist you … Goodbye for now… we shall meet again.

'But who are……..'

Before Phil could finish his question, the image vanished. A barrage of visions and sounds suddenly began to assault his psychic senses. The intertwined forms of himself, Vi and Esba spiralled down his screen of consciousness. The haunting melody of 'Hush Little Baby Don't Say A Word' echoed through his mind. A lucid Dickensian scene emerged: an old man, clad in a long black cloak, stooped over a desk, writing by candlelight, with a quill. *The man's face was a blur, indistinguishable.*

Suddenly, a rapid succession of scenes began to flit through Phil's mind. The wolf. The fawn. The butterfly. The celestial wheel. The gypsy lady. A seemingly never ending stream of images.

After a while, the psychic phenomena started to ease off, the images fading back into the nothingness. His internal screen became black once again. Yet, something remained. The warmth that had embraced him all evening suddenly gave way to a deep sadness. A coldness filled the air. He shuddered. Another shimmering form materialized in his mind's eye: an old lady, stooped and frail, grey shawl draped around her flagging shoulders, knotted grey hair tied back to reveal a tormented face. She beckoned him forward, gesturing with her hand. A voice laced with sorrow began to whisper through his mind.

She must tell George it wasn't his fault. They will both heal if they know the truth.

The scene dispersed in an instant. Phil sat upright - bewildered.

'I didn't recognise her physically, but that voice was unmistakable – Mary. Her son must be George - Vi's father…… I wonder why he's blaming himself?'

He mused over this conundrum for a while, then his thoughts shifted to the lady with the wolf-like eyes.

She implied she was one of my Soul family. That makes sense. I did feel an affinity with her. And, as she said, it's reputed we can absorb the attributes of our Soul sisters and brothers. This would explain why I feel she amplifies my psychic senses; I'm drawing on her energy... And what about Galfridus? What is his connection?...he appeared in Vi's past life regression...

... I'm getting the strangest sense that Vi, myself, G, Galfridus, the gypsy lady, Theodore and Esba are all intimately connected - Soul family. That celestial wheel connects us all – I know it. I'm also getting a strong sense that we're all working towards a common goal.

Chapter 17

Romantic Revelation

Phil and Vi sat drinking cappuccino in a quiet coffee bar. Vi was bubbling with excitement, eagerly relaying the events of Saturday night to Phil. After re-iterating the fact that her sister was pregnant again, she moved on to tell him about her unexpected reunion with her father.

'Over fifteen years, I've been to many family gatherings and my father hasn't attended one of them. I must admit, at the time, I was thankful. It would've been very uncomfortable. But now, just as I feel the time is right, he turns up on the doorstep! It's amazing Phil. There's no way this could have been a coincidence...

'..... As a result of working on my issues, I become ready for reconciliation. I send out intentions, asking the Universe to provide the circumstances. My father has no intentions of going to the party until he receives a signpost; a photograph falling from his drawer. The exact same picture you saw in your mind's eye the first time that Mary came through: the one of him pushing me around the garden on his motorbike.... Now, when we meet up, I see him in a totally different light. My anger towards him disperses and I feel compassion. Then, at the end of the night, I invite him around to my house for a meal, something I could never envisage happening in my wildest dreams. ..... What an extraordinary set of circumstances.'

'It doesn't end there either, Vi.' Interjected Phil.

'What do you mean?'

'Is your father's name George?'

'Yes it is.' She looked at him mystified. 'I've never mentioned that before?'

'I know. But on Saturday night I had another visitation from Mary. I saw her image this time and she looked really troubled. I feel she's desperately trying to get a message to your father. She's trapped between two worlds, reluctant to move on until he forgives himself.'

'Forgives himself for what?'

'I don't know. I was hoping that you might be able to shed some light on that. She just said, "you must tell George that it wasn't his fault." She added that you would both heal if you knew the truth.'

Vi looked perplexed.

'I haven't got a clue what she's talking about. But then no one ever mentions him much when I'm around.'

'Well keep it in mind. I feel it's very important. She seemed so desperate to give him this message.'

'I will - thank you, Phil.'

Vi proceeded with great insight.

'It's so strange, but since Saturday night, I've had the strongest sense that there's hidden design and purpose behind all our seemingly random interactions. It feels like the material world is a huge metaphor that shouldn't be taken literally; every physical event is somehow symbolic, designed to evolve our understanding and enable us to grow.'

Phil felt a growing sense of gratification. He could see that Vi was beginning to connect with the deeper mysteries of life.

'That's so true, Vi....We attract situations that are conducive to the lessons we're here to learn. When we have experiential knowledge of this phenomenon, life is never quite the same again - everything takes on new meaning.'

'You can say that again,' she replied, propitiously. 'Each dilemma becomes a challenge. Each heartache a stepping stone. They're all opportunities to grow. We just have to interpret them differently. Instead of sulking and complaining, we need to ask the right questions – "Why have I created this situation? What can I learn from it? What is its hidden meaning? How can it enhance my life?" - When we take this perspective, victimization is superfluous; we resume control and take back our power…. Take my own life for example. I can fester on my childhood experiences or turn them around and make use of them. They left me terrified of love and compassion, and yet, with insight, I can see that I'm here to learn about them: they're life's lessons of mine. I feel this strongly because I seem to be attracting situations that are testing my resolve to master them………How do you think it all works Phil?'

'Well, personally, I think there are two main aspects involved in the creation of reality. Firstly, as you know, we exist in an amorphous sea of intelligence, an ocean of thought in which everything is interconnected and interrelated. In truth, there's no space around us, just an invisible mosaic of intelligence; a spiritual tapestry that connects every realm of existence - just like a vast internet. When we send out intentions, the spirit world responds by manipulating the quantum field and making things happen: for instance, the timely falling of a photograph… Secondly, in the material sphere, *we* can manipulate the quantum field with our thoughts. Remember, the quantum field is not only the primordial clay from which everything material is sculptured, but the artist behind the sculptures is ourselves - the thoughts we pour into the quantum field have great influence in creating our circumstances. As this intelligence is non-judgmental, it doesn't determine whether our mental broadcasts are negative or positive, it just creates from what it receives - this is why it is so important for us to nurture our thoughts.'

Vi's brow furrowed.

'That scares me at times. Negative thoughts seem to arise in my mind of their own accord. The more I resist them, the more they seem to persist. It makes me wonder what I'm actually creating.'

'That's a pertinent point, Vi - let me elaborate. Through meditation, I've come to realise that we don't consciously choose all the thoughts that enter our minds. Many of them arise quite spontaneously. Remember we're just like radio sets, receiving signals from many different sources: our sub-personalities, society, personalities from past lives, our Uniqueness, our Soul and spirit guides. Our mind is an emporium through which a vast amount of information passes; a spectrum of frequencies containing both negative and positive vibrations. These faint impulses of intelligence have no causal power whatsoever until we amplify them; until we stamp our name on them and claim them as our own. If we simply observe a thought without attaching to it, then it will dissipate back into the silence from where it came. However, if we fuse with it, if our awareness becomes consumed by it, then it has the power to create. For example, if our awareness is consumed by the thought *nothing ever goes right in my life,* the quantum field will deliver exactly what we've ordered - remember, it is non-judgemental. On the other hand, if we adhere to the thought *I create whatever I desire,* then the field will respond in a positive way…. Belief is the key, Vi. We have to believe in our broadcasts with every rudiment of our being. It's no good believing half-heartedly - it won't work. Remember Theodore's four-point procedure: **Image – feel – radiate – and know the Universe is about to respond.**'

'So are you saying we don't control the thoughts that enter our mind, but we can select which ones become reality?'

'Exactly. We generate some thoughts, others we pick out of the ether. Each thought is like a train passing through the station of our mind. We might not control the schedule, but we do choose whether or not to get on board. Most people board the same train day-in, day-out, because they have a pass stamped "conditioning". They tend to sleep throughout the journey and end up back where they started. Others, who are wide awake, stand on the platform observing the trains of thought, until the right one arrives. These are true explorers, unphased by fear. They'll take many trains and explore many lands until they end up at their destiny…

'…..Our mind is an ocean of infinite possibilities, Vi. There's a never ending stream of thought to choose from. We just need to be selective. **Control our mind instead of letting our mind control us.** Attach to the inspirational thoughts that'll take us one stage nearer our destiny. Explore the ocean instead of swimming around in a puddle.. … ..can you see what I'm getting at?'

'Yes - I can. As you were talking, I got a mental picture, envisaging it like this …Our mind is a field of pure potential in which many seeds are planted. This field is divided into allotments. There's the garden of life's conditioning in which all our inhibiting seedlings are planted. There's the karmic garden in which all our past life seedlings are sprinkled. Then there's the inspirational garden, containing seedlings of pure creativity. We are the gardeners and have the power to cultivate any allotment. We might observe the negative seedlings but we don't have to germinate them. Within every seedling there is the potential of a forest, so we must choose wisely. If we germinate negative thoughts, we'll grow a jungle of discontentment. But if we develop nurturing ones, we'll cultivate a wonderful harvest…………so which flower am I going to choose I ask myself?'

'Exactly, Vi….. For me life is about realising our true potential. This inevitably involves vanquishing the spectres of our past and releasing the encumbrances of our accumulative karma. The Universe, in its infinite wisdom, provides the learning arena. It may seem that life is a series of random interactions in which we're permanently at the mercy of the external world, but in actuality, we have great influence over everything that happens to us. ***Every battle is really a battle with ourselves. Life's created from what's inside of us; our programming determines the situations we attract.*** If we want to change our external environment then we need to look deep within ourselves and identify the blockages that are being mirrored externally.'

'As within, so without,' injected Vi.

'Precisely. I truly believe that our Soul is responsible for placing certain conflicting thoughts into our minds. Our eternal essence dips into our memory bank and constantly reminds us of the rigid patterns we're here to break. This is how we are tested. This is how numerous pathways are opened up to us. Earth is a school of life and the curriculum is set by our Soul. We can choose to germinate our seedlings with tears of sadness and the heat of anger, or we can cultivate them with tears of joy and the sunshine of our hearts. We can opt for safety, fear and familiarity, or we can embrace the unknown with love and faith – the choice is entirely ours: **we are masters of our own destiny.**'

Two orbs of light suddenly swirled into the surrounding space. Vi began to drift, her mind regressing to the party on Saturday night. Theodore was drawing her attention to the fundamental reason for this meeting - she had something important to tell Phil?

Conflicting thoughts surfaced in her mind.

Should I tell him? – Or not?

Her inner assassins immediately locked horns with her Uniqueness in a quest to influence her decision.

Don't trust. Remember the past – speak the language of your heart. Welcome the future.

Which seedling would she germinate? She stood with one foot in the garden of her wounded child, the other in the pastures of her truth. One train would take her to purgatory, the other to a magical place, where she truly belongs.

She mulled over the offerings of her inner adversaries, vacillating from one polarity to the other. *Fate* or *fear*. *Heaven* or *hell*.

A scene entered her mind:

She stood on the platform with trains on adjacent lines, one bound for fear, the other for the place where she truly belongs. Magnetized by familiarity, yielding to conditioning, she inched towards the fear train. With one foot on board, she was distracted by voices whispering from the destiny train: a monk, an Indian, a jester and an old lady. A whistle sounded. The trains were about to leave. The doors hissed and started to close. With no time left, she threw caution to the wind and jumped on board the destiny train.

A crimson tint eclipsed her face and an endearing timidity came over her. Her heart chakra began to unfurl, allowing in the sunlight. The cordial quintessence of her true nature radiated loving undulations into the ether. Phil was totally captivated, not only by her gentle comportment, but by the enigmatic look in her eyes.

'Vi,' he whispered. 'Your heart is trying to speak but your throat is reticent …. What is it sweetheart?'

Her eyes averted, she fidgeted nervously. Her fingers drummed lightly on the table.

Let go and enjoy the journey - the panorama is beautiful, whispered her Uniqueness.

She fused with the thought; it consumed her awareness. A spark of truth arced from her heart vortex igniting her quiescent throat chakra. A sky blue wheel of shimmering light appeared in the hollow of her neck. Her heart had finally been given a voice. With face flushed, and voice edgy, the truth began to flow.

'I'm a bit nervous, Phil. So please bear with me.'

'Take your time, sweetheart.'

'….On Saturday night, after we'd finished talking on the phone.. I felt something that I've never felt before. All these feelings started in my stomach and spread throughout the whole of my body. It felt wonderful. I rushed downstairs, picked up Charlie and swung her around in circles. My family thought I'd gone mad. I danced and danced and danced….'

She paused again, mustering up the courage to finish her message.

'W-what I'm really trying to say,' she stammered, '…is that.. I know I have feelings for you.'

Silence.

More silence.

Phil pinched himself. *Is this dream? or am I in the midst of a tantalizing hallucination?*

When he realised that neither was true, a wide smile arced from cheek to cheek: an even bigger one across his heart. He felt himself suddenly expand. His sacral chakra soaked up Vi's loving emanations. Every cell in his body danced with delight.

He stared at her admiringly, noticing how her eyes glistened with truth. In the prevailing silence, their hearts expressed far more than words could ever say.

'Vi… I love you so much, sweetheart.' He eventually replied, softly. 'Thank you so much for having the courage to tell me… I know how difficult that must have been for you.'

An endearing innocence came over her. 'I thought about your courage, Phil, the day you declared your feelings for me; I thought it was about time I reciprocated.'

Phil slipped his hand across the table locking their fingers together. They were immediately engulfed in a molasses of blissful energy. Time seemed to suspend. 'I love you little lady,' he whispered.

*

That night Vi had a bizarre dream....

A stranger asked if she would meet up with him. She agreed. They met on a street corner and he invited her back to his home. She accepted. On arrival, he took off his clothes, stepped into the shower and asked her to strip naked. Once again, she agreed. Next, he asked her to dance for him. She thought, *why not.* As she danced, he gestured for her to join him in the shower. Again, she complied. As she put one foot in the shower, his appearance radically transformed and she found herself facing a frightening ogre. She immediately fled back to the safety of her home and life with Tom.

When she awoke, she was not only embarrassed but perplexed and frightened. She intuitively felt that the sexual theme was symbolic of something much deeper. The previous day she had entered unknown territory, baring her innermost self to Phil. She'd stripped away all her armour and revealed the naked truth. Was this dream telling her to be careful? Was her trust about to be abused? Were things going to turn nasty?...... Or were Theodore and Esba portraying another reality that lay deep within her?

Chapter 18

Synergy of worlds

Roma sat in the office clutching the remnants of a blood stained nylon shirt that belonged to a young boy. She had been commissioned by the Police on several occasions to help find missing persons. Her reputation for success stretched as far as Germany and the Czech republic where she had helped solve several horrific crimes. Although she found these experiences heart breaking and distressing, she fully accepted them as part of her life's work. She had been endowed with an extraordinary gift and was willing to use it in whatever capacity it was needed.

From a very early age she realised she was different from other children; she could sense things very strongly. She had inherited her gift from her father's side of the family who were of Romany heritage. During childhood she would often ask him why the other children made fun of her. He told her that she was different and one day her difference would make her special. His words couldn't have been more befitting. Her work had been very difficult at times, joyous at others, but always highly fulfilling and rewarding.

She clutched the torn shirt and closed her eyes, asking for the assistance of her spirit guide, then slowly drifted into deep trance.

The mental plane of existence.

Angelique stood beside a circular marble spa in the main hall of the crystal temple; she stared intently into the silver pool. As she sent intentions to the Universe, the divine intelligence began to respond.

A scene emerged on the mirror-like surface of the silver pool. Shreds of blood-stained clothing draped on thorn bushes. She focused intently and began to establish a telepathic connection with her incarnate Soul sister.

Back to earth.

Imagery started to appear in Roma's mind. She gestured to the sergeant to start the tape recorder.

'I see blood-stained strips of clothing hanging on some thorn bushes… there's a quarry nearby……I see a narrow path edged by lots of trees…there's a man… brown, dead-pan eyes…receding red hair…Vandyke beard…late thirties - early forties….he's leading the boy up towards the quarry… there's a reservoir ……'

Return to the mental plane.

Theodore and Esba were also in the crystal temple. They had fused together and were concentrating their thoughts on one of their Soul group – Robert. The quantum physicist was so scientifically minded that he dismissed subtle communication as nonsense – he had forgotten his roots. He claimed that people who believed in such things were naive and susceptible to their overactive imagination. Little did he know his decision to become a quantum physicist had been orchestrated from the higher realms. Theodore had been keen to persuade one of his personalities to enter this insightful realm of science for it was slowly uncovering the esoteric secrets of the Universe. Theo's plan had succeeded to a point: he had presented Robert with the appropriate signposts and his *intuition* had led him to become a physicist. However, Robert totally refused to acknowledge the spirit world. Everything had a scientific explanation. Theodore and Esba had a vested interest in him expanding his theories. They wanted him to integrate his scientific knowledge with spirituality and evolve people's understanding of the Great Mystery. This was his life's purpose, but he had veered off course. Their attempts to contact him directly had been to no avail, so they adopted new tactics, directing another member of the Soul group to act as an intermediary.

After formulating their plan and sending out intentions, they diverted their attention to Esba's forthcoming re-incarnation. A number of Theo's personalities were involved in a mission. As every personality is endowed with free will, success was highly dependent on them awakening and aligning with their purpose. If Theodore's initial plan was to succeed, Esba would re-incarnate and take part in the next stage in human form. They continued to monitor the progress of her potential parents with great interest.

Earth.

Roma continued to verbalize the imagery that Angelique was placing in her mind.

'….the boy is resisting but the man is overpowering him..he's dragging him along…the area is deserted…they're climbing some steps now… heading for a chasm cut out in the quarry….. it's going dark…Oh no. No!...No!'

She started trembling uncontrollably, her eyes burning like fire.

'He's beating the child with some sort of baton…..the child, he's slipping away…..oh God!....**Stop! Stop!**'

The police officer became increasingly concerned. 'Do you want to stop?' he inquired.

She appeared oblivious, deep in trance, continuing with voice broken and tears welling in her eyes.

'…..he's placing the body into a plastic bag….He's putting rocks in the bag.'

She snapped out of her trance and shot a disconcerting glance at the police officer.

'His body is at the bottom of the reservoir.'

Chapter 19

Growing Pains and Insight

The car serpentined down a country lane piercing the wisps of mist that drifted out of the darkness like wandering apparitions. Vi and Phil chatted excitedly about their Christmas night out. Tomorrow evening they planned to have dinner and visit the theatre. Vi was harbouring a second source of excitement but had postponed disclosing it until tonight's support group session.

G. was experiencing grave problems at home and in need of the support. Since stepping out of the submissive child role, the dynamics of his relationship had changed and things had started to deteriorate. Joan didn't know how to handle his newfound confidence and was rebelling - becoming highly erratic.

He appeared detached, gazing somberly out of the window. A transient cloud of mist glided by and seemingly transfigured into the spectre of Aristotle.

'*There is nothing wrong with anger. The trick is to get angry at the right person, at the right time, for the right reason,*' he whispered.

A pang of regret suddenly besieged G. as lucid images washed through his beleaguered mind....

...Joan and himself were engulfed in a tempest of explosive energy. A barrage of venomous expletives were being hurtled across the room. Their inner assassins were tearing strips of each other like savage dogs fighting for their lives.

'Who do you think you're talking to, you useless bastard,' Joan roared.

G. spat back like a cornered viper, clouds of toxic energy spewing out of his throat chakra. 'You, you fat old witch – I'm talking to you!'

'Drop dead, you good-for-nothing piece of shit.' She scowled.

'Go stick your 'ead up your arse, you sour faced old bint,' he countered.

The malevolent verbal onslaught continued for some time, G. ridding himself of a lifetime's worth of pent up anger.

Eventually, Joan found herself yielding, overwhelmed by his never-ending supply of ammunition. She re-positioned herself - adopted new tactics; her manipulative child stepped forward wielding a blade of culpability: a guilt edged sword that might just win the day.

'Why are you picking on me?' she snivelled, pathetically. 'I'm a pensioner. Do you get some sort of thrill out of bullying old women?'

Her tactics didn't work. G. spotted her maneuver and had no intentions of internalising her vindictive annotations. They belonged to her - not him; projection was in operation. He fired them straight back at her, externalised them and vehemently refused to succumb to her manipulation.

After the heat died down, G. felt a sense of triumphant gratification. At last he'd stood up for himself... His celebration was short lived, however. The impact of his actions slowly filtered through and remorse set in. Joan had inadvertently activated a volcano that had been lying dormant for years. Regrettably, she'd taken the full force.

She didn't deserve that. Much of my anger was attributed to my relationship with my mother – not Joan. I could've handled the situation much better. I should have removed myself, cooled down, and analyzed the facts. Then, if appropriate, confronted her from the analyst position, without the emotional charge of my inner assassins.

As he drifted deeper into a state of melancholy, an eerie silence pulled him back to the present. The music on the car radio was cut dead. The disk jockey announced a newsflash: the body of a missing ten-year-old boy had been recovered from the bottom of a nearby reservoir.

*

After a short attunement meditation, Phil opened the session and invited the others to talk. G. remained subdued, distant. So Vi took the opportunity to relay her latest insight.

'Things just seem to be accelerating,' she said, buoyantly. 'Last night I went to my mother's. She was really happy to see me making an effort with my dad. Despite their past, they've always maintained a degree of amicability. What she said next almost floored me. She started talking about his past. Apparently, his father was prone to violent outbursts and he became very protective towards his mother. When he was nine years old, his parents were divorced and he never set eyes on his father again. A couple of years later, Mary became very ill and he spent most of his time caring for her. One day some friends called and asked him to go out to play football. He refused, saying he had to tend to his mother. She overheard the conversation and insisted that he go. When he returned, less than two hours later, she was dead.'

She shot a glance at Phil.. 'Your message makes complete sense now – he's been blaming himself ever since!'

'I knew there was something,' Phil replied, thoughtfully. 'That message was so strong. It also explains why Mary said – "you'll both heal if you know the truth." Your father will heal as a result of your understanding and forgiveness, and your internal

conflict will lessen as a result of introjecting a new version of him..
….that's great news Vi.'

'Yes, it explains so much: his anger, his violence, his destructive drinking and the fact that Mary was trying to contact him; she couldn't move on until she'd reassured him he wasn't to blame.'

The trio continued to discuss the impact this event must have had on George. His character totally changed from that point on. He became very insular and depressed for many years. Vi felt a deep sense of compassion. He must have been crippled with guilt, she realised. She was astounded at the parallels of his childhood to that of her own: tending to mother, isolation, depression, angry outbursts. No wonder she felt such a bond with him. She also identified a repetitive dysfunctional pattern and part of her purpose was to break such patterns.

She expressed her gratitude for the signposts, realising that if they hadn't have happened, she would have probably condemned him for the rest of her life. Now she had an opportunity to heal the rift and was fully intent on taking it.

The trio took a coffee break. When they resumed, G. seemed in a much better frame of mind and started talking about his dilemma. As he churned his way through his torment, his voice was laced with contempt for himself. Phil intervened, pointing out that balance takes time and he should be aiming for improvement rather than perfection. He needed to nurture the child within - not condemn him. He brought G's attention to the fact that his own inner oppressor was now crucifying his inner child; scolding him needlessly, just like significant others had done all his life.

'Can you see how the messages we receive from others are internalised and form the structures of our inner saboteurs? In this case your own oppressor has turned in on your inner child. This will diminish your self worth, not improve it……Turn this event around big man, re-interpret it….. Perhaps you created this event to learn the virtue of balance?'

Phrasing things in this way caused something to shift within G. Insinuating that he had actually *created* the situation (at an unconscious level, of course) made sense. While the battle with his mother lay hidden deep inside, he couldn't access it. Re-creating it with Joan, enabled him to externalize it and work on it.

A welcomed sense of relief swept through him. He vowed to work on this inhibiting relationship with his mother as soon as possible. Phil offered to assist him. He now continued to describe the subsequent events.

'For the next couple of days she tried to force me back into submission, but I wasn't having any of it. Yesterday, when I came home from work, she informed me that she was filing for divorce. That didn't bother me too much; we've been estranged for many years anyway. I thought it was probably for the best. Then she dropped a bombshell: she informed me that she stood to acquire the house. I looked into the legal implications today and it seems she does have a case. She's much older than myself - a pensioner, and it seems the law falls in her favour. She has certain rights. What really infuriates me is that I've paid all the bills and the mortgage for years, and now, just as I've virtually paid for it, she stakes claim to the lot!'

'G.,' injected Phil, 'when we embark upon this path our worlds can be turned upside down. It's obvious you're feeling extremely insecure at the moment but things happen for a good reason. There is order behind all this seeming chaos. When we start to connect with our truth, it's almost inevitable that things will change: relationships can end, homes can go, employment can go, etcetera, but what's most important is that we adhere to our path. Be true to ourselves. Things will start to get better.. you'll see.. just give it time.'

'I will. Thanks very much, Phil.'

'As a matter of interest, what expectations have you been holding for the future? What areas of your life have you identified as warranting change?'

'The ones you've just mentioned: my relationship, my home and my employment. I'm not happy with any of them. My job doesn't fulfil me. My house is not a home. My relationship has been a farce from day one. The only reason I'm still there is that I need a place to live. So I've asked the Universe to lead me to my life's purpose, meaningful friendships, and my true home.'

Phil smiled inwardly. Things seemed to be making sense to him. 'It seems the Universe may already be responding. You're unhappy in your home and with your relationship, and now things are happening that may sever your ties with them. Remember G: signposts are not always welcome experiences, but if the Universe is trying to move you forward, don't fight it - have trust. These developments will ultimately lead to your destiny....Let go of the old and make space for the new.'

G. felt lifted. A radiant smile came to is face. 'I guess you're right, bro.'

He shot a glance at Phil, then Vi. 'The meaningful friendship part seems to be coming along just fine – doesn't it,' he beamed.

'It certainly does,' replied Phil, outstretching his arms and gesturing to them both to take his hands. The three formed a human circuit of love that generated a feeling of sheer harmony.

'Now G.,' Phil continued, genially, 'have you got any inclination into what your purpose may be?'

'Yes,' he stated, emphatically. 'I want to be involved in your project – the centre. I can't get the idea out of my mind lately, Phil. It grows every day. I think this is another source of frustration – I want it now.'

Phil was delighted.

'It'll be great to have you on board big man. It seems we're all searching for our true home and that centre will provide us with a haven. Let's finish this session by sending our intentions out loud and clear, setting our expectations high and asking that *our* centre actualizes just the way we've envisaged.'

After sending out their impulses of intent, nobody seemed in a hurry to leave. So Phil suggested that they review the events of the year. Each of them had kept a diary and a dream log. Phil had collated all the material and kept a complete record of it on computer. In addition, he had kept tape recordings of every channelling session they had held.

As they discussed the happenings of the year, the Dickensian image of the old man writing loomed vividly in Phil's mind: the material they were currently sifting through, the log of their journey, had something to do with the book?....Phil just hadn't realised it yet.

Chapter 20

Black Christmas

Christmas brought about mixed emotions for them all. G. retreated to the sanctuary of his converted attic room and spent most of the holiday in isolation: reading, meditating and listening to classical music. Although he enjoyed the solitude, he was besieged by pangs of loneliness as spectres of the past rose from the dark denizens of his mind. Nevertheless, he remained focused, sending out intentions daily. He was beginning to accept that the spiritual clay from which everything was moulded was intelligent and could be sculptured by the power of thought. He visualized himself in a number of scenarios: blissfully happy with his perfect romantic partner, fulfilled carrying out his life's purpose in the planned holistic development centre, and "at home" in a residence set in an area of great natural beauty. He let these visions expand in his mind until they felt real, generating a tremendous amount of joyous emotion. Without knowing it, he had become a vibrational match with the things he desired; he just had to maintain complete faith that the Universe would respond by manufacturing the signposts that would pave the way.

Phil travelled down South to spend the holiday with a close friend. Throughout the long train journey he was immersed in thoughts of Vi. Every intricate detail of their night out came flooding back: how the tables were adorned with flowers and candles, the subdued lighting and soft music that amplified the romantic ambience, Vi's radiant smile. The old lady who observed their deep bond from an adjacent table and commented to Vi on how she had observed Phil's love for her. (On that night, Vi couldn't help thinking that the

Universe had sent this little old dear to reassure her that Phil was the right person for her – she was a signpost).

After the meal, he handed her a gift and urged her to open it straight away. The friendship key ring had two bears embracing one heart. It detached in the centre leaving each bear nursing a segment of the heart on which a message was inscribed. Vi kept the segment saying 'one love' and handed him back the part saying 'two hearts'. For the rest of the evening they locked them back together so that the message befittingly read: 'two hearts – one love'.

Later in the evening, as the curtain descended on the musical, the atmosphere became subdued: neither of them wanted the night to end. En route home they hardly exchanged a word, yet their hearts spoke volumes. Phil put on some soft music and beckoned Vi to place her hand in his. He gently caressed it for the rest of the journey. As they approached her house, Eva Cassidy's 'Somewhere over the Rainbow' rang out from the CD player. Their eyes moistened. After an emotional exchange of farewells, she handed him back his segment of the key ring. He then watched as her forlorn silhouette disappeared into the darkness.

Since that night, everything associated with Christmas had sent his heart yearning for her: cosy movie scenes of lovers in front of log fires, choirs of children singing carols, playful children having snowball fights, cold moonlit nights. Although he'd abstained from relationships for some years, Christmas time always brought out the romanticist in him, and he longed to be with that someone special.

Apart from Christmas day, when he received a couple of affectionate text messages, he had heard very little from her. Inwardly he was upset. Yet these shifts from intimacy to diffidence epitomised their relationship. Once or twice he felt a surge of anger emerge as his programmed child leapt forward crying 'rejection,' but he had come to accept that life was about mastering emotions and refused to surrender to the destructive aspirations of his inner assailant. He counteracted his anger by absorbing deer medicine and arming himself with nothing but gentleness. He was now certain that one of his life lessons was that of unconditional love and Vi's role was instrumental in testing his resolve. This way of thinking enabled him to turn his insecurity into gratitude, highlighting the value of spiritual alchemy.

Vi's Christmas had been bleak, dogged by rocky emotions, her moods swinging like a pendulum. On Christmas day she felt totally numb – wondering what it was all about? She went through the niceties of giving and receiving, trying to make some sort of effort, but inside it all felt meaningless. On opening Phil's gift, she fled up the stairs in tears. Tom wondered what was going on. He had become accustomed to her angry outbursts, but in recent months she'd seemed much more stable. Now he couldn't fathom her out. One minute she was quiet and withdrawn, the next, sobbing and running to her bedroom. Her family and friends had also become very concerned.

The past few days had seen her feelings intensify, giving credence to the old adage 'absence makes the heart grow fonder'. This had given rise to an intrinsic melee. When she longed to be with Phil, her wounded child would form an alliance with her shadow and together they would broadcast destructive tapes in a desperate attempt to sabotage her thinking. 'Never become dependent on a man', 'don't trust', 'it will end in heartache'. Her Uniqueness and Soul child would respond by allowing her to feel the depth of Phil's love and reassure her of his integrity. They were determined to get her out of her head and into her heart.

Her energies ebbed and flowed between these two polarities: love and loyalty, safety and the unknown, resulting in an obvious imbalance. As she clung desperately to that crumbling cliff, her head became filled with contrasting questions.

What am I getting myself into? What are the consequences? What if I leave Tom and it all goes wrong? What if I stay with him and regret it for the rest of my life? Should I allow him to pull me back up to safety? If so, will I ever find happiness? If I let go will I drown in a sea of sorrow, or take to the skies just like the butterfly and find my true home.

*

Vi had gone to bed early this evening to get away from the festivities. She had always despised new year's eve - *what's the point in celebrating the beginning of another monotonous twelve months?* As this thought took precedence in her mind, a familiar energy pervaded her space and her hardened deportment began to soften.

Remember, my child, your future is carved by your thoughts. You are producer and director of your own life. The alchemist must be prepared to betray her ego to be true to her Soul... Your Soul's desire lies in your heart.

Her awareness heightened as she fused with the refined energy of her Uniqueness. She began to drift deep within, suddenly feeling herself being transported back through the centuries.

She found herself imprisoned in a tower after refusing to marry the knight. Galfridus appeared from the shadows, unlocked the door, and urged her to follow him. Her freedom was imminent, but then, something very strange happened. She froze. Her mind became immersed in fear and indecision. This was the only life she had ever known. Where would she go? What would she do? She had wealth and status; if she fled she would relinquish everything.

    The cell that imprisoned her was only symbolic of her state of mind. Outer reality was reflecting her internal state. A key to a locked door could not set her free; only

transformation of thinking could release her from her shackles.

Galfridus began to sing another ditty. She could see his mouth moving but could not hear the words.

Suddenly, she was jarred from her experience by the melodic tone of her mobile phone. She stared hazily at the envelope on the display. A fleeting thought rushed through her mind:

You create your own prisons, my child. Your thoughts construct the cell that incarcerates you. Imprisoned then, imprisoned now - what lessons can you learn?

She reached over for her phone. As she began to read the text message, Galfridus reappeared in her mind's eye. She was momentarily stunned: he seemed to be singing the ditty that was written in the text?

When indecision rules your mind

And answers are so hard to find

Place your trust within your heart

And all your fears will soon depart

Tides of change can ebb and flow

When you don't know which way to go

Call upon your Higher Power

She will lead you to your flower

May the next year bring you every happiness, sweetheart.

Love always, Phil. X

How can this happen? She mused. *I have a vision from the thirteenth century yet the message is re-enforced by somebody in the twenty-first century... Are Phil and Galfridus connected in a way that transcends time? If so, does it mean that past and present co-exist.*

Past, present and future co-exist, my child, answered her Uniqueness. *Time is an illusion: a psychological event; an artifact of the material Universe. In truth, everything happens in the eternal continuum of the present.*

'How can that be?' she murmured, hazily.

Your world is divided into time zones. If you go West you move back in time, if you move East you go forward. So, theoretically, people co-exist in your past and future. A similar principle is at work on a universal scale, only the veil that separates you from centuries past and centuries future is not one of time, it is one of vibrational frequency. Linear time does not exist, only domains of experience that are demarcated by frequency of vibration... Don't forget.. nothing happens in the way you think it happens: everything is an experience within consciousness.

Her mind became still. Although her intellect could not quite grasp this phenomenon, it resonated with something deep within.

If everything happens in consciousness and time doesn't really exist, then what I perceive as the past is actually happening right now, in another domain of experience; somewhere in the vast consciousness of the universal mind. WOW! She exclaimed, as an incredible insight hit her: this could mean that we're actually able to communicate directly with people existing in what we perceive to be the past and the future.

Something else suddenly struck her.

I wonder if it's possible for us to exist in two of these domains of experience simultaneously? Parallel lives. I felt incarcerated back in the thirteenth century and I feel incarcerated now; there is a common thread. Mm...I wonder, if I conquer my fears in the present, could it actually affect my other life and vice versa? If so, it not only means that the past affects the present, but the future does too... This is mind blowing.

She pondered a while longer, acknowledging the powerful effects of thoughts and how life lessons are carried over from one lifetime to another. She also thought about the concept of parallel lives: the possibility that we can exist in two domains of experience simultaneously. And how these experiences may impact on each other.

Eventually, she leant over to place her phone back onto the bedside table. As she did, she inadvertently knocked her keys to the floor. She got out of bed to retrieve them and noticed that one of her key rings had detached from the bunch. She peered down, transfixed on the heart which seemed to have a lustrous glow, everything else fading into insignificance. As the clock struck midnight and the new year commenced, the message was crystal clear - **one love.** (Some of you may think this a coincidence, but the two invisible orbs of light in her bedroom would fervently disagree!)

Chapter 21

Recap with a Disincarnate Entity

'Greetings, dear one.. yes.. you my child - the reader. At this point in the story, in order to heighten your awareness, I'd like to revisit some of the concepts and phenomena you have encountered... ...We will start by taking a look at what happened when Phil and Vi reunited after the Christmas break..'

Vi appeared detached and guarded once again, her New Year's Eve experience swallowed up by her internal quagmire of confusion. As Phil hugged her, wishing her happy new year, he felt a heavy gungey mess seeping in through his sacral chakra and immediately began to feel angry and irritable. He quickly recognised that he was absorbing her feelings (another aspect of clairsentience). His counselling training had taught him to monitor his feelings very carefully, particularly before and after a counselling session. If he felt differently afterwards, then it was highly likely that he'd absorbed his client's feelings. A simple recognition of this phenomenon was usually enough disperse it. However, if it went undetected, it could lead to problems.

'.... So my friends, let's take a closer look at this aspect of clairsentience. This energetical transaction is common in everyday life. When humans experience it, without recognising it, they can unwittingly carry another person's feelings for quite some time - What's up with me? Why am I feeling this way? Why am I weepy? Why am I furious? - they ask themselves, feeling this way for no apparent reason. They are literally carrying someone else's unwanted energies - just like a dirty sponge.......So I urge you, my dear one, be awake. Next time you suddenly feel heavy, irritable or angry, ask yourself - whose emotions am I carrying? And don't forget you can absorb joyous feelings

too!…… Now, let's further our insight and take a look at what happens when it goes undetected…

    '…When this aspect of clairsentience goes undetected it can lead to a reaction. Again, let's examine this morning's episode and elaborate… …Phil had absorbed Vi's anger and irritability which entered via his sacral chakra, the energy centre in which emotional energy is processed. Now, deep within his being, in the vast land of his unconscious, lay energetical recordings of all the thoughts and feelings affiliated with his past relationships. If, for example, he encountered a school teacher who was nasty and oppressive, this relationship would be swirling about within him. The anger and irritability absorbed from Vi may inadvertently aggravate and amplify this internal conflict and lead to an emotionally charged reaction; that is, her anger may tap into and trigger unresolved issues within him. This, in turn, may cause him to respond inappropriately to the current situation. He may shout, bawl, sulk, or revert to emotional blackmail, depending on which inner character dominates his response. … So be aware, my friends…don't let your unresolved issues impinge on your treasured relationships. Identify your internal saboteurs and expel them……Now, let's briefly return to the story……'

Thankfully, this morning, Phil recognised the adverse effects of clairsentience and didn't react. He invited Vi out for lunch, but she declined, saying she had to go shopping. Her defences were fully deployed; she was intent on pushing him away. The intimacy that had prevailed before Christmas seemed like a life time away. He intuited that part of her anger was directed at him. Before they had bonded, she was unhappy - but safe. Now her inner world had become fragmented and she was rebelling.

    '…In actuality, dear one, these episodes were part of a bigger picture – a learning process. They were both presenting circumstances through which the other could grow - then that's what Soul mates do! … Phil was experiencing rejection and his lesson was to tame the inner assailants that would normally dominate his response: the oppressor yelling "forget her, she isn't worth it anyway," the wounded child, crying, "she doesn't love me anymore."

The alleviation of these emotionally charged responses, my friend, is a fundamental part of spiritual growth. Shedding the demands of these intrinsic saboteurs enables your true essence to shine through, propelling you into the magic of your Uniqueness and taking you one step closer to your boundless nature...

'......*In addition to rejection, Phil was faced with another lesson this morning. He was unable to play "caretaker" - a role in which he thrived. When Vi was dependent on him, it fulfilled his need to be needed. But, when she was independent, the dynamic changed, and his need wasn't being met. From an earthly perspective, this would have put a strain on their relationship: the relationship fit, caretaker – child, would have been under pressure. When fundamental needs are not being met in relationships, they tend to dissolve or become problematic. From a spiritual perspective, however, these incidents are all tests: opportunities to relinquish the demands of your inner characters and evolve towards unconditional love...Thankfully, Phil recognised this....*

'......*Vi had been presented with a test, too. Phil had presented her with the opportunity to address her innermost fears. She had recognised she had to be prepared to become vulnerable if she wanted to form intimate relationships. Her history had left her with a serious lack of trust, so she was inclined to opt for safety. Now she had a chance to grow, re-establish trust and embrace intimacy – life lessons. ...The big question still remained...***which flower would she choose?** *Would she wither and die? Or would she flourish and blossom?...*

'......*Life is an excellent training ground, dear one, each nuance providing an opportunity to grow. Interpretation is the key to freedom. The difference between a good and bad experience is simply a matter of interpretation. If Phil had interpreted this morning's events through the eyes of his wounded child, then, as we have seen, either overt or covert conflict would have surely followed: aloofness, sulking, tantrums, verbal assassination of character, and so on. Yet, interpreting it through the lens of his Uniqueness, looking for the lesson behind the mask of matter, casts a whole new light on things. It now becomes a challenge, an opportunity to let go of the influences of the internal saboteurs whose happiness is extremely volatile; dependent on other* people acting in accordance with their rigid demands. This type of so called love - love based on needs - is an integral part of earthly life, yet, it can be so enslaving. **When you release that which you are not, the debris you have collected within your being during your earthly journey - the wounded child, the manipulative child, the controlling caretaker, the oppressor, the shadow, the mask, and the ego - then you will step into the magic of your Uniqueness...**

'...How do I jettison the demands of these inhibiting complexes of energy? I hear you ask. Simply by observing them: refrain from fusing with them, abstain from becoming them...

'...During your everyday interactions notice when, and in what situations, they emerge. Notice the dialectic interchange between yourself and others. For example, does your manipulative child emerge when you are faced with another person's oppressor? Does your wounded child step forth and counteract the love and affection of another's loving caretaker? You can learn much about yourself from this practice, dear one. You will almost certainly find that many of your interactions are distorted by the needs of your inner people...So now, let's recap on who these are:

*'**The wounded child** – a complex resulting from traumatic episodes in your life. Fear is the inhibiting force of this complex.*

*'**The manipulative child** – a complex that results from internalising past methods of getting your needs met: sulking, aloofness, tantrums, emotional blackmail, and so on.'*

(Both the aforementioned bundles of energy can be seen as the **programmed child**).

*'**The oppressor** – the critical, controlling, inauspicious, part of yourself.*

*'**The caretaker** – the loving, nurturing, encouraging, kind, giving, accepting part of yourself. But, don't forget, this complex can also be very controlling: love masquerading as manipulation.*

'***The analyst*** *– the part of yourself that is free from the emotionally charged responses of the aforementioned bundles of energy. The rational, analytical, logical, part of yourself....*

'*...Now finally...The spiritual elements of your inner world..*

'***The wonder child*** *– the unconditioned, free, explorative, adventurous, loving, accepting, fun-loving, creative part of yourself.*

'***Uniqueness*** *– a higher aspect of yourself that links you with your Soul: wise, enlightened, nurturing, creative, healing and loving. This is the aspect of yourself you aim to become during your journey home...*

'*...So, once again, I urge you –* **be awake.** *Monitor yourself and become aware of when your inhibiting complexes arise. Be prepared to let go of them. Don't waste your time trying to change others, attend to you own shortcomings. This practice will set you free. Ask yourself - "do I really want to be enslaved by the demands of my inhibiting inner complexes for the rest of my life? Can I really experience freedom when I'm enslaved to their whims?" If the answer is no, then exploit them, see them as trouble-makers and detach from them. With no life sustaining energy, they will eventually leave of their own accord. As alchemists turned base metals into gold, you will convert your slavery into freedom....you will become a spiritual alchemist...*

'*...At this point, you may be asking yourself – who is this voice that has suddenly emerged in the middle of the story?......time to quell your curiosity, my dear one...* **I am your Uniqueness***...and I am with you right now...yes, that's right... in the space surrounding you...I, and many other beings of light exist within this space...so, please, communicate with us...we are all working for a common purpose...* **we are all one***...*

'*...just before I depart, I must tell you that Vi did eventually go for lunch with Phil. At coffee break she poured her heart out, saying that she'd had a dreadful Christmas and didn't want to go through another one like it...*

'*...Over lunch, their attention diverted to an important event which is due to take place this forthcoming Saturday – Vi's meal with her father. She told Phil she had invited the whole family around in an attempt to restore harmony......*

'......Anyway, time to go ......don't forget to call on me and all the other beings of light whenever you need us. Use your higher senses to explore the space around you and listen attentively to the all knowing silence......It is now with love and light that I depart.'

Chapter 22

Abused From Beyond the Grave

Carla lay in bed. It was two thirty in the afternoon. The incessant ringing of the doorbell awoke her from her languid stupor.

'Go away - leave me alone,' she scowled, pulling the duvet further over her head.

The strident sound of the telephone caused her already shredded nerves to jangle even more. Nothing mattered anymore - absolutely nothing. How long she'd been there she didn't know. Furthermore, she just didn't care. It took the greatest of efforts to muster up the energy just to get to the bathroom. Even when the dull ache in her stomach caused her to make this short trip she quickly retreated to her darkened room and the oblivious state it induced - death by duvet.

Almost two years to the day, her ex-husband had been found slumped over the wheel of his fume filled car. She had divorced him eight years earlier for fear of her life. The history of abuse read like a catalogue: he had beaten her black and blue, threatened to cut her up, and tried to run her down in the street. His parting words when they were divorced were – 'I'll never let you go, I'll make your life hell.'

A cold shudder ran through her veins as she felt certain he was adhering to his final vow - even in death. The room began to take on an even more sinister atmosphere. Carla shuddered again as the temperature appeared to drop drastically. She wrapped her shroud-like duvet around her wracked and tormented body.

'Just let me die,' she screamed inwardly.

At that very instant, an animal-like roar of titanic force appeared to erupt from her chest. She froze.

Chapter 23

Synchronistic Science

G. was wandering through the corridors on his way home when something compelled him to take an alternate route through one of the lecture theatres (he was unaware of the two orbs of light in the surrounding space). A middle-aged man stood musing over a complex equation. The two stared at each other, having an uncanny sense that they had met somewhere before.

'Do I know you?' inquired G.

'I was just thinking the same thing,' replied the man. 'Can't think where though.'

'That looks daunting,' G. continued, turning his attention to the data scrawled on the whiteboard.'

'Quantum Physics,' replied the man. 'Isn't it fascinating to think that nothing physical exists until we observe it. We create physical reality purely by observation. As soon as we observe something it appears. Until then, it doesn't exist - at least not in the form we perceive it.'

'Yes – precisely,' replied G, enthusiastically. 'The magic of perception – everything is constructed in our head. The physical world is in here (pointing to his head), not out there.'

The physicist's eyebrows raised. He looked impressed. This guy had an insight into what he was talking about.

'I wonder what else is out there?' continued the scientist. 'Our brain processes a couple of thousand of bits of data a second, which sounds a lot, but considering billions of bits per second pass through, it makes you wonder what we're missing out on? What's out there that lies beyond the limitations of our physical senses or scientific measuring equipment? The Universe is mostly empty space. Even the nucleus of an atom is insubstantial. But we're finding this empty space is actually imbued with intelligence. So, what lies in this nothingness that we're unable to access?'

'Or can we access it,' injected G, 'through our subtle senses? And do we dismiss it as imagination?'

'Oh,' the man sighed, 'I don't know about all that stuff. Science will find the answers eventually.'

'But you just said that nothing exists until it's observed. Experiments have been carried out to find the observer. Every nook and cranny of the brain has been explored. But, no one can find the experiencer. They know the brain executes commands, but the big question is - where is the invisible intelligence that issues them? ....Our bodies are forever changing. We never step into the same cloak of matter twice. We are continually regenerating new cells; we are relentlessly metabolising bits and pieces of other people and the environment. Every cell within our body changes within two years, meaning we outlive its death. Our emotions are transient and our thoughts are fleeting. So, unquestionably, nothing's permanent. **Yet, we all have a sense of continuity. There's a part of us that lies beyond all this change. Something that observes this change, yet is impartial...** Explain that one Mister scientist?' G. said, triumphantly.

'I must admit, that one is an enigma... Maybe I've had my head in science books for too long.'

Theodore and Esba smiled at each other. Their plan was taking effect. Using G. as a signpost was a good idea. He'd got a thirst for spirituality and wasn't easily dissuaded. The physicist needed a prodding and the big man was just the chap to do it!

'Anyway, I must be getting along now,' said G. 'This has been a very interesting encounter - fancy pursuing it some other time?'

'Certainly do,' replied the physicist, holding out his hand. 'Robert's the name…and yours?'

'Graham, but most people call me G.'

'Right G., here's my card. Look me up and we'll continue our discussion soon.'

As they shook hands, a surge of energy arced between them. Again, they had an uncanny sense of familiarity.

Chapter 24

A Family Reunion

Phil paced up and down like an expectant father: turning on the television, then turning it off; running a bath, then draining the water; picking up a book, then lashing it to one side - he just could not settle. As tonight was the occasion of Vi's family reunion, the implications lay heavily on his mind. If all went well, not only the debilitating elements of her internal world could be alleviated, but the curative process may also lead to a synthesis of the family as a whole.

After a few more manic laps around the living room, Phil decided to put his excess energy to good use. He got out the iron board and began to tackle the mound of clothes that had accumulated. Whilst gliding the iron over his clothes, whistling like a demented budgerigar, the telephone began to ring. Still preoccupied with extraneous thoughts, he inadvertently mistook the apparatus in his hand for the telephone. He let out an excruciating cry as he placed the red hot iron to his ear.

'Hello….aaarrgghhhh…Shiiittttt!!!…..'

What followed was nothing short of a pantomime: an elaborate display of his extraordinary talents! First - the marsupial. Boing..boing..boing, he went, down the hall, into the lounge, and back into the living room. After coming to a sudden halt, an amazing transformation began to take place. His bottom protruded, his neck extended, his head developed a spasmodic twitch, and his arms began to flap. He had shape-shifted into the funky chicken and was now darting around the room. The finale was most entertaining. Phil suddenly winced. His knees buckled, and everything appeared to go into slow motion. He then stamped around the room as though performing some sort of ceremonial war dance, chanting expletives that most definitely do not have their roots in any ancient spiritual practice!

Vi sat, eyes closed, in her bedroom. She had prepared the family meal. Tom had gone to spend the night at his parents. And her guests wouldn't be arriving for a while. So, she decided to spend the quiet time in commune with the unseen realms.

'I know all this started as a means of healing my scars,' she murmured, earnestly. 'The internalised version of my father and my inner child, were in battle. And this inner turbulence was being projected onto my external world, severely damaging my relationships. But it's gone beyond that now. I feel real compassion for my dad and I want him to know it…. I ask the Universe to bring divine light into my home tonight and help heal my family. We've been through enough. It's time for harmony. I'm not too good with words in these situations, so let my father *see* and *feel* what's inside of me. Set him free. …Set me free….. Set our whole family free….. Make me a channel of your peace.'

Three orbs of light descended into the surrounding space in response to Vi's request. A gentle breeze began to caress her body, purifying and replenishing her. She bathed in the divine shower of light, drinking in the spiritual elixir with the thirst of a woman who'd been lost in the desert….An iridescent form suddenly slipped into her mind. The image resembled an unfocused photograph. As it became more pronounced, she was able to discern the figure of an old lady: stooped and frail, grey shawl draped around her flagging shoulders…*Tell him he was not to blame,* she whispered, pleadingly. Vi felt her words reaching deep within, penetrating a threshold to a once inaccessible land: a forgotten world where love and compassion are the only currency. 'I will

Mary... I promise you,' she replied, while continuing to drift deep inside herself.

Silence. Images of her father's childhood reeled through her mind; he too was a casualty of dysfunctionality. She observed and absorbed, gaining a very deep understanding of him. Her empathy levels rose and her heart chakra unfurled. A healing started to take place. A vibrant light cleansed the core of her being. Her vibration heightened. She felt herself expand. Expand. Expand. Expand. Time seemed to suspend. She entered the nothingness where everything exists: the realm of the all knowing silence. She felt herself to be nowhere – yet everywhere; nothing – yet everything; creation itself: omnipotent and omnipresent.

After what seemed like a lifetime in this euphoric state, she started to soar back to earth, re-entering the atmosphere like a triumphant astronaut in possession of new-found knowledge. Her eyelids fluttered. She hazily readjusted herself to the surroundings. Her eyes locked open. As they did, the room seemed to take on a fluorescent tint, everything appearing to shimmer in and out of focus. The sound of something falling caused her to resume normal awareness. A magazine had toppled from her book shelf. It lay open on the centre spread – an article on oceanography. A dolphin peered straight up at her; its eyes hypnotic. She was spellbound, somehow feeling she was conversing with it. In an inexplicable way she knew she was absorbing its healing powers; medicine that would help restore harmony in the family.

Phil lay on the couch, recovering nicely from his earlier mishap. Once again, he was immersed in thoughts of Vi, contemplating her healing process. As he reflected on his relationship with her, he started to question his motives. His attention started to ebb and flow between two contrasting polarities...

...Am I doing the right thing expressing my love for her? Or am I adding to her confusion?.... Are my intentions right?.... How much of my

interest is based on self? I am in love with her after all....Does she love me as much as I perceive? Or is projection in operation – am I being blinded by my own feelings and seeing them situated in her…... How much of it is dependency? Counselling situations give rise to dependency, not only for the client but for the counsellor too. Our relationship has that dynamic to it……If she is in love with me but determined to stay where she is - what should I do? That situation will inevitably be painful for both of us……. Should I back off? I've tried that on a few occasions but she seemed very upset. She perceived me as being cold. She already has abandonment issues and I don't want to add to them…. There are morals to be considered too. She is with another man, and it's not in my nature to mess around with other people's women…... But then if we're meant to be together…I must pursue her. It would be such a shame if something so special didn't get the opportunity to flourish…... And if her heart is with me, she'll be of little use to Tom anyway – they'll both be desperately unhappy.

His attention drifted to a succession of images that bombarded his mind a couple of days earlier. They had been eating away at him like a malignant cancer.

I saw their probable future together. They had a child but she was desperately unhappy – she felt totally imprisoned. Trapped. Suffocated…But how can I tell her?... I can't is the simple answer – it would appear manipulative…. My psychic senses are of very little use in this situation. I'm so deeply involved I can't be objective…... I need an outside perspective. Someone who can see the situation through neutral eyes.

He closed his eyes and sent out impulses of intent, asking the Universe to provide an outside source who could give an objective view of their relationship. Someone who could clarify the right course of action. Action that would resolve the situation in a way that considered the highest good of all concerned.

As the clock approached twelve thirty, his phone rang. He unnervingly scanned the room for the iron. After convincing himself it was actually the *phone* ringing - he answered it.

'Phil, you're my best friend ever,' a bubbly voice blurted. 'I've been wanting to text you all night, but I didn't get much of a chance. I did try to ring you earlier, before everyone came - were you out?'

'No, I was ironing my ear,' he replied.

'What!' she exclaimed.

'Never mind, I'll tell you later. I want to hear all about your night first.'

'It went so well, Phil,' she replied, excitedly. 'My father really enjoyed himself. It was difficult at first. I had to have a couple of glasses of wine to steady my nerves. My brothers and sister still have issues with him, so, understandably, I was a little tense beforehand. But they didn't get in the way tonight. Everyone enjoyed themselves. They were all surprisingly amicable. It makes you wonder doesn't it, Phil? Intentions.. and their power. You should have seen my dad with Charlie. He loves her to bits - and she loves him too. Obviously she doesn't know anything about the past. It was lovely to see them playing together… He was speechless when we gave him the cake. I thought he was going to cry - he nearly did……..And Phil…'

She went on to describe her mystical experience and brief encounter with Mary.

'I didn't know how I was going to give him a message from the spirit world,' she continued. 'You don't normally spring something like that on someone you haven't seen for years - but I did it. He was the last one to leave, so I got the perfect opportunity. Coincidence? - I think not. He's developed a deep interest in spirituality over the last couple of years. He said it was the only thing that could've stopped him drinking. He was delighted about the message, Phil. I emphasized that he mustn't blame himself and it seemed to sink in. To reassure him that the message was authentic, I told him that it initially came via a friend who couldn't have possibly known what happened. His face beamed. You were right, he did need to hear it.'

'Wonderful, Vi... I'm so pleased for you all... Perhaps Mary will go back to the Higher Astral plane in peace now.'

'Speaking of spirits and things, my mother has a psychic visiting next weekend. She's reputed to be excellent - so good that the police commission her to help solve cases – I'm going to have a reading myself.'

Phil lit up inside. The independent person he'd asked for had come forward. Even he was amazed at the speed of this result.

'Anyway, you'd better get to bed now.' Said Vi. 'You're off to your hypnotherapy convention early tomorrow morning - aren't you?'

'Yes - I am. I'm going to see if I can get treated for an Iron phobia.'

'What?' she replied.

Tears of laughter poured down her face as Phil relayed his unfortunate mishap.

'I've heard of steam coming out your ears – but that's ridiculous!'

'Thank you for your obvious concern, missy.' He laughed.

'Anyway, night night, and thanks so much for your help once again.'

'Sweet dreams, sweetheart. See you later in the week.'

Phil wasted no time whatsoever. As soon as he put down the phone, he went straight back to his meditation room and asked the Universe to enable this psychic to bring clarity to their situation. He appealed for the guides of Tom, Vi and himself to be present at the reading and influence it in a manner that revealed the truth. He concluded by asking that the outcome be for the highest good of all concerned.

Chapter 25

Devastating Effects of Psychic Abuse

Carla sat adding to her suicide note. Immersed in a seemingly never ending stream of heartache, she had reached the jumping off place. Having attended the doctors complaining of breathlessness and chest pains, a heart condition had been diagnosed and medication administered. Seeing her obvious depression, the GP persuaded her to see a psychologist. She attended a number of sessions, but nothing was improving. During the final session, she proclaimed she was going mad and beyond help.

Her boyfriend of twelve months had recently departed saying he couldn't bear to see what was happening to her. She had received an eviction notice from her landlord due to amassing rent arrears. Her beloved daughters had disowned her saying they didn't know who she was anymore. Her elderly parents were being persecuted by gangs of youths outside their home. And her father had recently gone into heart failure. In a last ditch attempt to save her sanity, she consulted a priest, but he was also unsuccessful.

As she scrawled her final words, draining the last remnants of her impoverished mind, the shrill of the doorbell caused her to jump. She huddled into a ball, like a frightened child, terrified of the least noise.

'Go away,' she scowled, under her breath. 'Leave me to die in peace.'

The person at the door was persistent, ringing and knocking relentlessly. Five minutes. Ten minutes. Nothing.

With patience wearing thin and anxiety levels rising, the caller reverted to bellowing through the letter box. 'Carla, open the door! It's me - Phil.....I'll stay here all night if I have to.'

She was taken aback. *Phil?... What's he doing here?*

After meeting in Alcoholics Anonymous many years ago, the two had helped each other through the most difficult of times. She was a tower of strength to him during his early days of recovery, always finding the right words at the right times. Over the years, they had kept in touch, but recently Phil's attempts to contact her had been to no avail. Being in close proximity of her home, attending a hypnotherapy convention, he decided to call in.

'Carla. Open the door. I know you're in there.' He bawled, as several curious neighbours peered through the windows.

Knowing how stubborn he could be, particularly when sensing that something was amiss, she stood up, her jittery legs hardly able to carry her. After flinging the suicide note into a drawer, she languorously traipsed her way to the door.

Phil was shocked when her pathetic figure eventually appeared: a former shadow of the woman he once knew. Aged beyond her years, hair dishevelled, face as white as a sheet, excruciatingly thin, and uncharacteristically unkempt. The air of confidence that was once a dominant feature of her personality had vanished, leaving a dithering wreck.

She stared at him through fiery eyes.

'My God, Carla, what happened to you?' he exclaimed.

Not wanting the prying neighbours to catch sight of her shabby appearance, she quickly ushered him in. He idled behind her as she wheezed, coughed and spluttered her way up hall. Although she was one of the most hospitable people he'd ever known, he felt he'd entered hostile territory: the atmosphere was unsettlingly eerie.

The rancid smell of cat urine infused with the pungent aroma of stale food caused him to wince as they entered the smoke filled lounge. Her living space had been reduced to nothing more than a squat: cold, half drunken, cups of coffee; scrunched up cigarette packets; scraps of discarded food and remnants of shredded paper lay strewn about the place. The sunlight palled as it filtered through the thick film of nicotine smearing the window panes. The reason Phil had been unable to contact her was now also clear - the phone lay smashed to smithereens on the floor.

Christ! What the hell happened here? He thought. *She was always such an impeccably clean person.*

Before he could sit down, tears started to flood from her sunken eyes. 'Phil,' she sobbed, 'he's back.'

He didn't need to ask who? She had expressed concern about strange goings on shortly after her ex-husband's suicide.

He wrapped his arms around her skeleton-like frame. 'It's okay, Carla....just calm down..... everything's going to be okay.'

She slumped into the armchair and started spitting out the catalogue of dreadful events that had brought her to her knees, claiming her deceased ex-husband, Jim, was behind it all. Judging by what he sensed, and knowing the Carla of old to be a very rational person, he was inclined to believe her. Initially, however, he didn't want to add to her already disturbed psychological state, so he suggested it may be her mind trying to make sense of her circumstances. She categorically refuted this explanation.

'No! No! No!' she bawled. 'He's here. We've got to get rid of him.'

Phil yielded to the suspicions of his subtle senses. 'Okay, Carla, I believe you. If that's the case you're going to have to let him know he's not welcome.'

'How the hell am I supposed to do that? – he's dead!' she barked.

'In exactly the same way you'd let any physical person know they're not welcome. Shout at him! Bawl! Scream! Generate as much anger as you possibly can and drive him away. In this dimension you're much more powerful than him. Don't forget that, you just have to let him know it.....If that fails, we'll find someone who's more experienced in these matters.'

Three testing days later, Phil left Blackpool. In that time he cleaned the house from top to bottom, sifting his way through grease, dust, rubbish and grime. Painstakingly, he listened to Carla's problems and gave her the benefit of his counselling experience. He almost force fed her until she re-established a meagre appetite. And then made an appointment for her with an organisation that counsel people for psychic abuse.

After a couple of days, when she had gathered enough strength, they bawled, screamed, stamped, banged and wailed, generating tremendous amounts of energy in a ploy to drive out the menacing entity.

On leaving, she was of a much more calm disposition; things appeared to have quietened down. Their efforts, however, had not been enough to drive out the menacing spirit. Anger was not a long-term answer. There was, nevertheless, one energy that *would* drive it away......as they would find out at a later date.

Chapter 26

Prophecy of a Romany

Vi and her mother sat chatting over tea and sandwiches. Sue, Vera's friend, was in the next room having her reading. Vera was telling Vi that Roma, the psychic, had a wealth of experience. Her C.V. included: ridding houses of unwanted spirits, spiritual healing, white witchery, and assisting the police to find missing persons.

'She even found the body of a ten-year-old boy that went missing late last year,' she exclaimed, eulogizing the extraordinary talents of the psychic medium. 'Val had a reading from her twelve months ago,' she continued, ' and she predicted she'd have another baby - what do you think about that? There wasn't much chance of it happening, and now she's pregnant again!'

'My friend, Phil, predicted it too.' Vi replied. 'He even foretold *when* it would happen,' she added, her voice intoned with pride.

'You never told me that,' replied her intrigued mother.

'I didn't want to build your hopes up, but then I should have known better; Phil is quite extraordinary,' she smiled, endearingly.

Vera noticed a glint in her eyes. Cocking her head to one side, she shot her a curious glance. 'You talk about Phil a lot, and with great fondness I might add. You're not holding back on me – are you?'

Vi's face flushed. Before she had a chance to respond, the sound of chattering voices disturbed them. Inwardly, Vi was relieved; the re-emergence of Sue saved her from any further embarrassment.

'That woman's frightening,' Sue exclaimed. 'She's just told the story of my life.'

As she sat down and started to tell Vera of her experience, Vi stood up: it was her turn next.

Roma sat motionless, entranced by a candle flame. Her long, jet black hair twisted down from beneath a silk head scarf and draped over one shoulder. Her features were sharp and tanned. Silver earrings, each holding a disc-shaped snowflake agate, dangled from her lobes. She wore agate to help foster, abundance, longevity, acceptance, courage, protection and balance.

As the silence continued, Vi observed the flamboyantly dressed medium with great curiosity. Her appearance had an air of eccentricity: a fuchsia, wrinkled-cotton gypsy skirt fell down to a pair of metallic lustre sandals; silver rings, inset with precious stones, adorned almost every finger. Another ring pierced her right nostril; her emerald green blouse, with flounced three quarter length sleeves, revealed a heavy silver charm bracelet.

After perusing Roma's garb, Vi's attention moved to a purple silk cloth on the table in which were wrapped Roma's Tarot cards. As she stared at it, she suddenly felt a strong presence: Phil's call had been answered – the guides were present.

Roma emerged from her trance-like state, flashing a penetrative gaze towards her. 'Come - sit.' She ordered, her mysterious, wolf-like eyes, scanning Vi from top to bottom.

Vi felt uneasy: intimidated. Yet she felt that beneath Roma's stern exterior, lay a gentle, caring Soul.

'My God,' said Roma, 'your abdomen is full of a gungey mess. Let's see if we can get you sorted out.' Then, as Vi sat down, quite spontaneously, Roma started making a very strange sound: one that was very familiar to Vi.

'Aaaaaarrrrrrggghhhh,' she gurgled, 'that tickles you doesn't it?' She enquired, tilting her head to one side, a trace of a smile coming to her face.

The tension immediately dispersed. Vi chortled. 'Yes it does,' she replied. 'A friend of mine often does Mr Bean impressions while we're out shopping.'

The first part of the reading was of little significance, names that didn't mean very much. The focus then shifted, centring on her martial arts, and one or two very pertinent points came to light. As it progressed, Roma started to uncover the intricate details. What ensued was nothing short of remarkable.

She described Vi's life as a real battle ground, tapping into her turbulent childhood. She then spoke of a break in her family history, picking up on another mother and father – her foster-parents. Slowly but surely, she pieced the fragments of Vi's life together to create a very comprehensive picture.

'You're deeply unhappy aren't you, my dear?' she continued.

Vi's gaze dropped to the floor.

'He drags you down, doesn't he?' she added.

Vi knew exactly who she was talking about – Tom.

She remained silent.

Roma turned another card. The atmosphere lightened.

'And who's this with the cheeky smile? A real monkey and I mean a monkey.'

Vi started to chuckle again, thinking of the ape impressions Phil often did. 'It's my friend, Phil - the Mr Bean impressionist!'

Roma's demeanour suddenly softened, her voice becoming low and purposeful. 'He offers you a lot of kindness doesn't he dear?'

'Yes,' Vi replied, her voice infused with affection.

Roma's sacral chakra began to unfurl and draw in Vi's emotional energy. She paused to contemplate. Then, her acute senses started to scan Vi's mind like a powerful search light, illuminating every dark corner. 'You'll be faced with a big decision in the near future,' she said, returning her gaze to the cards and carefully scrutinizing them. 'If this doesn't work out,' she continued, gesturing to the cards pertaining to Vi's relationship, 'then you'll end up here - with this person.'

Vi suddenly felt transparent. Her honesty threshold had been breached. Her wounded child leapt to her defence, vetoing Roma's prophecy. 'But Phil's just a friend!' she retorted.

Roma wasn't known for her subtlety when it came to important matters. She saw straight through Vi's armour. 'I'm telling you,' she roared, banging her hand down on the table. 'You're attached to this person by the heart.'

A strange silence suddenly descended, the atmosphere infused with an air of anticipation.

Roma tilted her head. 'What's that?' she said, communicating with a presence that lay beyond this world.

She reached for the tarot deck and flipped another card. Her intonation suddenly assuaged to a mystical whisper.

'Wait a minute…'

Pause.

'…….you aren't attached to this person by the heart..'

Pause.

Roma's voice now took on a real air of mysticism. 'There's only one heart here…..'

She glanced up at Vi. 'The two of you share only one heart.'

The image of the key ring suddenly flashed before Vi's eyes.

Two hearts – one love. Yet, the bears shared only one heart.

It all started to get a bit too much for Vi. Her defences deployed again and she retreated. 'But won't I ever find happiness where I am?' she murmured, now close to tears.

Roma became sensitized to her predicament. She softened her stance. 'Not unless there's radical change, sweetheart. But don't despair, if you go to this other person, I'm telling you right now, you'll never look back.'

Roma had unlocked the door, but Vi was not ready to walk. She felt a strong sense of déjà vu as remnants of another life rippled through her unconscious, stirring up her life-lessons.

Roma now started to sink into a deep trance-like state, relaxed but extremely concentrated. 'You mustn't have any children just yet my dear,' she murmured, driftily. 'They're giving me this, they're asking me to tell you this.... If you're to have children, it will be to this other person.' (Mary dissipated into the surrounding space, her mission accomplished).

As Roma continued this course of conversation, Vi became increasingly irritable. She longed for happiness and contentment but her roots were so deeply ingrained in safety, she was unwilling to explore other fields of possibility. However, although part of her was cocooned in a rigid shell of fear, another part was going through the process of metamorphosis. The big question still remained - would she ever sprout wings and fly?...... Roma's final words left the question open to deliberation.

'Another life awaits you my dear, a life beyond your wildest dreams.... Only you can make the choice.'

*

That night Vi lay in bed tossing and turning, the dream of her stripping in front of the stranger haunting her mind. Her interpretation suggested that she shouldn't be trusting. If she was to bare the naked truth, it would inevitably backfire and lead to heartache. She was better off where she was, in the safe sphere of familiarity.

Just before she fell asleep, she decided to ask for further guidance and clarity. 'Please show me my highest path during my sleep,' she uttered.

Phil stood menacingly at the bedroom door.

'You know you want it,' he said threateningly.

Vi sat nervously on the bed. 'I just want us to be good friends – what are you playing at?' she retorted.

'You knew full well what you were doing. Why on earth have you been leading me on?' he snapped.

'I thought you understood. I thought we were just good friends who cared deeply for each other.'

Phil glared at her in total disbelief, then walked away. He returned a couple minutes later.

'Why are you doing this, Vi? You know what you want it,' he bawled, inching closer to her.

She froze.

'Leave me alone, Phil, you've got it all wrong.'

He took another step forward. Her stomach churned. He moved his face close to hers. She recoiled; his deep blue penetrative eyes making her feel transparent.

'You want to get honest with yourself,' he roared, then disappeared slamming the door behind him.

Vi awoke with a jilt. Deeply upset, shaking, her thoughts flashing back to the abuse she suffered as a child.

I asked for guidance and it seems I've been given an answer — don't trust. Phil said that dreams portray realities, so this dream must be a prophecy. My other dream told me not to trust, and now this one relays the same message... But it doesn't make any sense. Phil's not like that. He'd never force himself on me. He's kind and gentle... But then so was my foster-father, and look what he did to me... These dreams are beginning to scare me.

Her thoughts began to race. She started to break out into a feverish sweat, tossing, turning and feeling nauseous. She never slept a wink for the rest of the night.

Chapter 27

Observations from the Unseen Realms

Vibrant clouds of energy poured forth from the void, each individual particle dancing in rhythm with Universe. Shafts of blinding light appeared, drinking in the particles then scattering them like stardust to form a shimmering template of celestial architecture. The crystal temple emerged from the iridescent form. Sunlight splashed through its stained glass windows sending streams of coloured light cascading through the main hall. Two iridescent embryos appeared, hovering near to the ceiling then gracefully descending towards the ground. Concentric circles of rapturous energy pulsated outwardly from each ellipse imbuing the air with harmonic vibrations. The shimmering figure of a monk appeared, followed by the glistening form of a native American Indian.

Welcome, my dear child, said Theodore, mentally. *The time nears for you to re-incarnate, but this future, as yet, is still at the stage of possibility. It is essential that you are born into a family were true love prevails, for your earthly mission is of great importance: unlike other earthly personalities, you will retain full access to your eternal memories. The wealth of wisdom you have accumulated over thousands of lifetimes, both on the earthly plane and other dimensions of existence, will be at your disposal. You will utilize your knowledge to awaken the collective consciousness of the planet. Your work will take place primarily at the proposed centre for holistic development. For you to maintain your eternal memories it is imperative that you are not immersed in chaos or turbulence; your parents must bathe you in love, recognise your gift, and give you their full support. They are being primed for this at this very moment…*

…Your potential parents have chosen some difficult lessons in this lifetime, ones that you have mastered through the course of your own evolution. Before you can re-incarnate, it is crucial that they follow your example and

awaken to truth: they must understand the true nature of love and be finely attuned to the unseen realms…

…Our collective mission is to relay a message to the occupants of the material world. A message that says:

We are all unique cells within one unified body, inimitable waves in the same ocean. Each of us has a singular purpose and that purpose is designed to serve the whole.

We are one.

Part one of our plan involves the manifestation of a book. The book is still writing itself, though, the author has not realised it yet. Experience is invaluable when writing. An author who writes from truth and experience, transforming his heart-felt emotions into creativity, will reach the collective consciousness of the planet. At this stage of our mission, it is looking highly probable that the book will materialize. It is also looking promising for the materialization of the centre. Stage three, however, is hanging in the balance. Should Phil and Vi succeed in integrating their final lessons then it will actualize: you will reincarnate and the world will witness the boundless potential of an enlightened human being…

…At present, Phil is beginning to awaken to the fact that memories are stored at the level of the Soul. Initially, they are stored in neural networks in the brain, but they are then transmitted to a large reservoir of accumulative karma that's held at the level of the Soul. The Soul then utilizes certain memories to test the earthly personality. If I highlight conflicting thoughts in the minds of any of my personalities, I offer them a choice. Their choices then determine whether they reach their destiny or not…

….As warriors of light, our children must conquer their fears. Phil has chosen the lessons of unconditional love and altruism and is making good progress. His objective is to have no conditions whatsoever on his love or good deeds. As yet, his actions are not purely altruistic. He's in love with Vi and therefore has an investment in being kind to her - he fears losing her. True

altruism is pure selflessness. At some point in the near future, he will encounter his ultimate test…

…She is in love with him also, but adheres to the belief that she is not. If she remains rigid and continues to push him away, then an opportunity will arise for him to prove the extent of his love. If he continues to love her whilst believing they have no future together, then his lesson will be over – he will have attained unconditional love and pure altruism. And, if she allows herself to become vulnerable and opens herself up to love, then she too will have achieved a major goal – trust. But first, she has to test Phil. They agreed on this before incarnation, though they won't remember that of course…

…They are not only evolving as individuals, Esba, but we are evolving as a collective consciousness – a Soul family, each providing lessons through which the others can grow. This can be done directly or indirectly. I can plant seeds in their minds, or use another personality to act as a vessel to direct them. We have used Graham as an instrument to awaken Robert. We have also used Galfridus as a vessel to reach Vi. Though it's impossible for humans to grasp intellectually, the past is not over in the way they perceive: past, present and future co-exist in the eternal continuum of the now. Past lives are over in the individuals experience and their residual energy, memories and feelings, are stored in a karmic reservoir at the level of the Soul. A handful of these memories can be accessed via the individual's Uniqueness. The reason that access is limited is that the memories that are accessible are biased towards the individual's current life's purpose; they predispose them to explore a certain direction. Future lives haven't happened in the individual's experience: but the past and future domains of experience continue to exist; they are on-going. This being so, it is quite possible for an entity to experience two realms of existence simultaneously; parallel lives as they are called. Using the vehicles of dreams, meditation, channelling, regression and progression an entity can bridge the frequency veil that separates these domains and commute between the two. In general, parallel lives impact on each other; making changes in one affects the other and vice versa. So, if Vi should free herself from the tower in the thirteenth century it will impact on her twenty-first century life, if this happens, I would make the suggestion that you make your final preparations for re-incarnation…

Our ultimate aim, Esha, is to bring peace to the earth. The power of intention holds the key; people just have to believe it. Collective thought is much more powerful than any nuclear weapon. Our hope is that your influence will prove this to the population of the Earth. We must convince like-minded people to converge and emanate their collective thoughts of peace. These radiations will have an impact on the Earth's collective consciousness. With perseverance, they will start to neutralize the fear vibrations and harmony will eventually prevail. ...So, let us now see how your potential family are progressing......

*

Vi was extremely cagey this morning. Roma had spoken of a life beyond her wildest dreams. Yet, her wildest dreams had prophesied impending catastrophe. Phil's inquiry about the reading was met with indifference. 'Oh.. it didn't live up to expectations,' she sighed, her aloofness infused with a marked sign of agitation.

Once again, her defences were fully deployed and the mask of deceit covered the face of reality. As the morning progressed, however, her protective veneer slowly began to crack. During coffee break she laughed as she told how Roma had described him as monkey and imitated his Mr Bean impression. She went on to say that Roma had given an accurate description of Tom and advised her to postpone having children for the time being.

The last comment rang through Phil's mind like the pure resonance of a crystal bowl. His intentions *had* been heard; she had received the contentious message that troubled him so much. Tears of sheer relief began to well in his eyes.

Vi angled her brows, a look of concern sweeping her face. 'What is it Phil?'

Pause.

Phil looked out of the window at the plethora of students traversing the campus.

'..I feel in an awful predicament, Vi,' he started, cautiously. 'A couple of weeks ago, I had visions of your future with Tom. They were vivid. You had a child, who you obviously loved, but you looked so empty. You looked as if you'd just received a life sentence; imprisoned with no escape route. I wanted to tell you, but how could I? It could've been perceived as manipulation. So before you had your reading, I asked the guides to relay it to you, if it was meant to be. And it seems they did.'

Phil's obvious concern endeared Vi. She empathized with his predicament. His whole demeanour exuded truth.

'Thank you, Phil. I understand.'

An investigative tone steeped her next statement, 'Roma said I'd be faced with a life changing decision in the near future. She said that if my domestic situation didn't radically improve, then I'd end up with you.'

She observed Phil's reaction carefully, looking for signs of approval, then added, 'she also said that, if this were to happen, I'd never look back.'

Phil's eyes glazed over again. He was just about to make a heart-felt comment when Vi cut him off. 'And…..if I was going to have a child, then it would be to you.'

A tide of emotion suddenly rushed through Phil, as both his love for Vi, and his adoration for his guides, came to the fore. 'Excuse me,' he said, standing up.

Overwhelmed by the revelation that his guides had acted in precise accordance with his intentions, coupled with the thought of having a child with Vi, he rushed to the toilet flooding with tears.

When he returned, he apologised and explained why he felt so emotional. Then, he stared at Vi lovingly. 'Vi, if things don't work out between Tom and yourself, I would welcome you with open arms.'

Silence.

Vi's Soul child had got the reaction she wanted; Phil was obviously very much in love with her, but now her wounded child felt threatened and jumped up to dominate her response. She recoiled, her face bereft of expression. The woman who sat before Phil only seconds ago had taken leave of absence. The train to fear had arrived and she'd stepped on board, leaving behind the inhibited aspirations of her inner saboteur.

'But Phil!' she exclaimed, 'I told her. It's not like that. You and I are just good friends who care deeply for each other.'

Phil felt like a priest at an exorcism, wanting to cast out the demon before him. He took a deep breath and composed himself. 'Maybe she was picking up on your feelings?' he challenged.

The wilderness returned to Vi's eyes. 'What feelings?' she retorted.

'The ones you spoke about a few months ago,' he countered.

'Phil, they were just friendly feelings. The only person I've ever had feelings for is Tom.' She replied, defensively.

A surge of anger fuelled by frustration erupted in Phil's sacral vortex, powering its way to his throat: his oppressor stood in readiness to attack. Then, the timely intervention of Esba's whisper, coupled with the vision of a fawn, overwhelmed his inner assailant and saved the day.

To win this battle you have to surrender. She is frightened. Gentleness, my friend.

He quickly calmed down. Thoughts of the lesson of unconditional love swept through his mind. He decided to use pacification as a neutralizing force. 'Okay, Vi, I apologise. I must have completely misunderstood.'

Inwardly Phil was thankful he'd booked a holiday for next week. It seemed they needed time apart. Nevertheless, her incongruence became apparent during the remainder of coffee break. She had spoken with disdain about her reading, and yet she eagerly anticipated getting home to listen to the tape again? If it was filled with things she did not want to hear, what was the attraction?

Chapter 28

The Physicist Awakens

G. and Robert were in deep conversation.

'So the building blocks of everything physical are atoms,' said G. 'When we break down the atom, we find there's nothing substantial there. It's mostly empty space. Now these minute particles are flickering in and out of existence at the speed of light; one moment they're there, the next they've gone – so where do they go? They're energy, they can't just disappear.'

'Good question,' replied Robert. 'Your guess is as good as mine.'

'And if we're made up of these particles,' G. continued, 'then we are flickering in and out of existence, too.'

'Precisely,' replied Robert, 'which explains the abstract concept of us being vibrational beings: these particles are not solid entities, they are fluctuations of information and energy moving in and out of time and space. The nearest thing we can compare them with is thought; thoughts are just fluctuations of information and energy, too. Considering that these "thoughts" make atoms, from which everything physical is comprised, then physicality isn't born of matter, it is born of thought: matter is crystallised thought.'

'Which reinforces the posit that everything is consciousness,' G. injected. 'Now if, as Einstein said, particles are influenced by the power of thought, and particles are also comprised of thought, then what's really happening is that thought is impacting upon thought: **consciousness is interacting with itself, and becoming aware of itself.** All things considered, our earthly selves are localised bundles of conditioned thoughts, so our influence on the quantum field is going to be coloured by our conditioning. If our energy field is clogged with negative vibrations: fears, phobias, mistrusts, worries and so on, we'll act like magnets, attracting negative circumstance. Our expectations will be very limited and the quantum field will respond to precisely what we radiate – it's non-judgemental. So we must get rid of our shit, take time out to get in touch with our destiny, and set our intentions loud and clear......... Robert, I know you're an intelligent man, but are you also stupid!.......'

Esba chortled to herself from the surrounding space. She had imbued G. with badger medicine. Badger has an aggressive streak, but uses its anger for creative and healing purposes. G. had been a passive man all his life and needed to be fired up. Not only was he now using this medicine to stand up for himself, but he was using it on behalf of Theodore to awaken Robert!

'...Nothing exists until it's observed,' he continued, 'yet no one can find the observer. Our bodies are flickering in and out of existence at the speed of light. Vast amounts of data are eluding our brain, everything in existence is simply the movement of thought.....So, don't you think there must be an orchestrating force behind all this activity. And don't you think that that force is spirit – what else can it be? The reason we are flickering in and out of time and space is that we are being projected into being from another dimension. Inhabitants of that dimension, in turn, are being projected into being from a higher level. Eventually, if we continue this process, we end up back at the pure potential of the Source. The Universe is a projection of consciousness cascading down through many levels of experience. Wake up man! We are all thoughts in the mind of God - it's obvious.'

As G. made this last statement, something ignited within Robert. A light switched on. A glow came to his face and he looked as though he had just struck gold. Unknown to Robert, G. was completely baffled. As soon as he stopped talking, something hit him: he'd never come across some of this information before? Unknown to G, he had just channelled his disincarnate Soul sister and spirit guide, Ellissia. She had just relayed the phenomena of Monads, Souls and personalities without labelling them as such. In the beginning was the pure potential energy of the Source: pure consciousness. The Source wanted to expand and explore and so It created Monads - super-beings - our primordial source of intelligence. Each Monad then projected a number of Souls into existence and consciousness cascaded down through the lower frequency domains. Finally, each Soul projected a number of personalities into existence and *we* are these personalities. The sub-atomic particles of which we are comprised repeatedly appear and disappear, in and out of the time / space continuum. This is because we are being projected into existence on a moment-to-moment basis by our Soul. We are thoughts in the mind of our Souls; Our Souls are thoughts in the mind of their Monads; and the Monads are thoughts in the mind of the Source: hence, **we are all thoughts in the mind of God. Everything happens within the consciousness of the Universal Mind. Ultimately we are all one: unique expressions of the one omnipotent intelligence.**

Chapter 29

Inner and Outer Direction

The car sauntered leisurely through Chania as Phil took in the eclectic mix of wonderful architecture that surrounded him. After following a long curve of Venetian houses that followed the harbour front, his attention was drawn to three distinguishing landmarks: a massive fort that pushed out into sea, an Ottoman mosque that stood at the harbour's edge, and an Egyptian lighthouse that looked out across the water.

After stopping for a light breakfast at a traditional taverna, he decided to take a walk. As he strolled through the network of alleys and courtyards that comprised the old town, the smell of basil and oregano cooking in earthenware pots filled his senses. He marvelled at the elaborately carved Venetian doorways and Ottoman style houses with overhanging wooden balconies that lined the narrow streets. The place was steeped in history: the Minoans, Byzantines, Venetians, Genoese, Turks, and Egyptians, had all left their mark here. After visiting the church of Agios Anargyroi and contemplating its mysterious icons and paintings, he decided to take to the road and explore the neighbouring countryside.

Though February is an unpredictable time of year for weather in Greece, the temperature was a pleasant sixty five degrees. The lustrous sheen cast over the surrounding mountains by the midday sun faded intermittently as a peppering of light cloud obscured the light. Many of the surrounding fields were dotted with women working amidst the lush olive and citrus groves.

As he continued his drive through Western Crete's Kisamos country, Phil passed through several small towns. Men with leather-like skin sat outside the kafenions languidly sipping coffee or Ouzo; some ate olives and feta cheese; others indulged in conversation or played Tavli. Women sat leisurely in the shade. Cats sprawled lazily in the sun. Several Byzantine churches dotted the route. The pace of life was slowed to a near standstill. The traditional Greek philoxenia (love of strangers) could be felt in a warm and welcoming way.

Phil appeared as free as a bird. Arm slumped out of the window, light breeze brushing through his hair, and relaxing music playing quietly in the background: the epitome of peace, or so external appearance would suggest. Behind his serene front lay a mind as dark as his sunglasses: his head was in search of a heart that refused to leave Lancaster. The romantic ambience of the Greek islands intensified his longing to be with the lady he loved so much. One question lay heavily on his mind - *Should I move on?*

His relationship with Vi being as it was, made decisions extremely difficult. The way in which she expressed her feelings for him left him in no doubt that she was in love with him. Though, her denial indicated a solemn resolution to cling on to what she had. If they were to continue seeing each other in the close confines of an office, the emotional entanglement would inevitably lead to pain for the both of them.

What should I do? He thought. *I love her so much, but I want to do the right thing; even if it means leaving her. What action will lead to the highest good of all being served?*

He vowed to hold this question in the forefront of his mind for the rest of the day, hoping that the Universe would respond with relevant signposts.

After driving through the small village of Topolia, the car angled right onto a narrow dirt track. The low-powered vehicle slowed to a snail's pace, screaming in protest, as it negotiated the steep incline. To Phil's relief, when the path eventually levelled out, the road widened and normal acceleration resumed.

Further up the road, a strange looking metallic star rose up from a nearby field. As he turned to take a closer look, the sunlight deflected from it, sending a dazzling beam towards his eyes. Wincing, he fumbled frantically for the visor. The vehicle snaked across the road. As it did, his squinting eyes locked onto the vague outline of something stepping into the road in front. With lightening speed he slammed on the breaks, sending clouds of dust into the air. The car skidded. Then, he heard a thud.

Silence.

Phil was filled with an impending sense of remorse.

A seemingly long minute or so passed. Then, shaking, he slowly lifted his head from the steering wheel, dreading what he might find. He peered out through the window, but everything was still hazy.

When the dust finally settled, a pair of beady eyes were staring straight back at him. The stray goat, no more than a foot away from the bumper, chewed happily on a few shoots of grass, completely unperturbed by its near death experience. With heart still pounding, Phil wondered what had caused the thud – he *had* hit something? A nauseous feeling gathered in his stomach. He jumped out of the car and rushed to the front. As he did, he breathed a huge sigh of relief; the car had veered into a mound of earth by the roadside. There was no noticeable damage.

Sitting on the bonnet, taking a few deep breaths to calm down, he began to contemplate the symbolic meaning of the goat. Historically, the goat has been used in ceremony, making it a symbol of both the sacred and the sacrificed. It is also widely known as a symbol of fertility.

Is this a signpost? He thought. *Am I to sacrifice my own personal desires for the higher desires of the Universe - am I to leave Vi? Or is the symbol of fertility connected with this illusionary child?*

Suddenly, something dawned on him.

The Goat also represents the Devil, and Theodore often refers to the Devil known as fear.

This goat is blocking my path. Symbolically this situation is saying that fear is blocking my path – Vi's fear. But what can I do about it?

With no clear cut answers, he decided to continue his drive. He jumped off the bonnet and was just about to open the car door, when a sign on the opposite side of the road caught his attention: it seemed to shimmer and hypnotize him - Elafonissi 25km. He stared at it fixatedly.

Be gentle. That sign is telling me to continue to be gentle with Vi. Elafonissi literally translated means 'Deer Island'.

*

Vi was desperately unhappy. She hadn't heard from Phil since he went away on holiday. Unknown to her, he had decided to leave his mobile phone at home.

She stared out of the window, a deep loneliness in her eyes, longing to be by his side. *The Greek island of Crete,* she thought. *Beautiful sunsets, turquoise oceans, golden sand beaches, ruins and monasteries, culture and history, romantic nights in open air candle lit restaurants…. I wonder what he's doing right now?*

Another thought rushed into her mind and her stomach suddenly dropped like a rapidly descending elevator. *I wonder if he's met anyone?*

Determined to keep control, she turned her focus back to her dreams. *I mustn't get involved. It'll only end in heartache. My dreams have told me so.*

On thinking this, the ambience of the room began to change. She felt as though a comfort blanket had been draped around her. Then, the vivid image of an owl appeared in her mind's eye. As it did, the gentle voice of her Uniqueness echoed through her mind.

All is not what it seems, my dear child – it is time to ingest some owl medicine. Many humans are afraid of the dark but owl is at home. As a symbol of wisdom, owl is able to see that which eludes others, which is the true nature of wisdom. Where others are deceived, owl sees the truth…

…The darkness of which you are afraid is your shadow. You are trying to repress a part of yourself of which you are fearful… This abandoned facet of yourself is seeking expression through your dreams… Your dream is an enigma, dear one, and cannot be interpreted at face value… There are two ways to interpret a dream: literally - at face value… and using projection, which is seeing one's own fears and anxieties embodied in another person…

…In this dream both characters are parts of yourself, sub-personalities that are locked in battle. Tell me… if you could use only one word to describe what Phil represents to you, what would it be?

Vi looked uncomfortable, embarrassed. 'Love,' she uttered, reluctantly.

Good… so we can say that in this dream, Phil was the embodiment of love… Now your own character - what did she represent?

'I was frightened to death…I suppose she represented fear.'

Right…so now we have the embodiment of love and the embodiment of fear portrayed by the two characters in the dream…now take a look at these two children.

The images of two little girls appeared on Vi's internal screen: one bedraggled and tearful, the other radiant and joyful.

Do you know who they are?

'One I recognise to be my wounded child.'

That is correct. The wounded child within, part of the programmed child that has learnt to adjust her feelings in response to the hostile external environment…The other is your Soul child. She is the infantile version of me, your Uniqueness, free from conditioning and in possession of the truth.

'What's all this got to do with my dream?' inquired Vi, getting agitated.

Watch…………

The bedroom scene suddenly materialized in her mind's eye once again. But this time, sat on the bed, and taking the place of herself, was her wounded child. And, standing at the door, taking Phil's position, was her Soul child. The dialogue began:

'You know you want it,' said the Soul child.

'I just want us to be good friends – what are you playing at?' Replied the wounded child.

'Why are you doing this? You know what you want it,' said the voice of her truth.

The Soul child inched threateningly close to the wounded child.

The wounded child froze.

'Leave me alone, you've got it all wrong,' she countered.

The scene dispersed.

So what does this dream reveal to you……what is the issue that is causing the conflict……what is the wounded child denying that your Soul child is so annoyed about?

'I don't know,' replied Vi, defensively.

Which part of you has just answered that question? Am I speaking to the voice of your truth or the voice of your wounded child?

'Stop being so inquisitive,' replied Vi, beginning to feel totally exposed.

Could it be that your impenetrable fortress has become vulnerable? Are you losing control? Are you falling in love?

'Don't be so ridiculous,' she snapped. 'I think the world of Phil, but I'm not in love with him.'

Then what were the feelings you spoke to him of?

'Friendly feelings….. just friendly feelings, that's all.'

And friendly feelings take courage to disclose do they?

The room fell into silence. Vi initially felt infuriated, her wounded child stepping forward to dominate her response. 'How dare she tell me I'm in love.' But then her Soul child prevailed, appealing to her innermost centre. She began to mellow. Deep down she knew this interpretation of the dream held the truth. Her energies were divided. And to suggest that the characters of Phil and herself in the dream were actually two warring parts of herself made absolute sense. It explained all her erratic behaviour. Her mood swings. Her instability…She gave a huge sigh of relief as she realised that Phil wasn't about to force himself on her. The dream wasn't a prophecy, but it did portray a reality: one that reflected her divided internal state.

Her thoughts drifted back to Phil.

*

Phil closed his eyes causing his pupils to dilate so he could see better in the dim light. On opening them, he realised that the cave was vast. Enormous variform stalactites hung from the ceiling and regal looking stalagmites projected upwards from the ground. A sense of wonder began to fill him as he thought about the legend of St George – the dragon slayer – connected with the cave. A wry smile came to his face. *He's not the only one slaying dragons!* He mused, somewhat affectionately.

He took a few more hesitant steps, his eyes continuing to adjust to the faint light. As he did, he noticed a little church etched into the rock; the cave wall serving as one of the church walls. For a brief instant, he had the endearing image of Vi and himself walking down the aisle.

Moving further in, the surroundings took on an air of mystique. The stalagmites offered a never-ending variety of shapes, ranging from exceptionally tall conical formations, to very short forms. In several places algae completely covered the rocks, leaving a dark-green, velvet-like coating.

He began to veer off from the handful of other tourists and started to explore the deeper chasms. As he did, his attention was caught by a combo rock and stalagmite formation that closely resembled the mythical unicorn. He began to drift and contemplate the origin and symbolic meaning of the mythical creature.

In the fourth century BC, he thought, *Greek historian Ctesias spoke of a wild animal with a spiralling horn on its head. The horn was believed to have magical healing powers. The Unicorn has many symbolic meanings: purity, innocence, healing, courage, gentleness and inner wisdom.*

For the next few minutes Phil drank in the energy of this powerful totem, hoping it might help him in his quest to find a solution to his dilemma.

Moving on, revering at natures delights, the spectrum of colours became more pronounced. The ground beneath his feet began to squelch and he noticed the moisture had given rise to the growth of several wild fig trees. Due to rising humidity, he took a seat on a rock. As he rested, he drifted into an altered state of awareness; the surroundings suddenly started to paint pictures of other worlds. A sad scene materialized in his mind.

Vi and himself walked hand-in-hand towards two cavernous tunnels. As they approached, their hands parted. She dejectedly moved towards one tunnel, and he, towards the other. Just before they entered, they glanced at each other, disconsolately. Then disappeared into their own separate dark worlds. The scene dispersed. Phil was left with an impending sense that Vi and himself were to part.

Emerging from the cave, the bright sunlight caused Phil's eyes to squint. After a short period of readjustment, he trudged dejectedly down a flight of spiralling steps, his mind a whirl of confusion.

Has the time arrived for me to let go? Vi's said she has no feelings for me and that vision portrayed a parting. I just can't accept she has no feelings for me, but I can see she's desperately fighting to cling onto what she has. Perhaps the time has come to honour her choice. If she is in love with me but determined to stay where she is, then it would explain why we both looked so down-hearted when separating during that vision. Perhaps the Universe is trying to tell me that what's 'meant' to be is not going to happen and the time has come to let go…

…I've always used my emotions as guiding forces. They tell me what I want and what I don't want from life. Presently, though, they seem to be telling me I want what I cannot have. It's so difficult when powerful emotions are involved, but then part of life is about mastering emotions. If I'm to let go, inevitably, it's going to be heart breaking. I need to move my awareness from my feelings and into my thoughts, analyse the facts without emotional bias and plan a strategy. It's impossible to switch off our emotions like a tap, but changing the way we think alters the way we feel, given time. If I start to 'think' that we have no future together and let this scenario grow in my mind, eventually I'll accept it; then my feelings will begin to stabilize. I know I'll continue to love her. I'll always love her. I wouldn't want it any other way. Even when I've felt rejection I've never stopped loving her. Rejection is just the temporary loss of self-esteem, like any other loss it needs to be mourned. But most people don't allow themselves this temporary mourning period, instead they defend themselves. The oppressor and wounded child complexes jump forward to prevent the ego from feeling loss; they defend and maintain the ego's status. When this happens the person who's been rejected generally attacks the other person. Love then quickly

turns to hate - which is such a shame. That will never happen with Vi and myself; I won't allow it...

...Other people die of a broken heart. Their attention dwells on the emotions that keep them harnessed to the object of their feelings; they feel that life is no longer worth living. When this happens, such people really do need to 'think' rather than 'feel'. I know it's difficult, but it does work...

...Another thing to consider is that many people who experience rejection look for their own faults – what's wrong with me? But we must remember that earthly attraction is based on unconscious needs. If this 'chemistry' isn't present then the relationship won't work. It's not down to a flaw in ourselves, it's just down to a difference: an unconscious dynamic that's missing....

...If Vi doesn't want to be with me then I must move my attention into my solar plexus vortex. Readjust my thinking and accept we have no future together. And I mustn't forget there's a higher reason for everything. I need to trust in the will of the Universe; trust I'm being supported by Mother Earth. Sometimes what we 'think' we need and what we 'actually' need are two completely different things. The Universe knows what's best for us so we must trust in the natural process..

...Through my relationship with Vi, I've learnt that I can give of myself in romantic relationships, something I've found very difficult in the past. I've obviously changed. Perhaps the time's arrived for me to seek a loving partner. Someone who does want to be with me. It's just so difficult to determine at present - I need help. I'd give anything to spend the rest of my life with Vi; I love her so much. But, I only want that to happen if she feels the same way. And, at present, I'm very confused about that...

...I ask the Universe to give me clarity. Am I meant to be with Vi? Or has the time come to find another partner? Please help me.

On reaching the bottom of the steps, he noticed a small shop selling souvenirs. Noticing they had a wide selection of hand made cards, he decided to go over and see if he could find one for Vi. The first one he picked up brought a smile to his face – a huge stone phallic symbol! *Maybe not*, he thought.

After browsing a while longer, still unable to find anything appropriate, he spun the rotating stand and left it to stop at will. When it came to a halt, a card immediately jumped out at him. He opened it to find a number of poems inside. One in particular caught his attention:

>
> **H**arvesting thought in a field of dreams
>
> **E**mbracing *that* which is not what it seems
>
> **A**spiring to freedom, dance to the sun
>
> **L**oving each other for in truth we are one

Perfect! Exactly what I'm looking for.

But there was something else about the card that captivated him. Yet, he wasn't sure what it was. He read it through again.

Still nothing.

He returned to the title on the front cover: Virtuous Insights Of Lost Entrusted Truths.

This was it - he sensed it. This title was trying to tell him something, but he couldn't decipher what it was. He scanned it back and forth, musing, wondering why it fascinated him so much. Then suddenly, it hit him - smack in the face.

Virtuous **I**nsights **O**f **L**ost **E**ntrusted **T**ruths.

Perhaps he'd just been given the answer to his question?

Chapter 30

Progression: A Journey into the Future

Phil returned from holiday to a convivial reception from Vi. Once again, the winds of change were blowing in his favour. As they walked through the corridors, en route to the coffee shop, the extent to which she had missed him became obvious. He could feel her heartfelt emotion seeping in through his sacral chakra; an energetical transaction with an endearing richness, bearing testament to the nature of her true feelings.

During coffee break, he told her how he had purposely left his mobile phone at home.

'Not a day went by without me wanting to make contact. Vi. Every time I passed a telephone kiosk, I wanted ring you. Every time somebody's mobile sounded with a text message, I thought of you. But before I went away, I thought you were closing down on me, pushing me away. So I thought it best we had no contact for a while.'

'I wasn't closing down, Phil; I was just preparing myself for you going away. One day while you were away, I felt so bad that I thought of flying out to you. If you'd have been there for a fortnight, I think I would've done.'

No feelings, but a week's absence has to be prepared for? It doesn't make sense, thought Phil.

'Phil,' Vi interrupted, 'there's something else that may explain things to you. I had a couple of lucid dreams that really frightened me.'

She went on to relay the contents of her dreams. An in-depth discussion ensued in which Phil reinforced the fact that characters in dreams often portray different facets of ourselves. This dream was helpful to Phil; it gave him an insight into what was *really* going on within her. Still, it didn't alleviate the problem: she was still faced with a very difficult decision.

'I really do need to spend some time alone, Phil,' she continued, 'to get in touch with my true feelings. I wish there was some way I could have a glimpse of the future, just to see what it holds for me.'

Phil looked at her tormented face. 'There is a way, Vi.' He replied.

'How?' she inquired, a sense of urgency in her voice.

'Well, you've experienced regression - travelling back to your past. But there's also a hypnotherapy technique known as progression that takes you into your future. But remember, our futures are not set in stone, they are flexible. We all have an infinite number of possible futures, but only one or two probable ones. These probable ones are based on our predispositions presently. But, as you already know, we can reprogram the software that drives us and create any future we want...

'...Progression can be of great therapeutic value. It can reveal our innermost desires and aspirations. Conversely, it can reveal our deepest fears. But you must remember that if you enter a future that you find distasteful, you can change it. Our thoughts create our futures - remember those seedlings? Our futures are dependent on the seedlings of thought we choose to germinate, and we can choose from an infinite number of possibilities.'

'Will you progress me, Phil? I want clarity. I'd like to see what the future holds if I stay with Tom. And I'd also like to explore the future with you.'

'If you're sure that's what you want, but remember, use it for guidance only. It is a projected future, a tool to determine your path. If you should experience disdain, then analyze what you can change presently and alter your course. Otherwise your experience can become a self-fulfilling prophecy. On a positive note, however, a good journey can help you actualize the life you want. Many of these positive progressions turn out to be true. People *will* them into existence.'

'When can we do it?' inquired Vi, impatiently.

'How about tonight? Would you like to have something to eat at my place then I'll progress you later?'

'Yes. Thank you, Phil.'

*

Vi went into a deep hypnotic state quite quickly. Phil instructed her to see herself in front of two oak panel doors: one marked Tom, the other simply marked alternative (he wanted to have no influence over her choice). She moved towards the one marked Tom and pushed it open with her mind.

'When you pass through the doorway, you will find yourself five years into the future.'

Her eyelids fluttered rapidly. She began to relay her experience.

'I have a diamond ring on the third finger of my left hand,' she said driftily. 'I'm engaged but not married. The house… it's different, we have moved. I thought things would change if we moved house.' Tears welled up in her eyes. 'But they haven't.. I'm very sad inside. Tom is a good man, he loves me... I know he

280

does… I love him too….but (she stalled) I'm not *in* love with him. He's just like a brother….There's a huge void inside of me. I feel almost robotic, going through the same monotonous routine day in, day out: it's all a pretense. There's been a lot of pressure on me from his side of the family. They want us to get married and have children. I want a child so much, but that would tie me to this life forever. I'm not ready. I haven't had a childhood of my own yet. The glow that was once inside of me, the feeling that someday something very special was going to happen, it's gone – extinguished. When Tom goes out, I go to my bedroom… I have a hidden drawer in which there is a bundle of cards and trinkets. I read through the cards and sob. I miss him so much. He used to write loving poems in the cards. I read them and hang onto every word… they are filled with so much love. There's a ring here too, an eternity ring. He asked me to marry him once. I wish I had now. But at the time, I couldn't leave Tom. I think it would have been better if I had. I'm not much use to him nowadays: I live in a world of my own, a grey world.'

She started to sob uncontrollably.

Phil intervened. 'Okay, Vi.' He whispered. 'Everything is going to be alright.. I want you to find the oak panel door again, can you do that?'

'Yes,' she replied, her voice low and filled with melancholy.

'Pull it open with your mind…. And as you pass through it, feel yourself coming back to the present…. That's good…..now rest for a few minutes. Staying deep in trance, relaxing in this peaceful state.'

A few minutes elapsed.

'Now bring the two oak panel doors back to mind…….Can you see them?'

'Yes,' she whispered.

'Walk towards the one marked "alternative"….push it open with your mind…. And when you pass through it, you will find yourself five years into your future, exploring an alternative path.'

Again her eyelids fluttered rapidly. But now, a radiant smile came to her face.

'They're beautiful.'

'What are?' Phil enquired.

'The puppies…Yin and Yang, our dogs. They have had five pups… They still have their eyes closed and are suckling Yin…. Phil is stroking the proud father – Yang….. This place is wonderful: fields and trees, wildlife and a lake. There are even some caravans. Phil works so hard, yet there's never a dull moment.. life is a real adventure. And the baby… she's beautiful, bonnie yet wise beyond her years. Saintly blue-grey eyes that are somehow not of this world…. G. is so good with her. He cares for her while Phil and I spend quality time together… and another lady too, Charlene..no Carla…she lives with us. She's so natural with children… Lots of people visit our home. The place has a very special feel. Phil, myself and the baby spend time in Crete. We have another place there. Phil says the Greek Islands breathe inspiration into him; he's writing his fifth book at present. But he's a real family man. He always puts me and the baby first. We play together just like three children. I really have been given my childhood back….and so much more.'

The scene began to fade.

When Vi emerged from the hypnotic state, she remembered both her journeys vividly.

'That alternative life was heaven, Phil. I can't describe how I felt inside.'

Phil did not want to have any influence over her decisions. She had explored two possible futures and the choice was now entirely up to herself. He made the suggestion that she took some time out and contemplated what she had just experienced. He then quickly shifted the emphasis of the conversation.

'Now, Vi, please tell me that you have no plans for this weekend.'

'Nothing I can't put off – why?'

'Would you accompany me to the caravan for the weekend – I really have missed you, and we get very little quality time together.'

'I'd love to.' She smiled.

Chapter 31

Ullswater – The Mystical Lady

Phil and Vi arrived at the caravan early evening. After settling in and making themselves comfortable, Phil seemed quite enthusiastic to get Vi out of the way. He used his powers of persuasion to encourage her to take a walk along the river.

When she returned, he ushered her into the lounge. He was acting very strange. Obviously up to something. He disappeared into the bedroom and quickly re-emerged beckoning her to go through.

On entering, she was overwhelmed by what confronted her. Sprinkled all over the bed were imitation petals amongst which lay a number of gift wrapped parcels. On the pillow lay a dozen red roses. To their side sat a huge cuddly dog bearing a heart displaying the words – 'I love you'. Central, lay an envelope on which was written:

Please open the gifts before reading me.

Vi's eyes reddened as the ballad 'three times a lady' sounded from the CD player.

She unwrapped the first gift and found a quartz crystal wand, the handle of which was fashioned in the shape of an angel. She made a wish.

'I wish to find the place where I truly belong.'

As she swished the wand, the music changed to the Irish ballad 'Danny Boy'. A shiver of emotion ran through her as Eva Cassidy's incredible voice pierced the air.

She reached for the next gift - a forever friends sleeping bear. The duck that lay on its back was holding a sign that said 'sweet dreams'. She smiled, affectionately, thinking of the many occasions when Phil had text these words to her just before she went to bed.

She continued to open every gift with great care, savouring every moment. Amongst the other presents she found a hand woven Indian dream-catcher, a set of angel audio tapes and a silver heart shaped jewellery box.

Finally, she came to the card. As she opened it, the music aptly changed to the song that had meant so much to them both throughout their journey – Somewhere Over the Rainbow. Teardrops began to drip onto the white dove that stared up at her from the cover of the card. When she opened it, she found a poem – one that was centred around all the gifts she had received.

A sweet little girl was once lost and confused

She was filled with despair and entirely bemused

the cute little thing has grown up through this year

I've shared all her heartbreak and every last tear

She's now reached a stage of extreme opportune

The gateway's now open so reach for the moon

Take hold of the wand and give it a swish

The angel upon it will grant every wish

In This World but Not of It — Paul Henderson

We made a wish about eight months ago
That is me and two beings of light that I know
We wished that the sun would set on your past
And you'd enter the life you deserved at long last

Dorothy followed a yellow brick road
And sought out a wizard to lighten her load
She followed a rainbow to her promised land
Your wizard's called Theo you must understand

You may think your journey has been rather slow
But you've travelled some distance this year you know
My friends heard you call from a world full of fog
And the rescue commenced as they sent in a dog

The dog is so faithful with such a big heart
He's saying 'I love you' so listen sweetheart
In your times of trouble, on him you depend
He's loving and loyal and will be your best friend.

Look at him closely, stare into his eyes
You'll see that he's someone you know in disguise
Whatever you want he shall fetch you at will
Just call him over, he answers to Phil.

In This World but Not of It   Paul Henderson

He watches intently with love in his eyes
He sees natural beauty, e-pit-o-mised
The face of an angel, a heart of pure gold
You're priceless my friend and can never be sold

The heart is for jewellery and beats with love 'true'
It's lined with warm velvet in which I'd place you
For you are a jewel, a diamond or pearl
The gemstone elite, are you, little girl

The tapes they're angelic, your mind they'll renew
An angel called Esba will see to it too
You'll walk through a gateway to heaven on earth
She'll act as a midwife and aid your rebirth

The original dreamcatcher was woven by hand
There's something about it you must understand
It catches sweet dreams from the ether around
Magical dreams of a life where you're bound

So sleep little cute bear a duck on your back
And capture that life where you'll never look back
Drift through glad tidings and wonderful themes
Arise in the morning to a life of sweet dreams

> The dove on this card once had low self esteem
>
> She awakened one day to her ultimate dream
>
> She flew off so gracefully to her paradise
>
> And when she arrived there she never thought twice
>
> When you awaken to your ideal world
>
> There's something I want you to know little girl
>
> Whether we're close or miles apart
>
> You'll always reside in a place in my heart

Phil paced around the lounge nervously awaiting her re-emergence. She had been in there for what seemed like a life-time. His heart pulsated, his stomach filled with butterflies. He sat down, then stood up - unable to settle.

The bedroom door finally opened and out came Vi, tears still dripping down her face, nose shining bright red and a beautiful purity radiating from her.

'Nobody's ever done anything like that for me in my entire life,' she sniffled.

Phil rushed over, cupped his hands around her tear-stained face, and stared into her eyes.

'I love you so much, little lady. And I intend to take every opportunity I get to give you back that childhood. When we're together, I'll make every day your birthday – I promise you.'

Her face began to glow; one or two shudders rippled through her body. They wrapped their arms around each other and a whirlwind of blissful energy bound them together. ***At that***

moment they had the experiential knowledge of sharing one heart.

The rest of that evening was filled with joy, love and laughter. Vi had brought her guitar and Phil encouraged her to learn some more. He was surprised at the ease at which she picked the instrument up (then she had been tutored back in the thirteenth century by a lute playing jester!) They performed a few songs together, Phil adding the intricate parts whilst Vi strummed the chords. He was astounded at the quality of her voice; she had a natural talent for singing. He persuaded her to accompany him in performing the song he had written (or someone had written?) And so they sang duet. After they perfected the song, he asked if she would consider recording it with him. A friend of his, from his music days, had a small recording studio back in Liverpool. She was reticent at first but he eventually talked her into it.

They finished the night by taking a stroll into the dark woods from where they could observe the canopy of stars that glistened in the velvet sky.

*

The next morning they visited Phil's spiritual home – Ullswater: a magnificent sprawling lake winding around a breathtaking backdrop of mountain scenery. A truly dramatic place made all the more memorable by Ullswater's mirrored surface and a gently curving shoreline of green fields, woodlands and sheer rock faces.

'Isn't she beautiful, Vi?'

'Absolutely,' she replied.

'The mystical lady I call her. She's enchanting, mysterious, refined and exudes tranquillity. There's something about the energy of this lake that is quite magical. I remember coming here when I was struggling with alcohol: my nerves were jittery, I was suffering panic attacks, I felt like my head was home to a thousand bees and my life was a total shambles. Yet when I came to this spot, I felt I'd returned home. An omnipotent healing presence seemed to pervade every cell, bone and tissue of my body. I felt something holding me in gentle repose, alleviating all my pain. Ever since that day I've made this spot my shrine. I believe it's a portal to the higher dimensions. When I'm here, I feel my senses amplified a thousand-fold. The silence speaks volumes.'

'I feel it too,' said Vi, ruminatively. 'I could feel it in the car as we approached. A deep serenity coupled with an impending sense of anticipation.'

'That's right…..Tell me, Vi….what's she whispering to you right now?'

Vi closed her eyes and began to drink in the intoxicating tranquillity. The air was absolutely still, the silence broken only by the gentle lapping of the water as it caressed the pebbly bank. She slowly drifted into oblivion. Capitulating to the voice of nature……
'She says….'

Words suddenly floated into her mind as she channelled a loving entity that was determined to help her.

'Within my depths, obscured from view,

a promised land awaits for you.

When stormy days, where shadows cast,

subside to bring the sun alas,

this world appears, from depths ascends,

and this is where your rainbow ends.'

She continued to drift. Drunk on peace, inebriated by the pervading serenity. Very slowly she returned, opened her eyes and turned to face Phil - mouth agape.

'……Did I just say what I think I said - or was I dreaming?' She said, in somewhat disbelief.

Phil returned an enigmatic smile. 'I told you she speaks.'

The iridescent form of Galfridus suddenly wisped through the trees and hovered playfully between them. His energy began to expand, enveloping them. Their awareness accentuated. Several other orbs of light shimmered in the surrounding space, stroking their clairsentient senses. The energy became all embracing. Synchronistically, as though in hypnotic trance, they both pivoted to face the lake, gently floating into a fourth dimension of existence. Their third-eye chakras began to unfurl, glowing like beacons, sending receptive emanations into the ether. Visions began to bombard their clairvoyant senses; identical images, entered their minds simultaneously. Past – lives. Many of them. Ancient Egypt. Medieval England. The Crimean war. They had shared many lifetimes together. Then, the visions changed. They found themselves entering the upper dimensions. The celestial wheel appeared vividly, revealing their Soul brothers and sisters. The image then vanished.

They stood rooted to the spot, speechless. After several minutes of silent euphoria they turned and walked towards each other. Clasping hands, eyes locked together, a song brushed through their minds.

We are one

We are unified, for all eternity

We are one

The essence of true love is simple unity

Ground your being in oneness and commence a new journey

Hand in hand with everyone we'll reach our destiny

The plants, the trees and animals, the planets and the stars

Are all extensions of ourselves they're relatives of ours............

When the song came to a conclusion, another phrase repeatedly echoed through the peripheries of Vi's mind: *move 'further to wolf', move 'further to wolf'*. Phil brushed a lock of hair from her face and kissed her gently on the cheek. Time seemed to suspend. Then, like a vivid dream that is banished from consciousness on awakening, the whole experience faded from memory.

Chapter 32

Destiny by Divination

Winter turned to spring and spring gave way to summer, the changing elements reflecting the diverse emotive forces that swept through Vi, G., and Phil: storms and sunlight, calms and squalls, clarity and confusion.

G's domestic situation remained difficult. Divorce proceedings thwart with legal implications and mounting solicitor's fees drained his finances. Due to this, he decided to represent himself at the forthcoming court-hearing over the property.

Through it all, however, he maintained great faith, trusting there was a much bigger picture to be considered. With the help of Phil, he conscientiously worked his way through the debilitating issues he had with his mother. Due to her being deceased, he couldn't dissolve his issues physically. So he wrote letters from his inner child, using his non-dominant hand, so the writing resembled that of a child. In these letters he relayed exactly how he felt as a child: unloved, abandoned, transparent, and imprisoned. The therapy was highly emotional; he flooded with tears on many occasions. Phil reassured him that his mother had done the best she could with the skills she had. After the cathartic release of emotion, Phil took him through a series of hypnotherapy sessions in which he reconciled his differences with his mother. The sessions were powerful and liberating; he was now at peace with his past. This had led to much improved relationships with women in general. Despite their problems, even his relationship with Joan had improved. Although he knew that reconciliation was out of the question, he accepted she had been put in his path for a reason: to enable him to evolve his understanding of the unconscious forces that severely inhibit human relationships. G. felt a rebirth had taken place; he had developed an exceptional thirst for spiritual knowledge, devouring many enlightening books and religiously meditating. During this time his spirit guide, Ellissia, had made herself known. Coalescing with this wise entity had given him a liberating sense of expansion: his destiny now called and he was about to embrace it.

Vi's family situation continued to steadily improve. Her relationship with her father exceeded all expectations. She visited him regularly, sent him cards, telephoned him and he even helped her with the decorating. She had set an example to the rest of the family and they too had become responsive. The healing process was taking place, spreading by contagion throughout the entire family: her mother was considering allowing her father back into the family home, her brothers angry outbursts were diminishing and they were stabilizing, the grand children were flourishing, and the new addition to the family, a baby boy of seven pounds nine ounces, had arrived a month ago.

Phil had decided to run some weekend workshops in preparation for the future. He advertised in a local Mind, Body, Spirit newsletter under the name of 'Synergy School of Holistic Development'. He held Reiki workshops and channelling development weekends once a month; G. and Vi assisted him. He had also been devising several other courses for the future. These included: past lives, future lives, unconscious attraction in relationships and healing through intent. Two months ago, he completed his Counselling Diploma and was now fully qualified. Two nights a week he counselled on a voluntary basis at a local counselling agency. The story-line for the book continued to elude him, yet he maintained great faith in Theodore. He was certain that one day it would materialize. Recently, Vi and himself had travelled down to Liverpool and recorded his song.

They had tremendous fun in the studio and the recording turned out to be very professional.

Their relationship had been a real emotional roller-coaster ride. Her energies remained divided, ebbing and flowing from one extreme to the other. At times, her wounded child would form an alliance with her shadow and she would be consumed by fear. On these occasions Phil found it very difficult. If he retreated, she would advance, and when he came forward, she would retreat. Yet throughout, he persisted in speaking the language of his heart and treating her with the gentleness of a fawn. His love was unfaltering. On other occasions, her Soul child would coalesce with her Uniqueness and override her fear. She would blossom and he would feel the intensity of her love. Those days were magical; the memories were locked in his heart forever. However, as rapturous intimacy was inevitably followed by vehement denial, and there was no prolonged stability between these erratic shifts, he was gradually beginning to feel the effects. Sadly, he had come to the conclusion that the probability of her making the transition from her head to her heart was highly unlikely. Diverging paths now seemed imminent. Pastures new were materializing for him and he contemplated exploring them - somewhat reluctantly it must be said. Looking for further confirmation, he requested a reading from Roma.

*

Phil stood outside the library waiting for Roma. Carla waited at his cottage. She had recently slipped back into desperation, her unwelcome squatter wreaking havoc once again. She contacted Phil a couple of days ago and told him of her dilemma. He told her to pack a bag immediately and come up to his place, telling her that Roma could help. He had recently found out that she was an experienced rescue medium.

He glanced across the busy thoroughfare. Hoards of people scurried in and out of the shops, desperate to snap up the last bargains of the summer sale. Amidst the crowd, he spotted a dark haired, middle-aged woman, serpentining her way through the crowd. A light luminescent mist appeared to envelope her. The Star of David around her neck glistened, having an hypnotic effect on him. He suddenly experienced a powerful sense of déjà vu.

'Roma,' he called, as his intuition revealed her identity.

The two stared into each other's familiar eyes; an instant feeling of homeliness transpired.

As they drove towards Phil's home, he told her that Carla was waiting for them. Roma immediately began to describe her physical characteristics with great exactitude.

'Oh my God,' she continued. 'The poor dear had a still born baby and blames herself.'

Phil couldn't confirm this. He thought he knew all there was to know about Carla, but she had never mentioned this child.

Further into the journey a vacant look fell upon Roma's face. 'Jim,' she said, 'he's back.'

When they arrived at the cottage, Roma's findings were confirmed. Carla had indeed had a still born baby. Seeing she was highly distressed, Roma decided to read her first.

During the hour that followed, she uncovered everything, relaying the events of Carla's life as though reading them from a biography. She also identified that she was writing a suicide note and adding to it each day. When they re-emerged, she told Phil that he mustn't let her out of his sight. She intended to rid her home of the destructive presence once and for all.

Before Phil's reading commenced, Roma was distracted by a photograph of his niece.

'There's tears in that girl's eyes,' she said. 'She's been getting bullied at school.'

The truth of this was confirmed at a later date. Another photograph then intrigued her - Phil in his stage outfit, holding his guitar.

'You'll do some more of that in the future too. Not in the same capacity as before, but music will play an important role in your life.'

The reading began with Roma providing ample proof of the accuracy of her extraordinary psychic abilities. She picked out things from Phil's past which she couldn't have possibly known. She also picked up on his psychic abilities and urged him to put them to good use.

'You've been through a lot,' she continued. 'Oh my goodness, ouch! You really have hit the deck – a few times. You will draw on these experiences, they will become your strength…. The second half of your life will be rewarding and fulfilling. You must remain focused.'

She turned another card. '….you're contemplating a move aren't you?'

'Yes,' replied Phil, subdued.

'You must follow your destiny…. I can see this decision brings with it much heartache.'

Phil confirmed.

'You must go…don't despair… she will come to you.'

'Who?' Phil inquired, testing Roma's abilities to the limit.

She just smiled, knowingly, and dismissed his question.

'Oh, the poor dear. Her life has been a real battle ground…. She's very confused. But, I'm telling you right now…you will be together one day – one hundred percent… Give her time.'

She closed her eyes and slipped into a trance-like state. 'I see a child.'

Phil felt the hairs on the back of his neck stand to attention.

'A boy, no a girl, definitely a girl. She's a very spiritual child.'

Her voice transformed, becoming very low and gentle. She paused. Her eyes opened and she stared at Phil intently. A real sense of mysticism infused the air….. 'This child is very special,' she continued, closing her eyes again, 'and when she's born…. you'll know the reason why.'

The last statement sent a tingling sensation right throughout Phil's body. His eyes glazed. The rhyme 'Hush Little Baby' rang through his mind, along with the image of Esba cradling the new born child.

'I see a book,' Roma continued, 'a book that holds the key to your destiny.. you must write it now.' She glanced at Phil's blank expression. 'What's the problem?'

'I've known about this book for years, but the story-line is a mystery.'

'You already have the story…just look a bit deeper and watch out for the jester.'

Phil couldn't believe his ears.

After the reading, Phil and Roma reassured Carla that everything would work out okay. She had to be strong. She was more powerful than Jim and had to let him know so. If things didn't improve over the next couple of months, she offered to visit Carla's home and perform a spirit clearance. Carla readily accepted.

Chapter 33

Two People – One Heart

The cold winter chills arrived. Vi and Phil decided to take the afternoon off work and re-visit the place of their first rendezvous. They ambled along the winding path taking in the crisp, invigorating air. The afternoon sun glistened off the snow blanketed fields which nestled amidst a backdrop of roving pearl hills. A billowing cloud drifted lazily through the clear blue sky like a serene spirit floating through the heavens.

Phil smiled endearingly as he observed Vi's face, reddened by the biting cold, peering out from underneath a woollen hat. As her breath suffused into the frigid air, he could see that her teeth were chattering. He went over, put his arm around her shoulders, and pulled her up close. She, quite naturally, if not somewhat uncharacteristically, reciprocated by putting an arm around his waist and snuggling up to him. They continued their walk looking like a couple completely devoted to each other.

On reaching the lake the sunrays splintered off the ice-covered surface, sending slithers of silver into the distance. Phil pulled out two carrier bags from his coat pocket and placed them on the fallen oak tree.

'Save getting our bums wet,' he quipped, his forced smile masking a deep sadness.

They sat down and he drifted off, staring ruminatively at a sprawling maze of branches belonging to a nearby tree. He contemplated how they reflected the numerous pathways of life: the divergences, the entanglements, the rigidness, the flexibility, the ups, the downs: the *choices*. But, most of all, he observed that only one branch led to the top – this path he needed to discern and pursue.

Vi felt a growing sense of trepidation. Phil seemed strangely subdued, his diffident comportment hinting of impending revelation.

He stood up and moved to the water's edge. As his eyes lifted skyward, an escalating sense of unease became apparent.

Vi's brows angled. 'You don't seem your usual self today?' she probed.

Silence.

'Phil - what is it?' she pressed.

With eyes still elevated to the heavens, Phil broke the silence, his voice laced with despondency. 'Vi, I think the time's arrived for us to part ways, sweetheart.'

Her stomach dropped. She shot him a disconcerting look. 'What d'you mean?'

He paused a moment, then turned to face her. '..I'm considering moving down south. I made enquiries about a counselling post last time I visited my parents. I received a phone call yesterday offering me the position - I have until January to decide.'

Her face turned waxen, swearing testament to the true nature of her feelings. 'Ar-Are you going to accept?' she stammered, staring at him anxiously.

Phil dropped his gaze to the floor. 'Look, Vi,' he sighed. 'Right throughout our journey I've been encouraged to speak the language of my heart and I don't intend to stop now. I love you so much, little lady, and I've the strangest feeling that I always have. I'd like nothing better than to spend the rest of my life with you. But, let's be honest, Vi, circumstance doesn't permit our friendship to realise its full potential. We have precious little quality time together and that's highly unlikely to change. You're trying to settle with Tom, which I understand, and I must pursue my destiny; this job is a step in the right direction; so – yes, I'm seriously considering taking it.'

A fire came to Vi's eyes. 'I'm *not* settling with Tom,' she retorted. 'I'm still very unhappy and I *will* make a move if things don't improve.'

Phil's momentary rush of hope quickly transformed into a deep sinking feeling. 'But will that really change things, Vi?' he sighed. 'Recently, you've suggested that you wouldn't want to be with me even if you were single.'

She was caught off guard. She *had* implied such things, but they held no truth: mechanisms to stop her vulnerability threshold being breached; a firewall to keep out the infectious threat of true love; a ploy to negate the insidious peril of volatility and stay in control.

She opted for denial and looked at him perplexed. 'I don't understand…I've *told* you….you're everything I've ever wanted.'

He stared at the ground, reluctant to respond, his frustration pinnacling.

Yes, he thought, *that's true. You have said I'm everything you've ever wanted, but you omitted the subsequent disclaimer – 'the only thing that's missing is feelings'. Denial inevitably follows these declarations of truth.*

A kaleidoscope of conflicting thoughts and images began to fill his mind: her endearing innocence when she disclosed her feelings for him; the expressionless stranger that denied them; the sanctity of oneness that bound them together; the wall of fear that prized them apart; the unspoken yearning that blazed in her eyes; the stern veneer of her defensive, wounded child - the impressions spooled on and on.

During this prolonged period of uncomfortable silence, Phil was drawn to Vi's energy field. Swarthy squalls of vapour twisted turbulently like indomitable whirlwinds set on destroying newly planted crops: astaticism prevailed as the forces of change battled fiercely with the obdurate power of fear. Though this maelstrom of activity wreaked havoc within her, externally, she looked numb. A grey band of protection guarded the circumference of her emotional body, cutting her off from feeling, leaving her displaying typical symptoms of depression. Her radiance had once again been eclipsed by a grey pallor.

This can't go on, thought Phil, *it's liable to destroy her: it's liable to destroy us both. This journey is about healing, not pain. What should I do? What's the best course of action? What action serves the highest good of all concerned?*

After a further period of silence in which his attention circled his mind like an eagle stalking its prey, he could draw only one conclusion. She loved him, of this he was certain. And his love for her transcended anything he'd ever experienced before. But she was petrified of the unknown. Although her energies remained divided, and today the pendulum swung in favour of truth, realistically, the transitionary threshold seemed insurmountable: destiny was ushering them together, but fear was prizing them apart. It was seeming increasingly unlikely that she'd ever renounce the familiar. If they continued to see each other under these circumstances, then pain was inevitable. The strain of being so close, yet never fully able to embrace each other's love, would surely take its toll - he had to go.

Looking to the sky, he asked for strength. Then, turning to face Vi, a sense of foreboding suddenly loomed; he watched as she removed a tissue from her coat pocket and dabbed her watery eyes. As he did, a nauseous feeling swilled through is stomach. His resolve weakened. And he turned away.

I've got to do this, it's best for both of us, he urged.

After taking a few deep breaths, he turned towards her again, poising himself to speak. But this time he was rendered mute.

The words would not materialize: a debilitating sense of apprehension gripped him.

Come on, have courage, he urged, inwardly.

As he tussled with himself, he asked for strength and guidance. His request evoked an immediate response. A wise energy came spiralling out of the nothingness. As it did, a funnel of violet light blazed from the top of his head and drew in the celestial light; the energy took residence in his aura. As he fused with his ground of being - his Soul - his awareness immediately accentuated. His attention rose from the mental fog of his solar plexus chakra to the clear sphere of his heart vortex. Confusion subsided. A liberating sense of expansion transpired and a scene emerged in his mind's eye.

17th century. The desert.

A seventeen-year-old boy despaired after plunging his sword into another young boy during battle. Filled with remorse and self-hatred, he had opted for self-imposed exile. It was early evening. The sun was setting. The lonesome figure of a young woman approached. As she neared, he could hear her soft and gentle voice whispering '*all your future battles will be fought with love, my friend.*' She oozed compassion and appeared to have a very deep understanding of him. After securing his trust, she took him by the hand and they walked towards the sunset. The sunlight transformed into a radiant white light into which they both dissolved.

The scene dispersed. Phil was momentarily ungrounded and off centre. He called his awareness back behind the windows of his eyes and envisaged two thick chords anchoring his feet to the earth.

Gradually, his dizziness subsided. When it did, he began to integrate his experience.

Battle scars run deep, he thought.

Again, a carousel of images circled his mind. Vi's past: the abuse, the poverty, the persecution, the vicious taunts, the hopelessness, the despair.

He glanced over at her forlorn figure. *Another casualty of war,* he mused, *different era, different scenario, different weapons, but identical results - emotional and spiritual bankruptcy resulting from the demands and poisoned belief systems of a fear-filled world.*

A deep sadness gripped him.

She looks exactly how I did back in the seventeenth century – lonely and desolate.

His awareness reached deeper into the mysteries of past life connections.

She took me by the hand and led me out of the darkness back then. I was immersed in fear and guilt and she led me to freedom...... Now I'm contemplating abandoning her – why? Is it really because I think it's best for both of us, or am I afraid – afraid of sticking around and watching someone I love so much hurting. Or am I running away to protect myself from any further rejection?...these are conditioned responses, based on fear – not courage and love......we are Soul mates...we don't run off and leave our spiritual family incarcerated ... we find the key to their freedom and release them.

Within an instant, a thought etched itself into his mind. *I'm already in possession of the key - I have the love and understanding.*

A knowing smile suddenly lit his face. As it did, a blaze of multi-coloured light whooshed from his aura. Theodore had enlightened him; he now dispersed back into the nothingness.

Phil continued to contemplate, driftily. *All your future battles will be fought with love, my friend,* he thought. His insight deepened. As it did, a look of resolve came to his large blue eyes. *It's my turn to set her free now.*

Suddenly in no doubt as to the right course of action, he turned his attention back to the clear blue sky. 'Thank you,' he whispered.

Without averting his gaze, he gently broke the silence. 'So..you say I'm everything you've ever wanted?' he enquired, affectionately.

'Yes,' Vi sniffled.

He turned and walked across to her. On reaching her, he removed her hat and swept a lock of hair from her face. With the gentleness of a fawn, he cupped his hands around her reddened cheeks and stared directly into her eyes.

'Okay…,' he murmured, 'if that's the case then…'

Moving his lips close to her ear, he whispered two words that had eluded him all his life.

'….marry me.'

Silence.

More silence

Slowly, a look of adulation infused with a sprinkling of disbelief washed the sadness from Vi's eyes. A radiant smile broke through. She glowed, emanating a beautiful innocence.

Phil hugged her again, moving his lips back to her ear. 'With the sunshine of that smile reflecting on all those tears, a beautiful rainbow's sure to emerge,' he whispered, before cupping his hands back around her face and staring into her eyes. 'I'll never accept you have no feelings for me, little lady,' he continued, 'but I know you have your reasons for denying them… The face I'm looking at right now answers all my questions.'

Her face flushed. 'I know,' she uttered, almost inaudibly.

He took her by the hand, his voice steeped with sincerity. 'I've battled with myself for months, Vi, never really knowing the right thing to do. All I could ever be certain about is that we're two people who are very much in love with each other.'

Her look of enchantment offered no resistance to this statement. Her glistening eyes unquestionably confirmed it.

'I know you can't answer my question today,' Phil continued, 'and I have no intentions of rushing you. Whether I take the job or not, the offer is open to you. Should you decide to stay with Tom, then I'll respect your decision and love you regardless. But if you feel we have a future together, then I want you to be my wife - the answer lies in your heart, Vi….. in the meantime I'd like you to have this…'

He pulled a small jewellery box from his pocket. 'I intended to give it to you today as a token of my love.'

After removing the gold eternity ring from the box, he slipped it onto the third finger of her *right* hand – it fitted perfectly. 'If you should decide we have a future together, then I'll buy you another for the other hand,' he smiled.

She outstretched her arm, watching as the ring glistened in the sunlight. 'It's beautiful,' she replied, admiringly.

They embraced again, and this time, she moved her lips towards his ear. 'Maybe that baby will be born after all,' she whispered.

A passionate flame engulfed Phil's sacral vortex; he felt exhilarated. Yet, as he stepped back to look her in the eye, a peculiar smile came to his face. 'Yes,' he replied, 'and it will have to be a *very* special child.'

She looked at him with amusing bewilderment. 'What do you mean?'

'Well, I've only ever kissed you on the cheek – it will have to be the immaculate conception!' he jibed.

Laughter.

'Unless…….' he added, moving menacingly towards her, scanning her trim body up and down, a promiscuous glint in his eyes. 'You know you want it!' he taunted, reciting the script from her infamous dream.

'No!' she screamed as he chased her up the path and off into the distance.

Chapter 34

Spirit Clearance

Roma slowly ascended the stairs, a cruciform in one hand, a sodium stone dangling from a silver chain in the other. As she reached half way, the stone began to gyrate denoting the presence of a spirit. With each subsequent step, the movement increased. She began to sense a sinister form lurking in the surrounding space. Hostile vibrations permeated the air and an eerie chill swept through her.

On reaching the top, the stone started to spin frantically. Her eyes became transfixed on the bedroom door. She sensed the dark entity prowled somewhere behind it. An acrid smell assaulted her senses. She paused for a moment, calling for the help of her guides and the presence of Archangel Michael. Three points of light immediately entered the surrounding space. She began to recite the prayer of Saint Francis:

'Lord make me a channel of your peace.

Where there is hatred, I may bring love.

Where there is wrong, I may bring the spirit of forgiveness

Where there is discord, I may bring harmony……..'

She slowly approached the door, grounding her being in love with every step, emphasizing her intentions by repeating the next line of the prayer over and over.

'Where there are shadows, let me bring light.

WHERE THERE ARE SHADOWS, LET ME BRING LIGHT.
WHERE THERE ARE SHADOWS, LET ME BRING LIGHT.'

She opened the door. A blast of ice-cold air engulfed her. A grey cast eclipsed the morgue-like surroundings. The energy of the menacing presence became tangible.

'My name is Roma. I am a rescue medium. Make yourself known.'

Nothing.

'**My name is Roma. I am a rescue medium. Make yourself known,**' she said with increasing force.

A frame containing a photograph of Carla and her parents suddenly began to rock to and fro. Roma didn't flinch. She remained completely focused, unperturbed.

'I know you're here to cause harm,' she continued. 'This is a house of love. You are not welcome. Go!... Go now.... Go into the light. There are people waiting to help you.'

The photograph toppled over. Roma's voice took on more authority. 'GO... I DEMAND YOU TO GO - **NOW**..... THIS IS A HOUSE OF LOVE...WAKE UP....ACCEPT YOUR DEATH AND GO INTO THE LIGHT.'

The presence seemed undeterred. The atmosphere remained dank and threatening. The spirit was rebellious - but Roma was wise. She placed the cruciform on the bed and removed a small bottle from her pocket. The water it contained had been self blessed following an old tradition. She began to sprinkle it about the room whilst simultaneously reciting the prayer. As she neared the bedside table, the toppled photograph appeared to take on a lustrous sheen – it called out to her. She tilted her head to listen intently to the whispers that echoed through her mind.

'You loved these people once, didn't you,' she continued, as she restored the photograph to its original position, '....and they loved you, too.'

The atmosphere stilled. The entity recoiled. She had hit a fearful note - love.

'This is a house of love…. If you persist on staying then you must succumb to the harmony of this household.'

The three points of light in the surrounding space began to expand, suffusing their collective energy into the atmosphere. The intimidating vibrations began to disperse. Roma felt the entity shrivel, overcome by the increasing sense of unity.

A scene emerged in her mind's eye. A portal opened: a twisting, curling funnel of light. The three divine beings encircled the lost spectre. They moved closer, emanating a powerful spirit of love. Chants of 'peace', 'harmony' and 'love' wisped through Roma's clairaudient senses. The entity retracted further, withering in their light. The chants continued repeatedly. Finally, cornered, with no apparent escape root, the invisible squatter retreated into the portal and vanished.

The grey veil shrouding the room began to lift. The colours and textures sprang back to life and a peaceful ambience suffused throughout. Roma's job was completed.

Phil was still in a deep meditative state when she descended from the bedroom. He had been radiating loving intentions to the lost entity. Carla looked dishevelled, the contents of the ashtray revealing the state of her shredded nerves.

'He's gone, my dear,' Roma said, triumphantly.

Carla looked concerned.

'What will happen to him now?..... there was a time when I loved him dearly.'

'I know sweetheart,' she replied. 'In all probability, he will now enter a world created by a higher part of himself – his Soul. This sphere of existence is an illusion, though he won't realise it. If he continues to deny his true nature and remains self-absorbed, then in all likelihood, he will continue to inflict harm on others. However, the characters that occupy his new world are illusory and can therefore feel no pain. All his misdeeds will rebound and he will feel the effects personally. He will feel every ounce of pain that he inflicts on others. In the meantime, his Soul group will radiate loving intentions towards him, urging him to awaken. When his true nature emerges from the garbage he accumulated on earth, he'll be lifted up to the Higher Astral level. On arrival, he will be greeted by loved ones. They, and other highly evolved entities, will assist him to review his life. He will re-experience everything as though he is re-living it and it will occur at the speed of light. Viewing his last incarnation in this manner, through the lens of his Higher Self, will fill him with guilt and remorse. Remember we do still feel emotion at this level. In all probability, he will choose to re-incarnate and rectify his mistakes. In this future life, circumstances will prevail through which he can learn the lessons that he failed to learn the last time around.'

'So he isn't condemned to hell for eternity?'

'No!' injected Phil, his response filled with emotional charge. 'As a young impressionable child, I was forced to attend a church. On the wall, above the altar, was a gothic image: two grotesque gargoyle figures dangling a man over some flames. It terrified me. The narrow-minded priest was telling us how bad we all were and how we had been born sinners. That terrifying image portrayed what happened to sinners. I was five years old! In my eyes that's an inexcusable use of power. For years after, I questioned every miniscule detail of my behaviour. Was it a sin? Would I be condemned to hell for an eternity? I berated myself, forever thinking I was wrong. I'm absolutely certain that this played a major role in my destructive drinking – a self-inflicted punishment. I wish these people in influential roles would wake up and realise the potential damage they're causing. Admittedly we all have both good and bad traits, but to instill that type of fear into youngsters is inexcusable.'

'Jim had some wonderful attributes in the early days. He would buy me flowers and wine and dine me. He could be very romantic at times.'

'Then send him your love, my dear. Assist him to awaken and enter the harmonic realms.'

Before leaving, Roma took some precautionary measures. She placed tape measures across the door and window of Carla's bedroom. She had found that restless spirits were afraid of them. The numbers suggested levels of being and lost entities wouldn't cross them. In addition, she placed a tea light candle in every room to remind unwanted complexes of energy that this was a house of love and light.

Phil had brought some crystals. He placed a piece of tourmaline on her bedside table to provide a protective shield, a piece of amber in her living room to draw out negative energies and purify the atmosphere, and azurite in her kitchen to cleanse and heal.

Later that evening Carla expressed a desire to burn her suicide note. They went into the back garden and Phil performed a short ceremony. As every last remnant of the note was reduced to ash, he asked that it signify the end of her past and make way for a new beginning. He spent the remainder of the evening comforting her, during which time she agreed to seek help with the inhibiting residues of her past.

Chapter 35

Radical Transformation of a Dedicated Human Being

G's life continued to steadily improve. He was now on very amicable terms with *ex*-wife Joan. After receiving their decree nisi, she decided to drop her claim for the house, agreeing they should split the proceeds. It seemed strange, but in the final part of their marriage a radical transformation had taken place. The couple had eradicated the internal saboteurs that hindered their ability to converse. G. had spoken about the programmed child and oppressor modes of operation and Joan had been surprisingly enlightened. The identification of her own shortcomings had enabled her to open her heart. She could now see clearly why she was apt to operate from the oppressor position – she had an ingrained need to be in control. Unknown to G, she was bullied and singled out as a child and quickly learnt that oppression was the best form of defence. She criticised others in a ploy to feel better about herself. In reality, she was suffering from very low self-esteem, internally berating herself.

G. felt a great sense of compassion as she revealed the extent to which she had been bullied. She had taken on the persona of her role models in order to protect herself and nullify her pain.

They had also spoken about relationship fits. He had explained that perhaps they were initially attracted to each other for reasons that eluded their conscious awareness. Joan eventually came to the conclusion that her attraction to him was based on his gentleness. He acted as a container for the timidity and softness that life's circumstance had prohibited her from embracing. She, in turn, released the anger that he was unable to express. So the fit was that of opposites. However, as G. had correctly identified, he also had the added fit of unresolved childhood issues. Joan was oppressive, just like his mother, and he was unconsciously trying to dissolve the issues he had with her. Now the issues had been resolved, and G. had learned to stand up for himself (helped by Esba's badger medicine), Joan had begun to soften; their collective energies had balanced out. They both agreed that they had learned valuable lessons from each other: she had softened and faced her demons; he had learned to express his 'forbidden' emotions. In the past two months, they had achieved what had eluded them for sixteen years - harmony. They also agreed that they had come to the end of their journey together, but would always remain friends. G. offered to help her find alternative accommodation and help with any decoration.

This had been the start of an exciting new era for G. Three weeks ago, quite unexpectedly, he met a lady whilst taking a walk in the park. They got so engrossed in conversation that several hours passed by without them noticing. They had many things in common: classical music, architecture, spiritual beliefs and walking, to name but a few. It turned out that she had divorced eighteen months ago after her husband had been unfaithful. The pair had established a very intimate friendship in the short time they had known each other and things looked set to last: perhaps it was because she was his Soul sister, Ann Marie?

It would seem that the Universe had honoured G's requests. In the face of adversity, he had assimilated the precious life lessons of empathy, compassion, understanding and love; now he stood to reap the rewards. His friendships were flourishing. He was letting go of his old way of life with love and gratitude. And his purpose had become crystal clear: he had come to the conclusion that his teacher training had been part of a much bigger picture. Through his conversations with Robert and Phil, and the knowledge he had acquired experientially, he had become intent on bringing the domains of spirituality and science together. He was determined to provide people with an insight into the mechanics of consciousness. And, it would seem the higher realms were supporting his choice, quite 'coincidently', Ann Marie was not only his Soul sister but also a physics teacher!

The raison d'être of life had paved a pathway to his destiny and he was walking it with great faith. He knew that, one day, he would teach at a centre situated in a place of great natural beauty - a very special place, where reputedly, rainbows end.

Tonight was the trio's meeting night. They intended to have a discussion about quantum physics and spirituality. G. had the opportunity to put his teaching skills into action; he embraced it with great passion.

'So these wisps of energy and information that comprise the quantum field can be likened to thought. But these thoughts are fleeting in and out of time and space continuously. These vibrations are leaping in and out of existence at speeds so great that we don't even notice. This has led some, myself included, to believe that we are being projected into being by our Soul on a moment-to-moment basis. Think about it, these fluctuations of energy and information that continuously appear then disappear, form atoms, which form molecules, which comprise the physical body. So the physical body is a hierarchy of these vibrations and therefore must also be blinking in and out of existence. This means that the physical body is crystallised energy vibrations, or solidified thought: energy is matter masquerading under another guise. This is what Einstein's famous equation, $E = MC^2$, is telling us. E = energy, M = mass and C = the speed of light. Energy is mass vibrating at the speed of light squared.

If the raw fabric of the material Universe is energy imprinted with information, and the nearest thing we can compare it with is thought, then everything we perceive as physical is simply the movement of thought. This gives great credence to the proposal that consciousness is the ground of all being. And that we're all thoughts in the mind of God.

Behind the shroud of physicality there is an orchestrating force that is causing all this movement to happen: the thinker behind the thought, so to speak. I firmly believe that this force is the Soul, hence the name "causal body" - the foundation of our eternal existence which is thinking us into existence.

Our Soul weaves together the fabric of our earthly spacesuit from the quantum field, providing us with a vehicle of experience. From this mosaic of intelligence, a body consciousness is born - our earthly self - an appendage of consciousness that will act as a container for our lifetime's experience. This will house our ego and all the other complexes of subconscious and unconscious energy that orbit it; a singular world within a collective world.

Our Soul allocates another part of itself to reside over this child: our Uniqueness. While the body consciousness is busy becoming saturated with conditioning, absorbing the software that presents our challenges, our Uniqueness remains detached and observes. So now we have an observer and that which is being observed. But our Uniqueness has another function: it retains certain past-life memories from which our current life purpose emerges - conditioning that has resulted from past-life experience, leaving us with a propensity towards our life's lessons.

So we embark on the process of life. Our body consciousness begins to house our sub-personalities and our awareness, the lens through which we experience, starts to identify with scripts. Subsequently a veil obscures our view of our true essence and we believe that we are our Ego. Now, we either become lost in all this chaos, or we use it to our advantage. Embedded within chaos is perfection. When we awaken, we realise that every emotion has a richness and every thought provides an opportunity. The underlying principle behind every thought and emotion is growth. In concordance with Phil's belief, I believe that our Soul has great influence over the thoughts we experience. Undoubtedly, our primary source of thought in the secular sphere is memory, which stems from external stimuli. And initially memories are stored in neural networks in the brain. But this is only a temporary holding space. All our memories end up in a large data bank of accumulative karma which is stored as vibrations at the level of our Soul. If we closely monitor our thoughts we start to realise that *we* don't choose many of them, they emerge and dissipate of their own accord - randomly and spontaneously. I know we can recall memory through intent, for instance, when we sit an exam. And that association can trigger a string of thoughts. But what about all the other thoughts? It's my belief that perfection lies beneath this seemingly random phenomenon. I believe that when we experience conflicting thoughts it's our Souls way of testing us. Our Soul utilizes the experiences we've stored in our accumulative memory bank and feeds them back to our mind in order to present us with choice. When we have experiential knowledge of this, then a profound insight emerges. Let's take an example to clarify things: I have two conflicting thoughts, the first of which says, 'you are going to be a spiritual healer and teacher'; the second says 'people like you don't achieve such things'. Both are seedlings which lead to different destinations. If I have faith in my abilities and harness my inherent creativity, then I might germinate the first seedling. We germinate seedlings of thought by directing a flow of energy at them; this movement of energy is commonly called attention. Now this seedling has the potential to grow into a beautiful landscape – my destiny. By contrast, if I choose to fertilize the second thought and remain anchored by my conditioning, then it's likely that I'll remain in a small plant pot until the day I die; worse still, I may cultivate a garden of thorns. If I accept that my Soul is testing my resolve by placing these conflicting thoughts into my mind, then the game of life takes on a sense of adventure. ***I may not consciously choose my thoughts but I can choose the thoughts I meld*** *with.* Thoughts create reality; therefore, I should treat them with respect. The determining factor in any choice should be my heart's desire. Why? Because my Soul wants me to be happy and fulfilled.

Life can be seen as a journey through the chakras. We start at the base, our ego strengthens and we experience a sense of singularity. We grow towards the sacral vortex and affiliation with others - relationships. Through relationships we encounter many opportunities to evolve. As we enter the solar plexus, we enter the realm of thought, the platform through which our Soul tests us.

When we awaken, we begin to realise that everything imparts wisdom: nature, the elements, the animals, and other human beings. We just have to extract the hidden meaning behind our encounters. When we connect with this phenomenon, through experiential knowledge, then we begin to feel a great affinity with everything. This is the realm of the heart vortex; the bridge to our transpersonal selves.

As we move upwards towards the throat and the third eye chakras, we enter the unseen realms and communicate naturally with our disincarnate friends; our child-like innocence returns and we enter the Great Mystery. We connect with the hidden forces that reside in the space around us and take one step closer to home.

The whole process culminates in the crown chakra where we experience unity and enlightenment – the gift of which is freedom.

To sum up, our true selves are limitless, formless, timeless, inexorable bundles of infinite potential. We can traverse any domain of experience within the inexhaustible playground of energy known as the Universal mind. In essence, God is an omnipresent consciousness that is differentiating into an infinite number of observers and objects of observation. A supreme mind which is continually becoming aware of *itself;* forever expanding, creating worlds within worlds, domains within domains of experience. It has no beginning and will never end because all this is happening in the eternal continuum of the present, where past, present and future co-exist.'

Silence.

Phil and Vi just stood in awe of G., acknowledging his radical transformation. He was beaming: living proof of what a dedicated human being can achieve.

'I'd like to place a reservation on your services right now big man. I'm going to need people like you when our centre transpires…. Come here, both of you, and let's have a group hug,' said Phil.

They all huddled together, radiating and receiving a heart-felt love. 'Well folks, on that inspiring note, another enlightening year draws to a close.'

Christmas was just a few days away. Phil had to give some serious consideration to the counselling post and a move down south. Presently, he was reluctant to go; Vi and himself had become almost inseparable once again.

Yesterday evening they had their Christmas night out. After the meal he caressed her hand and expressed his love for her, promising to abide by any decision she should make about her future.

The meal was followed by a visit to a local cinema, which was showing classic films. Being that the rainbow had been such an important symbol throughout their journey, they decided to go and see the Wizard of Oz. Phil taunted Vi by saying she had certain attributes of the Wicked Witch of the West! Remembering the episode at Watendlath, when she covered him in hay, she retorted by likening him to the scarecrow - complete with no brain!

Despite their arduous journey, Dorothy and the rest of the clan found their way to the rainbow's end. Phil wondered would their story come to a similar conclusion. His heartfelt wishes had been thwarted by re-occurring visions of them parting; all his senses indicated that a storm was brewing. However, behind every rain cloud lays a golden sun, and the potential of a rainbow - A rainbow that might just lead to their promised land.

Chapter 36

Engaged in Fear

The car sped up the motorway heading for southern Scotland. Tom hadn't disclosed the exact location. Vi appeared distant, gazing out of the window at the snow covered hills. Her heart was torn in two. The reality of her situation had hit home and fear and uncertainty had set in once again. She took a sideways glance at Tom.

I don't know whether I could ever leave him. We've been together such a long time. We've nearly parted on a couple of occasions and I've never been able to go through with it. I know he loves me and I love him - in some sort of way.

As they travelled up over the Shap, the light snow fall turned to drizzle and a faint rainbow appeared over the hills. Her thoughts turned to Phil. They had made this journey several times en route to the Lake District. This was the precise spot where he would hand her a gift wrapped parcel and a card and wish her happy birthday – regardless of the date. The rainbow reminded her of their special times together. Her confusion deepened. She thought about his proposal.

But what if I should accept and it all goes wrong? I'd be left with nothing. Finding someone else would be so difficult. It takes me such a long time to gain trust. By his own admittance, Phil finds it difficult to sustain relationships. Maybe I've been living in cuckoo land and had an idealistic view of an unrealistic future. We have been living in a somewhat perfect bubble – what if it bursts? But then I know how much he loves me. I feel it every time I'm with him. I've never felt love like that from anyone before. And then there's been those times when we've been together, that I've felt things that I've never felt before in my life. On those days I felt as though I was floating on air and couldn't be happier. I know I love him and I know I deny it to myself at times. Sometimes I deny it so vehemently that I actually believe it.

She glanced at Tom again.

But how can I hurt him? He's making such an effort. I think he fears losing me……Oh (she sighed)…..I just don't know……'

'Are you okay?' Tom inquired, noticing how distant she was.

'Yes,' she replied, her forced smile revealing quite the opposite.

A sickly feeling began to gather in her stomach. Tom wasn't his usual self today. He was up to something. But she had no idea what it was.

Shortly after crossing the Scottish border Tom took a slip road off the motorway.

'Where are we going?' inquired Vi.

Tom nodded in the direction of a sign that read **Gretna.** Vi glared at him; her fears began to heighten.

Gretna Green is the marriage capital of the world. The history of Gretna weddings is surrounded by romance. Located on the old coaching route between London and Edinburgh, Gretna Green was the first village reached once you entered Scotland. Young couples used to elope over the border to Gretna Green, where they could be married at 16 years of age. English law did not allow them to marry until they were 18 without their parents consent. In popular folklore, the local blacksmith and his anvil have become the lasting symbols of Gretna Green weddings. As a "forger", the blacksmith marries hot metal to metal over the anvil. In the same way the anvil priests forged a union between couples who had eloped in love. To this day the old wedding traditions are preserved and thousands of couples travel from all over the world to get married at Gretna Green.

'Why are we going there?' Vi inquired.

'I thought it would be nice to have a look around. You said you wanted to get out more often.'

'Oh, okay,' she replied, somewhat suspiciously.

Tom pulled the car over near to the grounds of Gretna hall.

'Come on let's go and have a look around,' he said.

They made their way to a cobbled courtyard dating back to 1710, the home of the lord of the manor until 1792 when it became a coaching inn. After having a look around, they headed for the landscape gardens which took on exceptional beauty in the snow. They stopped at a pond and watched as the geese slid towards them on the ice-covered surface. Vi laughed inwardly as she thought of Phil's encounter with the geese at Watendlath.

After a while, they ambled across to the picturesque grounds of The Mill Forge, visiting the Fountain Garden and The Rose Garden. An air of romance enveloped Vi. She thought of the magical weekend at the caravan when Phil had covered the bed with petals and gifts. The song 'Danny Boy' rang through her mind.

The penultimate stop was at the kissing gate: a place where couples stopped for photographs after they were wed. Vi felt Phil kiss her gently on the cheek and whisper the words 'I love you little lady' into her ear. Her face started to glow bright red, as it always did when he kissed her.

'Shall we move on?' said Tom, appearing enthusiastic to get her to the main building.

Built in the design of a Scottish chapel, The Mill Forge was a place where many anvil weddings had taken place.

They entered the churchlike entrance and walked up the aisle towards the anvil. Tom started to look a little uncomfortable and held back, fumbling in his pocket for something. When Vi reached the anvil, she could almost hear Phil's voice whispering 'will you marry me, sweetheart'. She started to drift off, envisaging all the weddings that had taken place there.

When she snapped back to the present, she realised the place had fallen into complete silence. *What had happened to Tom?* She turned around to look for him and suddenly froze. Totally immobilized.

He was kneeling before her clutching a small jewellery box.

'Will you marry me?' he said, nervously.

She was speechless, unable to utter a word.

She looked down at his forlorn figure, his outstretched hand clutching the jewellery box.

How can I hurt him? He's been so understanding over the years. I must make a decision. I can't go on as I am.

It took several minutes before she broke the silence in which time her thoughts oscillated from one extreme to the other.

'Do you mean today?' she eventually replied, not really knowing how to respond.

'No, Vi. Not today. Maybe next year. I'd just like you to accept this engagement ring today.'

He opened the jewellery box and gazed up at her.

I do love him… I suppose. And I really can't envisage life without him; it's been such a long time.

She paused a while longer.

'Okay….if that's what you want,' she finally replied.

Tom got up and slipped the ring onto her finger. The atmosphere became subdued. Tears began to trickle down Vi's cheeks which Tom found endearing. However, they were not tears of joy: they were tears of sheer sadness and frustration.

Over the Christmas period, Vi set about convincing herself that she had made the right decision. Truthfully, she didn't really know what to make of the situation – it had all happened so fast. Since their engagement, Tom had seemed different – happier. Yet she wouldn't allow herself to believe that this was a permanent change. He had promised to change before, when they had almost parted. He did change for a while but it was always short lived. Within a few weeks he would revert back to his old ways.

As well as her concerns over Tom, she was confronted by another major problem: she still hadn't broken the news to Phil – she didn't know how to.

Chapter 37

Happiness to Heart-Ache:
A Lesson in Unconditional Love

Phil had travelled down south to spend the holiday with his family. His parents had moved from Liverpool a couple of years ago to be near their grand-children. They were a close knit family, but the four hundred miles separating them prevented regular visits. So, they had not seen much of each other lately. They were delighted to have him home for the festive season.

His two nieces, now in their late teens, and his ten-year-old nephew, thought he was crazy. He was always up to some mischief and making them laugh. This Christmas he was particularly buoyant; his effervescence fuelled by thoughts of spending the rest of his life with the person whom he loved with a passion.

Today he was playing cowboys and Indians with his nephew, Mark. His nieces had painted his face with lipstick and, as he had no headdress, they strapped some imitation flowers to his head with a belt!

Mark was getting infuriated with him. He had shot him several times but Phil refused to die. He just carried on riding around the living room on his mop! As he rode out of town and into the dining room, his phone sounded and an envelope popped up on the screen. He dismounted his mop and tied it to the door handle. 'Stay boy,' he ordered, as his nieces gave him some very strange looks. To their embarrassment, he asked one of their boyfriends to feed and water his mop while he have heap big pow-wow with big chief little horn!

His heart fluttered when he noticed the text was from Vi. Her image appeared vividly in his mind's eye. As he began to read the text, however, all the joy drained out of his face.

> **Phil I'm so sorry to give you this news via a text message, but I can't get any privacy to phone you. I have made a decision. Tom bought me a diamond ring for Christmas and asked me to get engaged. I've accepted. I think it's the right thing to do. I hope you understand.**
>
> **Love Vi. Xx**

He was devastated. The smile in his heart quickly transformed into a dull ache. A tear trickled down his face smudging his feigned war paint. The crack sounding from his nephew's cap-gun had no effect; he had already been slain by the might of love. He had to get out. He felt claustrophobic: nauseous. The life force that had sustained him five minutes earlier had suddenly been exhausted and he felt himself choking.

He trudged, head down, along the beach, his shoes sinking deep into the rain sodden sand. Dark clouds roared with thunderous contempt and waves crashed in as the ocean swelled with the intensity of the storm. He carried on oblivious, walking for miles, saturated to the skin, vision blurred by the squalls of torrential rain and savage winds. Each streak of fork lightening felt like a dagger piercing his heart. An emptiness of enormous magnitude filled his being. He asked himself a thousand questions.

What brought about this sudden change of heart? Is she really happy? Has the whole thing been manufactured to enable me to grow towards unconditional love? Is this a test of my resolve and integrity?.......Right now I'm hurting, but I will sustain my love for her - I'll always love her.

Tears started to trickle down his face as distant echoes of the past formulated in his mind:

You have emerged from a beautiful ocean of consciousness, dear one, and one day you will return to that blissful state. For now you must anchor yourself deep in this ocean of love for the surface is about to become tempestuous. This maelstrom emanates from the great inhibitor fear and can only be annulled by the light of love.

Chapter 38

A Child is Born

Later that evening, after many hours of emotional turbulence and mental deliberation, Phil returned Vi's text, wishing her and Tom every happiness. Nothing was rhyming, but he felt it was the only thing to do. She replied and agreed to meet, away from work, on the evening of their first day back at work. As Phil had preparations to make, and feeling unable to face Vi under work conditions, he intended to take that day as an emergency day's holiday.

Deciding to take the job offer, he asked his parents if they would mind putting him up for a while. They were delighted. The whole family would be in close proximity of each other for the first time in years. Phil was grateful; the timely exit from Lancaster meant he could start the inevitable process of mourning.

He now lay on the bed, eyes dilated, staring vacuously at the ceiling, slowly slipping into a deep state of melancholy. Vi's poignant text haunted his mind like an epitaph bearing his own name. Fits of nausea exploded in his stomach like depth charges pounding his sunken hopes. The elevator of life had once again plummeted to the basement of bad dreams and the prevailing blackout had left him in a place of darkened despair.

Curling into the embryo position, he wrapped his arms around himself in an attempt to reassure his wounded child. A couple of long hours passed in which time he tossed and turned, jerked and shuddered, relentlessly sieving his mind for answers. No matter how much he searched, the biting reality remained: Vi was now the fiancée of a partner she'd been desperately unhappy with for years.

After a while, and with emotional and cognitive energy totally depleted, his eyelids leadened and he slipped into the realms of unconsciousness.

Thirteenth century. Medieval England.

A woman of obvious status, donning conical hat and dripping in jewellery, strolled through a crowded courtyard, arm in arm with a stern-faced, oppressive, looking brute. Her eyes burned with contempt as he scowled and shoved a young peasant boy out of their way. She glanced down at the ornate ring on the third finger of her left hand and cringed, mortified at the thought of marrying the tyrant.

A crowd of people laughed heartily as a brightly clad jester entertained them with humorous odes. As she passed, the jester turned and looked towards her. She returned a longing gaze, finding refuge in his deep blue eyes.

Phil awoke rubbing his eyes, his dream banished from consciousness. And yet, initially, the jester's face remained emblazoned in his mind. Throughout his torpid re-entry into the land of the living, the image began to fade. Nevertheless, he was left with an inexplicable sense of hope.

Lacing his fingers behind his head, he quietly contemplated the relevance of the jester. As he did, another image loomed - a phoenix rising from its ashes. A puzzling thought transpired... *Life is going to emerge from my mourning?*

Suddenly, and with colourful flamboyancy, Galfridus came dancing back into his mind singing a ditty that sent shivers through his body:

Through life's experience the stories given
Birth your child and wake the living
On journey's new you now embark
Take heed of signposts in the dark.

The surrounding space became a hive of activity. Theodore, Esba, Mary and Galfridus wisped through the ether, fusing together, then disbanding, emanating their collective energies in every direction. As a result, Phil's sense of well-being intensified and a surge of expectancy coursed through him.

Murmuring to himself, and hanging on every word, he began to dissect the ode.

'Through.. life's.. experience.. the.. stories.. given.'

His body suddenly jilted with fright as the Dickensian image strobed before his eyes. Flash. Flash. Flash. Vanish.

After momentary shock, he resumed his quest…. 'The book.. the book's been given?' he intuited. 'But how?'

Somewhat perplexed, he moved on to the next line.

'Birth.. your.. child.. and.. wake.. the.. living.'

Esba's form now appeared, smiling, nursing a new born baby.

Phil was totally baffled. His eyes angled left and up towards the ceiling as he continued to deliberate. 'Baby - story?..Baby - story?' His mind vacillated back and forth, but he couldn't fathom the answer, so he moved on to the next line.'

'On..journeys.. new.. you.. now.. embark.'

Okay. That makes sense. Significant changes are taking place.

'Take.. heed.. of.. whispers.. in.. the.. dark.'

On uttering the last line, a rapid succession of images fired through his mind. He suddenly found himself reliving every intricate detail of his journey with Vi and G: the interactions, the dreams, the signposts, the joy, the sorrow, the tension, the intense love affair. The frames reeled on and on, until, eventually, a black screen signalled the end.

He sat up with a jilt. A moment of revelation!

'Of course!' he exclaimed. 'The book *has* been given - the story of our journey together. It never was going to be handed to me on a plate. That would've been meaningless. I had to live it; I had to go through the whole learning process. That's why I was compelled to keep a record of everything - I've been writing it all along!..

'..... And the baby,' he mused, 'the very special child - it's the book. Of course, a book that's been birthed by Vi and myself… Oh! And not forgetting uncle G., of course .... A very special book that will take my work into forthcoming generations…it's beginning to happen, all the promises are beginning to materialize…things are beginning to make complete sense now…'

His awareness leapt from his mental body and embedded itself deep within his heart chakra. He felt a deep sense of affinity with everything. His mourning temporarily subsided as he fully accepted he was eternally bonded to Vi – he vowed to marry her in the next life time, or the one after that. *Unity will always prevail between us,* he thought, *and where there's unity, separation can't exist.*

An overwhelming sense of gratitude emerged. 'Thank you, Theodore. Thank you, Esba. Thank you, Vi, G, Roma, Galfridus, Mary… THANK YOU UNIVERSE.'

His voice upsurged from a murmur to a muffled roar as a tide of inspiration began to flow through him. Pulsating with excitement, he jumped off the bed. After retrieving his laptop, he lit some candles. Then, eyes closed, he performed a short ceremony:

'I dedicate this book to my two dearest friends, my Soul brother G., and the one true love of my life - Violet Rowan; go in peace, little lady. I love you, and I always will.'

At that precise moment, he had assimilated a major life's lesson - in the face of adversity, his love had not faltered: he had attained unconditional love. Theodore and Esba observed from the surrounding space with great pride.

As Phil started tapping rapidly at the keyboard, the Dickensian image loomed vividly in his mind's eye once again. He felt a great affinity with the man. As the blurred face started to become more pronounced, he realised the reason why – it was himself: a past life personality.

IN THIS WORLD BUT NOT OF IT:

A Journey from Enslavement to Enlightenment

By Phil Harrison

Chapter one

Violet's Demise

Vi gazed nonchalantly out of the window…………

And so his child was born - **or so he thought?**

Chapter 39

Soul Mates Separate

The night was dark and dank, the lake barely visible under the subdued street lighting. Phil sat on a park bench, nervously awaiting the arrival of Vi. He watched as his breath suffused into the cold night air. The pounding of his heart sounded like the rapid succession of canon fire, ceasing only as a silhouette emerged from the shroud of mist that had descended.

He took a few deep breaths, attempting to calm himself down, each exhalation sounding more like a disconcerting sigh. An image appeared in his mind, Vi and himself sitting in this very spot, loving and laughing, planning a future that would never materialize. His stomach went into free fall.

Unable to settle, he stood up and walked over to the lakeside where, nestling amidst the long grass, was a male and female mallard. They huddled closely together, finding refuge in each other's warmth. A deep sadness washed over Phil as thoughts of what might have been poured into his mind. His eyes began to glaze. He could almost feel the texture of Vi's skin as she snuggled up to him on that unforgettable day when he proposed.

Just as he felt himself slipping further into a dark abyss, a voice reeled through his mind. *You must love her, you must nurture her.* Mary, it would seem, was not yet ready to return to the higher realms.

He returned his gaze to the devoted ducks. As he did, a lustrous glow appeared to envelope them. His gaze transformed into an hypnotic trance, everything else fading into insignificance. Galfridus' voice echoed through his mind:

> When darkened nights bring winter chills
> birds share their warmth for coldness kills
> as people sharing just one heart
> should pool their warmth and never part

The sound of light footsteps caused him to return to normal awareness. A deep sense of trepidation coursed through him. Though the air was infused with an icy chill, his palms began to sweat profusely. As the frequency of the tapping of footsteps accelerated, so did the frequency of his pulse. A vague outline emerged from the mist. He squinted and tried to make out the figure, yet his senses had pre-empted him - he knew who it was.

Vi's familiar form came into view. As she drew closer, he could see she looked drawn and upset. The sight of her engagement ring caused his stomach to lurch.

They hugged and exchanged pleasantries, then took a seat on the bench. An air of diffidence descended — neither of them knowing quite what to say. Phil felt like a little lost boy whistling nervously in the dark; Vi, like a widow attending the cremation of her own heart.

After a short period of uncomfortable silence, he took hold of her hand. 'It's nice.' He said, looking at her diamond ring. 'Can I be best man?'

She returned an awkward smile. 'I'm so sorry it had to be this way, Phil,' she replied, before turning to avoid eye contact.

He suddenly felt choked, struggling to keep himself together. 'I understand, Vi. I made you a promise. I said my love for you is unconditional, and so it is - I will always love you.'

Tiny red veins appeared in the whites of her eyes as the tears started to trickle. 'When are you leaving?' she sniffled, knowing without being told, it was imminent.

'Tomorrow,' he replied, his voice faltering.

'So soon?' She said, running her cuff over her dampened eyes.

'Yes, I made a brief visit to work this morning and handed in my notice. We came to an amicable arrangement whereby I use my holiday entitlement to cover my notice period – so I won't be coming back.'

'What about your cottage?'

'I've arranged for it to be valued. G. said he'd act on my behalf in my absence. He's helping me to tie up the loose ends.'

Vi stared dejectedly at the floor. 'Will we see each other again?'

Phil's eyes lifted to the dark sky. 'I dearly hope so, I really do. But maybe it's best if we have no contact for a while? I feel I need some time. I'm sure you understand.'

'I do, Phil. Perhaps it's best for both of us.'

Silence.

They both stared nonchalantly into space. Then Phil took hold of her hand again. 'We *will* give birth to a very special child, though.' he said, trying desperately to hold back his tears. 'The child is the book, Vi. Can I have your permission to write the story of our journey together?'

'You have my blessing. You deserve every success and I'll do anything I can to help.'

'Thank you. Thank you for everything, sweetheart. I promise I'll send you a copy of the manuscript as soon as it's finished. I've already written sixteen chapters....and Vi,' He turned her head gently towards him and cupped his hands around her face. 'I wish you and Tom every happiness.'

They left the park hand in hand, neither of them able to utter another word. As the mist began to lift, Phil stared up at the moon which was intermittently eclipsed by transient clouds. As he did, he felt it was sending him a message. As a card of the Major Arcana in the Tarot deck, the moon represents deception – he had a nagging feeling that Vi was still deceiving herself. Yet, there was absolutely nothing he could do about it.

Their final farewell was heart rendering: locked together, standing at the park gates, sobbing, and neither of them wanting to let go. One final thought drifted through Phil's mind: *to win this battle you have to surrender.*

Chapter 40

Destined to Deliver

Phil worked feverishly. Every minute of his free time was dedicated to the book. As he relived every intricate detail of their journey together, his emotions ranged from sheer joy to severe heartache. These emotive forces became his allies, his creative essence, finding expression through words and fuelling the passion behind his writing. As winter turned to spring and new born lambs appeared in the fields, the book was very near completion – his child was about to be born?

Not a day went by without him yearning for Vi. Temptation got so great that he removed her numbers from his contact list and changed his own number. Though heartbroken, he had come to the conclusion that if they were to see each other again, the Universe would provide the platform. He had to trust in the natural process - surrender his will completely.

The signposts were coming fast and furious. He made a sizeable profit on his cottage which he invested in a vacant shop premises; a place that would be ideal to start his venture. The alterations came expensive. The sales area had been converted into a meeting room, the stores divided into two therapy rooms, and the office had been refurbished. The upstairs living quarters still needed attention and he wanted to landscape the sizeable garden at the rear of the premises.

As his money began to dwindle, his parents inherited a half share in an estate. Old Bob had died at the ripe old age ninety-one. He had no family, so Phil's parents tended to him for years; he had become an adopted member of the family. On receiving their inheritance, they handed him a cheque for twenty thousand pounds and told him that old Bob would be pleased to help in his venture. He was a very spiritual man and had a great belief in the esoteric. They suggested that by investing some of the old man's estate in Phil's venture, his spirit would live on. Phil was extremely grateful. He promised to put up a commemorative plaque bearing Bob's name - now he had the finances to complete the remaining work.

Tonight, Phil was about to start the last few chapters of the book. Up until this point, the story had been written from true life experience. Now he was going to have to project an ending. For this he needed the assistance of his guides.

He retreated to his bedroom, lay on the bed, and focused intently; then mentally called for the presence of Theodore and Esba. The ambience of the room immediately changed and his awareness accentuated. He felt warm and comforted.

'Show me the ending,' he said aloud, whilst stimulating his third-eye chakra with the middle finger of his right hand.

Images started to appear in his mind's eye. The nature of these visions left him a little perplexed. He could not fathom whether they were projections of his heart's desire or channelled prophecies of a probable future. After much deliberation, he decided it didn't matter. He was going to put into words exactly what he was seeing. He felt this was the way it was *meant* to be. As Theodore had once reminded him, things that are *meant* to be don't necessarily happen. The final choice rests with the individual.

Chapter 41

Freedom

A Jester holds The Key

Vi gazed nonchalantly out of the window into the garden. It was a beautiful summer's day. The flowers and plants were covered in a morning dew. Each dew drop sparkled like a diamond as it reflected the sunlight. A tall tree reached out into the clear blue sky and the birds sang with the joy of a new day.

Vi perceived this scene as grey and dreary, reflecting the way she felt inside – desperately unhappy. Since Phil's departure, she had gone into steady decline. Externally, everything appeared to be falling into place: her family life had vastly improved; her father was residing with her mother; her brothers and sister, and their families, were flourishing; her relationship with Tom had improved, she had exposed the destructive aspirations of her inner assailants and, as a result, the automatic responses that once dogged their relationship (the rages, the aloofness, the criticisms, the emotionally charged responses) had subsided and a degree of amicability had been sustained. Nevertheless, she was left with a huge void inside, feeling as if she was just going through the motions. A vast amount of cognitive energy had been expended trying to stifle the real cause of her problem: love. This had led to her feeling drained and depleted. Depression, the nullification of emotion, had resulted from her trying to continually deny her feelings, and now she was back in that desolate place.

'Why didn't I tell him how I truly felt?' she sniffled as shudders of sorrow ran through her body. 'He was always so honest with me.'

She turned and stared at the manuscript on the table.

Is it too late? Have I lost him forever?

As this thought arose, a movie screen appeared in her mind's eye. On it, she saw herself as she was right now. The film began to rapidly reverse, taking her back in time. Twenty-first century. Twentieth. Nineteenth. Eighteenth. Seventeenth. Sixteenth. Fifteenth. Fourteenth. Thirteenth..........

She was back imprisoned in the tower. Galfridus entered and opened the door. They gazed longingly at each other, finding sanctuary in each other's eyes. This time she had no hesitation: she wanted her freedom as much as the air she breathed. They crept down a spiral staircase and made their way through the packed courtyard. Galfridus had two horses waiting. They galloped off, riding for days, stopping only to rest and eat. Their journey ended in a wood. Galfridus helped her down off the horse. Two flowers lay before her. One withered - one blossoming. Galfridus began to sing his ditty.

> **'See with owl's eyes**
>
> **for in darkness you roam**
>
> **Move 'further to wolf'**
>
> **and you'll find your true home.'**

The white chrysanthemum before her took on a luminescent glow…. The words 'further to wolf' became firmly imprinted in her mind. Suddenly, the letters began to mysteriously *move* around. Initially they spelt utter gibberish.

Werofl fo tutrh

Twertr of hut

Vi was perplexed. *What's happening?* She thought. Then, something quite extraordinary happened. She stood with mouth agape. The letters had rearranged themselves one final time and the answer to the conundrum had finally been revealed.

Flower of truth

She snapped back to her ordinary state of awareness – astounded.

The white chrysanthemum - it represents truth, she thought. *The flower I was supposed to choose, the one that would lead me to the very special place where I truly belong....is the flower of truth. I have been denying the truth all along. Let go of fear, embrace the truth, and I will grow towards the light: that was the message all along!*

The ambience of the room began to change and a familiar voice returned.

Are you prepared to go through the full life cycle, my dear friend?

'Yes, I am. Though, I don't know how I'm going to tell Tom - I feel I'm betraying him'

Sometimes we have to betray others to be true to ourselves, my child. In the long run, everyone benefits. Be free – it's time to fly into the new world.

Visions began to fill Vi's mind. She saw herself walking up the aisle towards the anvil arm and arm with her father; bridesmaids Charlie and Val followed closely behind. Phil stood ahead looking pristine with best man G. Eva Cassidy's 'Somewhere Over The Rainbow' echoed through the Mill. The scene changed. They were now locked together under the kissing gate. Phil whispered words of love in her ear. The crowd threw confetti over them. Their song, 'We Are One', played befittingly in the background......

....Suddenly, from the crowd, emerged a young girl with eyes that were not of this world. Her arms unfurled towards her. 'Mummy,' she said, in a voice that conveyed wisdom beyond her years...

Vi snapped back to the present. Four points of light entered the surrounding space. Theo, Esba, Galfridus and Mary looked on in anticipation. She turned to the manuscript again. This time it took on a luminescent glow. She picked it up and began to read the ending that Phil had projected.

When she'd finished, she gently kissed the cover. 'That's the way it has to be – my true home is by his side.'

Chapter 42

The Homecoming

Phil was frantic, running around like a headless chicken. He had arranged to pick G. up from the station within the hour, but all hell had broken loose. His book had been published two months ago and word was spreading like wildfire. He advertised the Synergy School of Holistic Development in the appendix, along with all the courses he would facilitate, and his phone had never stopped ringing. He'd secured bookings for the next year. In addition, many people were asking about his song, We Are One, and he was desperately trying to organize more copies. Along with all this, he had set up his own counselling practice and it was extremely busy.

Now, Yin and Yang, his two golden retriever pups, had decided to cause mayhem in the garden. Yang had jumped into the fish pond and was worrying the male and female mallard that had inexplicably found sanctuary there? Yin yapped at her brother from the edge. Phil dragged the dripping wet pup out of the pond, took him inside and was towelling him dry, when Yin decided to go to the bathroom - on the carpet!

I need help desperately. Thank God G's on his way. Maybe he's found his true home and life's purpose, but he doesn't know what he's letting himself in for!

The train was delayed, so Phil decided to go for coffee. As he sipped at his latte, his stomach sank as an overwhelming sense of sadness descended; the whole environment reminded him of Vi. His eyes glazed over as he thought of their many meetings in such places. Though he had yearned for her every single day, he had refrained from making contact; if she was truly happy, he didn't want to disturb the equilibrium. However, daily, without fail, he sent her loving intentions. His faith in spirituality was so great that he was certain that the Universe would provide the platform if they were meant to meet again.

Images of her started to appear in his mind's eye: her child-like smile, her radiance, her beauty, her humour, her face when he proposed, their last loving embrace.

These were followed by other images as well as sounds brushing through his clairaudient senses: a heart shaped musical box; the nursery rhyme, Hush Little Baby Don't Say A Word; Esba cradling a new born baby. Then, Esba's face transfigured into that of Roma's. *'When she's born you will know why,'* she whispered, mystically.

Phil was jolted from his experience as the station tannoy announced the imminent arrival of the train from Edinburgh - G's train. Wanting to give the big man a warm, welcoming homecoming, he quickly finished his coffee and rushed to the platform. A sense of excitement began to course through him. He was about to be reunified with his Soul brother.

The train entered the station and screeched to a halt. The platform became crowded as many people disembarked. But, G. was nowhere to be seen? Phil looked around, frantically trying to find him. People dispersed, but he was still nowhere in sight?

Suddenly, there was a tap on his shoulder.

He turned around.

'I've been asked to give you this sir,' said the porter.

An impending sense of disappointment loomed as he thanked the porter and began to open the envelope. When he set eyes on the contents, his heart stopped.

> **In darkness I no longer roam**
>
> **For I have found my rightful home**
>
> **I've broken through my shell of fear**
>
> **And flown to you my gentle deer**
>
> **Nothing's ever manifest**
>
> **Until observed, so they profess**
>
> **so turn around and magically**
>
> **make our dream reality**

He stood with mouth agape, momentarily immobilized. Then, closing his eyes, he slowly turned through one hundred and eighty degrees. As he did, he sent out intentions.

'Please, please, let this be,' he whispered, as waves of love rippled through his body.

Everything became absolutely still. He nervously opened his eyes. As he did, the surroundings seemed distinctly different: the whole scene took on a magical iridescence; colours seemed brighter, textures enriched, and the air filled with mystique. But the station was deserted - not a Soul in site?

As he felt himself deflating, a voice wisped through his mind.

> *Surrender has brought about victory, dear one. You forfeited your own will for the will of the Universe, despite the heart-ache it entailed. Through Sacrificing your own personal desires for the desires of the Universe, you have learned the lessons of faith, trust, altruism and unconditional love. Now I can reveal that the will of the Universe coincides with your own will - it was always for the highest good of all concerned.*

A major insight can be gained from this, dear one. When intentions are biased towards a particular outcome - an outcome that has been discerned by your earthly self - then, should your wishes manifest, they may not bring about sustained happiness. It is only when your earthly will is in alignment with the will of the Universe that true happiness is guaranteed. So I urge you to encourage people to make intentions, but influence them to leave the outcome to the Universe. This way, whatever happens, will be in the highest interest of the individual concerned.

As the voice dissipated, a solitary figure emerged from the corridor beside the waiting room. Echoes of past lives gave Phil a strong sense of déjà vu. The Universe *had* provided the platform - literally. Vi *had* boarded the train marked destiny.

With nose shining bright red and tears falling, she walked towards him. Streams of energy rocketed to and fro like magnetic pulses drawing them together. They embraced, collapsing into a oneness that surpassed anything they had ever felt before.

'Welcome home, princess,' Phil whispered, as tears of joy danced down their faces. 'How did you find m…..'

'G.' she gently interrupted. 'He came to me and handed me his ticket, saying "go to him." ….Then,' she paused and smiled at him, 'nothing was ever going to stop me.'

As the last words left her lips, she was mesmerized by the sight before her.

'What is it?' enquired Phil, noticing she'd become distant.

'Look,' she replied, driftily, staring hypnotically over his shoulder.

He turned around.

Silence.

A rainbow arced across the sky accompanied by its mirror image: two rainbows.

'Rainbows, Vi,' uttered Phil, 'at the end of which lies our true home.'

Another train arrived. People came and went, but Phil and Vi remained oblivious - locked together as one and this time they would never let go.

Epilogue

Rebirth at Rainbow's End

A year passed by and book sales surpassed all expectations. The demand for courses was so great that they had to find alternative premises. After rejecting several sites, they secured a five acre plot of land in an area of great natural beauty. The huge old barn, which was to be used as both their home and the headquarters of the Synergy School of Holistic Development, was currently being restored. Everything was just as they imagined. Within the grounds was a lake and a sizeable woodland where they spent many hours communing with nature. Phil decided to keep in line with tradition and had a dozen caravans sited in a field adjacent to the barn; these were to be used to house people attending courses. Out of pure sentiment, he had his old caravan transported down from the Lake District to take centre stage. That caravan held so many memories, he couldn't let go of it.

G. had joined them a couple of weeks after Vi had arrived; the time had arrived for the trio to reunify and recognise their destiny. In addition, Phil had plans for Roma, Ann Marie (who was to join them soon), Carla, and Robert, the quantum physicists who had recently taken a great interest in combining his scientific work with spiritual concepts.

The trio watched with sheer delight as the building work progressed. Presently, they were working from their old premises and living in the caravans.

Phil stood between Vi and G and put his arms around them both.

'Thank God we followed the signposts,' he said, triumphantly. 'Our baby has been born: the book, and the centre, will take our work into forthcoming generations.'

That very instant, the rhyme, 'Hush Little Baby' sang through his mind. A wrenching feeling gripped his stomach and a tear came to his eye. Someone was trying to tell him something?

G. peered around him and stared at Vi - a knowing smile on his face.

Vi was glowing.

Phil looked at them puzzled. 'Are you two holding back on me?' he inquired.

She smiled at him adoringly. 'The book *isn't* the child, Phil.' Her glow brightened and a twinkle came to her eye.

'You mean…..'

'Yes - I'm pregnant!'

Silence.

The delightful news took a minute to sink in. Phil drifted off to cloud nine.

'The immaculate conception has happened,' he said, staring at the sky, unsure whether he was about to laugh or cry. 'I have planted my seed with a kiss on the cheek.' He continued, now winking at G. through tear stained eyes.

He floated over to the expectant mother and embraced her so tight that she had to ask him to loosen his hold. Then he gestured to G. to join them. The three - sorry four! - huddled together basking in each other's harmonic vibrations, tears of delight dancing down everyone's cheeks.

One of the four orbs of light occupying the surrounding space dispersed into the nothingness: Mary whispered her farewells and happily disappeared to join her family on the Higher Astral plane.

Galfridus left next, heading back to the thirteenth century where he was about to wed his beloved - Emily. Since freeing her from the tyrannical grip of her father and fiancée, she had recognized her destiny and become a nurse. She now (or then?) tended to the poor.

In a parallel life - year 2006 of the twenty-first century - Galfridus was also about to wed his beloved – Violet Rowan. The venue – Gretna Green. But don't worry, bigamy is not a crime when one weds in two separate domains of experience simultaneously. Anyhow - he was marrying the same woman!

Theodore departed next, dissipating into the ether as he thought himself back to the crystal temple. He had a meeting with his spiritual mentor – his Monad. Something to do with the second phase of a plan that involved the re-incarnation of a highly evolved personality.

Only Esba remained, observing her future family with great delight.

One chapter was about to close and a new one begin. Could the trio's forthcoming adventure be the story-line for Phil's next book? In truth, their real work was only just about to begin…..

OTHER BOOKS BY THE AUTHOR:

Alcoholic to Alchemist

Paul Henderson once drank two bottles of spirits a day, plus anything else he could lay his hands on. As his habit progressed, this included surgical spirits, methylated spirits, and after shave.

Homeless, penniless, and desperate, he spent his nights on a rat-infested railway embankment. The extent of his deterioration was shocking: emaciated body, yellow complexion, eyes sunken, jittery and unkempt. At twenty five years of age, the former fun-loving entertainer resembled an old man - bereft of meaning and emotionally bankrupt.

His constant battle with alcohol and the fear, futility, guilt, and paranoia it evoked, finally became too much. Paul took a lethal cocktail of painkillers and alcohol, only to have his life saved by the swift response and expertise of hospital staff. Death seemed imminent: almost welcoming. The destructive force that possessed him was relentless, intent on propelling him towards a liquid last supper.

Today, Paul is an inspirational speaker and author who embraces the infinite possibilities that life has to offer. At fifty years of age he is in the pinnacle of health. On reaching rock bottom, a powerful force emerged from the depths of his psyche and led him on a journey of radical transformation: this force he refers to as the *archetypal alchemist*. Alchemy is the art of transforming one's mental and emotional debris into the invaluable treasures of insight, inspiration, motivation, direction, prosperity and abundance: **Alchemy promotes life.**

As a result of implementing this programme, Paul experienced a radical shift in consciousness: a profound awakening. Subsequently, he pledged to develop and document his powerful antidote to alcoholism. Eighteen years of dedication and continuing development on a personal and transpersonal level has culminated in this much needed resource.

The information herein is not designed solely to liberate you from the clutches of alcoholism, although it will certainly do that if you adhere to the suggested principles, it is designed to enable you to reach your true potential and transform your life beyond recognition.

Alcoholism is a *mind-set*; a destructive way of thinking, the answer to which is a profound shift in consciousness. This Alcoholic to Alchemist programme combines ancient wisdom, thought-provoking philosophy, and practical psychology in a way that educates, inspires, encourages, enlightens, empowers and evokes an incredible shift in thinking. If you are struggling with alcohol and seek answers, then come and join the ever-growing number of people who have transformed their lives the Alcoholic to Alchemist way.

About the Author

After a life-threatening battle with alcohol in the 1980s, Paul Henderson developed a deep interest in the workings of the human mind. Subsequently, he qualified as a clinical hypnotherapist and psychodynamic counsellor, before embarking on a Bachelor's Degree and specializing in Child Development and Social Psychology.

Dedicated to promoting diversity and flexibility in the field of applied therapy, Paul recently founded the **United Kingdom Association of Integrative Therapy** (UKAIT), and its associated training school - the **United Kingdom Academy of Integrative Therapy**.

In addition to teaching psychology, Paul travels the country conducting workshops and speaking on a wide array of subjects, including Vedic Science, the Mechanisms of Consciousness, and Past-Life Therapy. His interest in the transpersonal led to his first novel *'IN THIS WORLD BUT NOT OF IT,'* a compelling read which combines psychology, philosophy, modern science and spirituality in a way that is inspiring, challenging and transformative.

Visit Paul's Website:
www.al2al.com

In This World but Not of It — Paul Henderson